Interprofessional Social Work: Effective collaborative approaches

ANNE QUINNEY
TRISH HAFFORD-LETCHFIELD

Series Editors: Jonathan Parker and Greta Bradley

$SAGE | **LearningMatters**

Los Angeles | London | New Delhi
Singapore | Washington DC

Learning Matters
An imprint of SAGE Publications Ltd
1 Oliver's Yard
55 City Road
London EC1Y 1SP

SAGE Publications Inc.
2455 Teller Road
Thousand Oaks, California 91320

SAGE Publications India Pvt Ltd 150
B 1/I 1 Mohan Cooperative Industrial Area
Mathura Road
New Delhi 110 044

SAGE Publications Asia-Pacific Pte Ltd
3 Chuch Street
#10–04 Samsung Hub
Singapore 049483

Editor: Luke Block
Development Editor: Kate Lodge
Production Controller: Chris Marke
Project Management: Deer Park Productions,
Tavistock, Devon
Marketing Manager: Tamara Navaratnam
Cover Design: Code 5
Typeset by: Pantek Media, Maidstone, Kent
Printed by: MPG Books Group, Bodmin, Cornwall

Library of Congress Control Number:
2012941844

British Library Cataloguing in Publication Data

A catalogue record for this book is available from
the British Library.

ISBN: 978 0 85725 826 7 (hbk)
ISBN: 978 1 84445 379 5 (pbk)

Contents

About the authors

Anne Quinney is a senior lecturer at Bournemouth University and is the editor of the peer-reviewed journal *Practice: Social work in action*. Prior to working in higher education Anne worked as a teacher, youth worker and social worker in Sudan, Scotland and England. Anne's research interests are in technology-enhanced learning, and she has undertaken research projects into staff and student experiences of interprofessional learning using a virtual community, and the use of arts and humanities materials and online assessment in transprofessional learning. Anne is also interested in how students develop research-mindedness. She is one of the authors of the multimedia learning resources produced for the Social Care Institute for Excellence on *Interprofessional and interagency collaboration*.

Dr Trish Hafford-Letchfield is the Director of Programmes for Social Work at Middlesex University, London. Trish is a qualified nurse and social worker and has had a long career in social work including more than ten years of managing social work and social care services in a statutory organisation including supported housing. Trish has a wide range of experiences in interprofessional leadership and management development and has developed a range of initiatives in practice. Within higher education she has led and taught on interprofessional leadership programmes for a number of years and is widely published in this area. Trish's research interests lie in educational gerontology and social care, the use of the arts in learning and teaching, widening participation in education, sexuality and intimacy in social work and social care, leadership and organisational development. She is interested particularly in how social work draws on other social science disciplines to enhance their knowledge and practice.

Series editors' preface

Collaboration and interprofessional, interdisciplinary or multi-professional working have been sported almost as a talisman which, once touched, will rid the world of social work, health care and other human services of the narrow, tribal and often damaging practices that are held responsible for social tragedies.

National and global perturbations have continued to influence and mould social and health policy developments, which often determine the ways in which they are applied in social work practice. The UK faces numerous challenges over forthcoming years, many of which, perhaps, have been heightened following the 2007 fiscal crisis and its lasting ramifications. These include dealing with the impact of an increasingly ageing population, with its cognate health and social care needs, housing and support service needs, education and leisure services and so forth. Collaboration with other professionals and para-professionals is also set centre stage as we work with the financial implications that a changing demography, including lower fertility rates alongside population ageing, brings. This book adds to our knowledge and understanding of the complexities of social work practice in which collaboration with and respect for others is central.

Migration has increased as a global phenomenon and we now live and work with the implications of international issues in our everyday and local lives. Often these issues influence how we construct our social services and determine what services we need to offer. It is likely that as a social worker you will work with a diverse range of people throughout your career, many of whom have experienced significant, even traumatic, events that require a professional and caring response grounded, of course, in the laws and social policies that have developed as a result. As well as working with individuals, however, you may be required to respond to the needs of a particular community disadvantaged by world events or excluded within local communities because of assumptions made about them, and you may be embroiled in some of the tensions that arise from implementing policy-based approaches that may conflict with professional values. What is clear within these contexts is that you may be working with a range of people who are often at the margins of society, socially excluded or in need of protection and safeguarding. You will not always be the person or service who can meet the needs of the diverse population you will meet. This text provides important knowledge and information to help you become aware of the roles others play in helping in human situations, and to respond appropriately and make referrals to other professions when faced with challenging situations.

Reflection, revision and reform allow us to focus clearly on what knowledge is useful to engage with in learning to be a social worker. The focus on 'statutory' social work and, by dint of that, involuntary clients, brings to the fore the need for social workers to be well versed in the mechanisms and nuances of legislation that can be interpreted and applied to empower, protect and assist, but also to understand the social policy arena in which practice is forged. The books in this series respond to the agendas driven by changes brought about by professional body, government and disciplinary review. They aim to build on and offer introductory texts based on up-to-date knowledge and social policy development and to help communicate this in an accessible way, preparing the ground for future study as you develop your social work career. The books are written by people passionate about social work and social services and aim to instil that passion in others. The knowledge introduced in this book is important for all social workers in all fields of practice as they seek to reaffirm social work's commitment to those it serves.

Professor Jonathan Parker, Bournemouth University
Greta Bradley, University of York

Acknowledgements

I would like to dedicate this book to all the students I have worked with. They have helped me to stay tuned to social work practice and continually reinforced my passion for being involved in social work education.

Anne Quinney

For my dad, Peter Hafford; you are always with me.

Trish Hafford-Letchfield

Introduction

This book is written for student social workers who are beginning to develop their skills and understanding of the requirements for practice. The book will also appeal to people considering a career in social work or social care but not yet studying for a social work degree. Nurses, occupational therapists and other health and social care professionals will be able to gain an insight into the requirements demanded of social workers. Experienced and qualified social workers, especially those contributing to practice learning, will also be able to use this book for consultation, teaching, revision and to gain an insight into the expectations raised by the qualifying degree in social work.

A vision for social work operating in complex human situations has been adopted. This is reflected in the following definition from the International Association of Schools of Social Work and International Federation of Social Workers 2000:

> The social work profession promotes social change, problem solving in human relationships and the empowerment and liberation of people to enhance well-being.
>
> Utilising theories of human behaviour and social systems, social work intervenes at the points where people interact with their environments. Principles of human rights and social justice are fundamental to social work.

While there is a great deal packed into this definition it encapsulates the notion that social work concerns individual people and wider society. Social workers practise with people who are vulnerable, who are struggling in some way to participate fully in society. Social workers walk that tightrope between the marginalised individual and the social and political environment that may have contributed to their marginalisation.

Book structure

Learning features

The book is interactive. You are encouraged to work through the book as an active participant, taking responsibility for your learning, in order to increase your knowledge, understanding and ability to apply this learning to practice. You will be expected to reflect on your current learning and how your professional learning can be developed in your future career.

Case studies throughout the book will help you to examine theories, models or scenarios for social work practice. Activities have been devised that require you to reflect on experiences, situations and events and help you to review and summarise learning undertaken.

In this way your knowledge will become deeply embedded as part of your development. When you embark on practice learning in an agency the work and reflection undertaken here will help you to improve and hone your skills and knowledge.

This book will introduce knowledge and learning activities for you as a student social worker concerning the central processes relating to issues of daily practice in all areas of the discipline. Suggestions for further reading will be made at the end of each chapter.

Professional development and reflective practice

Great emphasis is placed on developing skills of reflection about, in and on practice. This has developed over many years in social work. This book will assist you in developing a questioning approach that looks in a critical way at your thoughts, experiences and practice and seeks to heighten your skills in refining your practice as a result of these deliberations. Reflection is central to good social work practice, but only if action results from that reflection.

Reflecting about, in and on your practice is not only important during your education to become a social worker; it is considered key to continued professional development. As we move to a profession that acknowledges lifelong learning as a way of keeping up to date, ensuring that research informs practice and in honing skills and values for practice, it is important to begin the process at the outset of your development.

In the first chapter you will be introduced to some of the key terms and definitions associated with both working and learning with people from other professions to enable you to develop a baseline understanding of, for example, interprofessional and inter-agency working, partnership, collaboration and interprofessional education. Interprofessional learning as a preparation for interprofessional working will be considered. This chapter will help you to understand the policy and service delivery context, from the Beveridge Report of 1942 to the present day, to set the scene for consideration of a range of 'branches' of the welfare state in Chapters 3 to 7.

In Chapter 2 we consider how you can prepare for working effectively with other professionals and work in partnership with service users. Recommendations from inquiries, for example the high-profile inquiries into the death of Victoria Climbié and Peter Connolly, and the recent Munro Review, will be considered to illustrate the ways in which working interprofessionally has become a clear government-driven policy focus. The tensions between breaking down barriers and building new understanding between professional groups will be considered, along with a discussion of the importance of maintaining a sound professional base and demonstrating core social work values while working across and within professional groups and agency settings. We will consider what helps and what hinders effective interprofessional and inter-agency working.

Chapter 3 addresses working with professionals involved in delivering youth work services. The common debates in social work and youth work will be explored along with key aspects of the youth worker roles.

In Chapter 4 we will focus on the health context. This will include material and activities to support developing an understanding of, for example, the ways in which health services are organised and delivered. Health inequalities will be considered, along with the current radical changes to the NHS. Values, professional identity and professional roles will be discussed and we will review policy documents and policy initiatives.

In Chapter 5 the focus will be on the education context, where structures relating to the delivery of education services will be explained, including Early Years (pre-school) education and formal education in schools and lifelong learning. Inequalities will be highlighted and we will consider the role of the education welfare officer. Recent policies and initiatives will be discussed in terms of their implications for working collaboratively.

Chapter 6 provides the opportunity to consider working in the housing and neighbourhood context. The chapter will include material to help you understand the problems associated with social exclusion and we will explore the professional roles and identity of those employed in organisations which are concerned with housing issues. Inequalities in housing and homelessness will be considered. Examples from recent policy initiatives will provide the framework for exploring current issues that have an impact on the work of social workers and on the experiences of the service users and carers that they are working with.

Chapter 7 will focus on the justice context and provide you with the opportunity to consider the implications of working with Cafcass and Youth Justice services as well as the police, probation and legal professions. This will build on material in the text in this series written by Robert Johns, *Using the law in social work*.

Concluding remarks and signposts will be offered at the end of the book and at this stage you will be invited to review the learning outcomes in each of the chapters and you will be encouraged to chart and monitor your learning in order to increase your knowledge, understanding and ability to apply this learning to your practice. You will be expected to reflect creatively on how your immediate learning needs can be met when working with other professionals in your practice learning experiences in agency settings and how your continuous professional development can be maintained in your future career.

Case studies throughout the book will help you to examine the material presented and activities have been devised to help you reflect on experiences, situations and events and help you to review and summarise learning undertaken. In this way your knowledge will become deeply embedded as part of your development. When you arrive at the point on your course when you undertake practice learning in an agency, the work and reflection undertaken as you work though this book will help you to improve and hone your skills and knowledge.

As with all other books in the series, this book will introduce knowledge and learning activities for you as a student social worker concerning the central processes relating to issues of daily practice in all areas of the discipline. Suggestions for further reading will be made at the end of each chapter.

This book has been carefully mapped to the new Professional Capabilities Framework for Social Workers in England and will help you to develop the appropriate standards at the right level. These standards are as follows.

- **Professionalism**

  Identify and behave as a professional social worker committed to professional development.

- **Values and ethics**

  Apply social work ethical principles and values to guide professional practice.

- **Diversity**

  Recognise diversity and apply anti-discriminatory and anti-oppressive principles in practice.

- **Rights, justice and economic well-being**

  Advance human rights and promote social justice and economic well-being.

- **Knowledge**

  Apply knowledge of social sciences, law and social work practice theory.

- **Judgement**

  Use judgement and authority to intervene with individuals, families and communities to promote independence, provide support and prevent harm, neglect and abuse.

- **Critical reflection and analysis**

  Apply critical reflection and analysis to inform and provide a rationale for professional decision-making.

- **Contexts and organisations**

  Engage with, inform and adapt to changing contexts that shape practice. Operate effectively within your own organisational frameworks and contribute to the development of services and organisations. Operate effectively within multi-agency and interprofessional settings.

- **Professional leadership**

  Take responsibility for the professional learning and development of others through supervision, mentoring, assessing, research, teaching, leadership and management.

References to these standards will be made throughout the text and you will find a diagram of the Professional Capabilities Framework in Appendix 1.

Chapter 1

The importance of interprofessional and inter-agency practice

Introduction

In this chapter we will be considering the factors that create the framework for the renewed emphasis on, and importance of, interprofessional and inter-agency working and for developing effective collaborative approaches. You will also be introduced to some of the key terms and models developed to explain and describe the concepts that underpin working with other professionals in order to prepare for effective practice in this area. We identify the relevant aspects of the Professional Capability Framework (College of Social Work 2012) and the Benchmarks for Social Work (QAA 2008). These sources emphasise the importance of learning about interprofessional and interagency social work practice as part of your social work qualifying course, for example:

Contemporary social work increasingly takes place in an inter-agency context, and social workers work collaboratively with others towards interdisciplinary and cross-professional objectives.

(QAA 2008 para 3.7)

In addition students are expected to develop

accurate knowledge about the respective responsibilities of social welfare agencies, including those in the public, voluntary/independent and private sectors, and acquire skills in effective collaborative practice.

(QAA 2008 para 3.7)

In the workplace setting collaborative social work practice which seeks to develop effective working across agency boundaries continues to receive a great deal of attention. This approach was embodied in the 'joined-up' and 'cross-cutting' approaches taken by the New Labour administration in its attempt to develop an integrated approach to the organisation and delivery of services to reduce inequalities and social exclusion, break down barriers between agencies and encourage the forging of new partnerships. Changes were made to education, health and social services structures in an attempt to focus on the service user and their need for a seamless service rather than having to negotiate the traditional service boundaries that are neither helpful to, nor easily understood by, the person in need of services. Examples of integrated approaches developed were Sure Start projects, Youth Offending Teams and Community Mental Health Teams.

When social workers are working with service users whose needs are complex the opportunities to work across traditional service boundaries are increasingly seen as one of the strategies for meeting complex and multiple needs. As a social work student you may find that you undertake a practice learning placement in an agency where there are workers from a range of professional backgrounds as well as social work and where a collaborative approach to the needs of service users and carers is taken.

This is represented in the Professional Capability Framework (PCF) (see Appendix 1) in the domain of contexts and organisations, by the statement that at the point of qualification students must 'Understand the inter-agency, multi-disciplinary and interprofessional dimensions to practice and demonstrate effective partnership working.'

The changing landscape of social work

Evidence from a wide range of sources, and in particular the Laming Report (2003) into the circumstances surrounding the death of Victoria Climbié, and the subsequent Laming Report (2009) into the death of Peter Connolly has highlighted the importance of working closely with people from other professional groups and with a wide range of agencies in the effective delivery of social work services, in order to protect and safeguard vulnerable children.

In particular, the following statements from the first Laming Report (2003) emphasise this:

> *It is clear that the safeguarding of children will continue to depend upon services such as health, education, housing, police and social services working together.*

> (para 17.112)

> *The skills involved in working successfully across organisational boundaries must be given proper recognition in both the basic training and in the continuing training of staff. It cannot be left only to those individuals who have the motivation to do it. Working across boundaries should be an expectation placed on all staff, and it must be reflected in training programmes.*

> (para 17.113)

Following the publication of Lord Laming's Report the Secretary of State for Health at the time, Alan Milburn, addressed the House of Commons emphasising how services providing care for children must work together rather than in conflict. (The Guardian 2003). He drew attention to the need for closer co-operation, co-ordination and communication across and between services, to prevent a reoccurrence of the administrative, managerial and professional failures by social workers, police and health professionals that contributed to Victoria's death. The second Laming Report (2009 para 4.1) after the death of Peter Connolly included the following observation in the section which specifically addresses inter-agency working.

> *It is clear that most staff in social work, youth work, education, police, health and other frontline services are committed to the principle of interagency working, and recognise that children can only be protected effectively when all agencies pool information, expertise and resources so that a full picture of the child's life is better understood. Cooperative working is increasingly becoming the normal way of working*

However, while it is clear that a lack of collaborative working can contribute to failures to protect vulnerable people there is not yet a body of research evidence to demonstrate when and how learning and working together with other professionals leads to more effective and safer practice.

The Social Work Taskforce and Social Work Reform Board

With the remit to *undertake a comprehensive review of frontline social work practice*, the Social Work Taskforce was created by the Department for Children, Families and Schools and the Department of Health in January 2009, chaired by Moira Gibb, Chief Executive of the London Borough of Camden. Following the publication of the Taskforce recommendations in 2009 for social work practice and social work education, the Social Work Reform Board was established in January 2010, in order to implement the Taskforce recommendations. All 15 recommendations were accepted by the government and five key areas of reform were identified.

- An overarching Professional Standards Framework.

- Standards for employers and a supervision framework.

- Principles that should underpin a continuing professional development framework.

- Proposed requirements for social work education.

- Proposals for effective partnership working.

The proposals for partnership working between employers and universities are informed by principles that should underpin all forms of partnership working.

The Social Work Reform Board was made up of representatives from higher education, the social work profession, social work employers, service user organisations and government, and addresses all aspects of children's and adults' services. An important theme was the raising of the profile of the positive role social workers play with the public, service users, the media and other professions. Parallel to these developments, the Secretary of State for Education and the Children and Families Minister established the Munro Review in July 2010 with the remit to improve child protection, including interprofessional working.

In order to improve the gap between expectations and actual standards the previous New Labour government had identified six areas to be addressed. These were:

- *protection* of vulnerable children and adults;

- *co-ordination* between agencies and authorities;

- *flexibility* to ensure the delivery of person-centred services;

- *clarity of role* with greater understanding of the role social services should undertake;

- *consistency* of service delivery across the country;

- *efficiency* of service delivery, to ensure best use of public money.

(Horner 2012)

These themes continue to be central to effective collaborative working with other professionals and are recurring themes in this book.

It is clear from the statements in the PCF and the Benchmarks that social workers are expected to know how to work effectively with other professions from a range of agencies in order to provide effective and appropriate services. In addition, as social workers are increasingly employed in a range of diverse settings in statutory, voluntary and independent organisations and agencies, social work students are expected to learn how to practise social work effectively and maintain a strong professional identity when social workers may be in the minority in that organisation or team, and how to work with people from a range of professional backgrounds in those organisations.

Defining the terms

As you have already seen in the chapter so far, a wide range of terms are used to describe the process of working together with other professions, including joint working, interprofessional working, multi-disciplinary working and inter-agency working, and collaborative practice. Hodgson (2005) reminds us that in some situations, *multi*-disciplinary working may conjure up images of many different professions being involved and that *inter*-professional implies a range of different professionals involved who collaborate in terms of discussion and planning.

These terms are further detailed by Whittington (2003 p15) in what he describes as the *lexicon of partnership and collaboration*. In Figure 1.1 you will see some of the common terms used to describe people from different professional groups working and learning together. There are some blank ones for you to add any other terms you have come across.

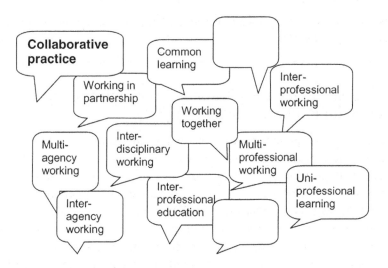

Figure 1.1 The lexicon of terms

Although some of the terms are often seen as interchangeable, Whittington (2003) distinguishes between them in the following ways. 'Working in partnership' refers to formal ways of 'working together' and is often described as:

- working together to achieve 'joined up' services;

- addressing service user needs through services provided by more than one organisation or professional group;

- arrangements between a service provider and those in receipt of it, for example in planning or monitoring the service.

'Working in collaboration' refers to knowledge, skills and values utilised when putting this into practice. Whittington (2003 p16) goes on to offer the following definitions:

Partnership is a state of relationships, at organisational, group, professional or inter-professional level, to be achieved, maintained and reviewed and *collaboration is an active process of partnership in action.* In a suite of open-access multimedia learning materials commissioned by the Social Care Institute for Excellence for the social work degree (Quinney et al. 2009; Thomas et al. 2009; Whittington et al. 2009) the term developed by the authors to represent this way of working was *interprofessional and interagency collaboration (IPIAC).*

ACTIVITY 1.1

Thinking about the range of terms you have read about in the section above, identify those that you have come across in the agencies/organisations you are familiar with.

- *In what ways do the terms accurately reflect the work undertaken?*

- *In what ways do you think they reflect the culture of the agency/organisation?*

- *Are there other terms, from those explained above, that would more closely describe the work being undertaken?*

Inter-professional learning in social work education as a preparation for interprofessional working

On the social work programme that you are following you are likely to learn about the context of the work of other professionals who are employed in the various sectors of the welfare state, possibly by learning about the history of the welfare state or in an area of study that considers current policy developments in relation to, for example, the National Health Service, education services, criminal justice services, housing and income maintenance services. These units or modules of study may also be offered on other professional courses in your university or college, where elements of a common curriculum are followed. Social work students may learn about the work of other professions but not meet students of these professions. This learning is sometimes described as uni-professional learning.

Social work students will often experience learning together with students from another professional group as part of their social work programme, with the range of other professions often determined by the professionally qualifying programmes offered by that particular college or university. This might include learning with students following a health-related course such as nursing, midwifery, occupational therapy or physiotherapy, or from other courses including teaching, probation or youth and community work.

The term 'multi-professional or common' learning is used where social work students learn alongside students following another professional programme, for example by attending lectures with students from other programmes on a common area of the curriculum. When learning by interacting with students from other professional programmes is experienced, or working and learning with people from other professions in placement, this is referred to as interprofessional learning. Learning may be organised around service user and carer issues, for example child protection, acute or enduring mental health problems, or may focus on personal and professional skills, for example communication skills, managing small-scale projects or practice development skills.

The UK Centre for the Advancement of Interprofessional Education (CAIPE 1997) uses the following definitions.

- Multi-professional education – where two or more professions learn side by side for whatever reason.

- Interprofessional education – where two or more professions learn from and about each other to develop skills and knowledge for collaboration and to improve the quality of care.

Their website www.caipe.org.uk contains useful information to support working with other professions.

ACTIVITY **1.2**

Visit the website of CAIPE and find out about its purpose and the resources available from the website. How could you use this centre to support your learning and practice?

Working collaboratively – policy-driven or evidence-driven?

Despite the strong evidence to demonstrate that a failure to work effectively together or communicate with other professionals can have tragic consequences for individuals (for example the findings from a number of child death enquiries from the Colwell Report in 1974 to the Laming Reports in 2003 and in 2009), there is less evidence to demonstrate that the face-to-face sharing of ideas and the development of an awareness of the role and values of other professions through interprofessional education and training actually promote closer collaboration. Barr (2002 p6) reminds us that *definition has been lacking, semantics bewildering, evaluations few and the evidence base elusive* and provides a useful overview of the history of interprofessional education.

Nevertheless there is a clear policy drive from central government to encourage partnership working and collaborative practice and for social workers it is incorporated into the PCF and must be evidenced in practice learning settings as part of the process of achieving a social work qualification.

Case studies from social work programmes

There follow some examples of the experiences of students on social work programmes where opportunities for learning with other professionals are provided. This experience will vary between programmes and will be influenced by the presence of other students following professionally qualifying courses and the structure of the programmes of study. Where learning with other professionals during the university-based elements of the social work programme is not possible, students often have the opportunity of learning with students from other professionally qualifying programmes during practice placements.

There may be other students on placement in the agency, organisation or locality where you are undertaking the placement from other professions providing the opportunity to carry out joint planning or joint working, to explore different viewpoints influenced by professional codes of conduct, or to learn informally from one another by sharing opinions, experiences and resources.

You may have the opportunity to work in co-operation with other professionals and, with the importance of continuous professional development being emphasised in the PCF, be in a position to contribute to the ongoing learning and development of colleagues by sharing your learning experiences from your social work studies. In these situations students may be working in a team or agency consisting of people from a range of professional backgrounds, or be undertaking joint working or close liaison with other professionals employed by a range of agencies where effective service delivery depends on the involvement of more than one agency.

The wide variation in the examples of interprofessional education mirrors the wide range and diversity of interprofessional organisations, environments and situations where social workers will be working in partnership and collaboration with staff from other professions. In all of these learning situations there are opportunities to extend your practice skills and develop a sound value base. Learning together can provide situations that prepare for the realities and challenges of working together.

Example 1. Social work students from two universities are experiencing learning with students from seven health-related professional courses at all three levels of the degree by undertaking problem-based group work projects, in both the university-based and practice-based areas of the course. This includes learning with medical students, nursing students, occupational therapy students and pharmacy students.

Example 2. Social work students are involved in shared learning with youth and community work students in a taught unit on 'working with diversity and difference'.

Example 3. Social work students are offered the opportunity to undertake a practice learning placement in a school working alongside teachers, in a primary care setting working with health visitors and nursing students undertaking their placement, in a prison working with a range of professionals and in a housing association working with a range of professionals.

ACTIVITY 1.3

Part 1:

With the examples above in mind and thinking about the programme of study that you are following, what are the opportunities for learning with students following other professional courses? You may find it helpful to make notes to refer back to later.

- *What are these professional groups?*

- *What do you think the benefits of learning together are?*

- *What do you think the challenges and difficulties of learning together are?*

Continued

ACTIVITY **1.3** *continued*

- *How will you use this knowledge and experience in your assignments and in your practice?*

- *What are the benefits for service users and carers?*

Part 2:

Thinking about the course you are following, are there opportunities during the practice learning experience in agency settings to work with other professionals, either students or qualified practitioners?

Consider again the questions set out above. In what ways are the issues the same or different?

COMMENT

Some of the things you have noted down might include the following.

- *Ethical issues, professional codes and values*

   You may have considered the difficulties and tensions that can arise when your professional values do not align with those of another professional group and started to consider why these differences occur and how these tensions can be addressed to provide effective and responsive services.

- *Roles and responsibilities*

   You may have considered how stereotypes can be challenged and how mutual understanding and respect can be built by learning about the remit of other agencies and the breadth and depth of work undertaken by the staff from other professional groups who work in them.

- *Sharing and developing knowledge and skills*

   You may have discovered new resources, learned about your strengths and identified areas where there are gaps in your knowledge about service users' experiences and appropriate interventions and services.

- *Providing a more effective service*

   You may have developed a better understanding of how this learning can support practice that delivers an improved experience for service users and carers.

Values and ethical issues

It would be useful at this stage to read in more detail about social work values and reflect on how these are, or will become, central to your professional identity.

ACTIVITY **1.4**

- *Review the teaching and learning on values and ethical issues you have experienced on the course you are following.*

- *What are the key learning points for you?*

- *What further reading do you need to undertake to provide a sound base for this learning?*

- *Draw up an outline action plan that will help you to continually review and reflect on your personal values and how they fit with the values set out in the Professional Competency Framework. It is helpful here to remind yourself that your assignments and practice should be underpinned by awareness of social work values and anti-oppressive practice.*

- *You might find it helpful to include a section on values in your Personal Development Plan and to discuss your growing understanding of values and anti-oppressive practice with your personal tutor/academic advisor.*

COMMENT

The works of Clark (2000), Banks (2006) and Parrott (2006) are a good starting point for reading about values. Clark describes the principles that help to define values and the 'rules' for good practice. Banks (2006 p13) identifies four types of issues that social workers report as resulting in ethical dilemmas: issues around individual rights and welfare...issues around public welfare...issues around inequality and structural oppression...and issues around professional role, boundaries and relationships *and provides case examples to illustrate these. Because social workers deal with some of the most vulnerable people in our society at times of greatest stress (Smith 2002 pi) when intervention, or the lack of it, has wide-reaching implications and impact, it is important that they work from a standpoint that is informed by clear values. A useful summary of values and anti-oppressive practice in relation to practice learning can be found in the book by Jonathan Parker,* Effective practice learning in social work (2nd edn) *in this series. It is in the context of practice learning when you are likely to have the opportunity to experience working in collaboration with other professionals. In later chapters we will be considering the value bases of other professionals that you are likely to come into contact with in order to understand how these may determine their responsibilities and actions.*

A key feature of the social work professional identity is the emphasis on structural issues and their impact on the experiences of service users. It is this aspect of social work that may lead to a degree of tension when working collaboratively with others and the need for negotiation skills to be employed to reach a common understanding. The definition of social work adopted by the International Federation of Social Workers (2000) makes clear the political dimension of social work that distinguishes it from other professional groups:

> *Social work has grown out of humanitarian and democratic ideals. Its value base is about respect for the dignity and equality and worth of all people. The main aim of social work is to alleviate poverty, to liberate vulnerable and oppressed people with the ultimate aim to promote social inclusion.*

The work of Dominelli (2002) is important in locating social work within an anti-oppressive framework. The work of Fook (2012) is important in developing a critical approach to practice.

Developing effective education and training to support interprofessional working

It is important to be aware that exposure to a learning environment or learning opportunities will not necessarily in itself result in interprofessional learning and the development from that of more effective services. The situation is more complex and involves an exploration and understanding of what effective learning for collaborative practice might consist of and how this can be supported and achieved.

Barr (2002 p33) recommends that, in order to be effective, interprofessional education must meet the following requirements.

- Put service users at the centre.

- Promote collaboration.

- Reconcile competing objectives.

- Reinforce collaborative competence.

- Relate collaboration in learning and practice in a coherent rationale.

- Incorporate inter-professional values.

- Include both common and comparative learning.

- Employ a range of interactive learning methods.

- Count towards qualification.

He also recommends that:

- Programmes should be evaluated;

- Findings should be disseminated.

RESEARCH SUMMARY

As recommended by Barr (2002), academics at the University of the West of England have published their findings from an evaluation of their interprofessional education programme in which social work students take part (Barrett 2003; Pollard and Miers 2008; Pollard et al. 2008). The experiences of staff and students, including social work students, engaged in interprofessional education at Bournemouth University have also been captured and published (Scammell et al. 2008; Quinney et al. 2008).

ACTIVITY 1.5

Thinking of the course that you are following, how do these recommendations match with your experience?

- *How are service users and carers placed 'at the centre'?*

- *How can you use your knowledge, skills and values to contribute to the development of improved understanding between students from the professional groups involved and improve the experience of service users and carers?*

- *Would you add anything further to this list from your own experience?*

COMMENT

Some of what you have noted about your own experience may be reflected in the following description of interprofessional working developed at a conference involving health and social care professionals.

In this book we will be considering the experience of social workers when working with a range of different professionals, including those from health, education, criminal justice, youth and community work, income maintenance and housing. We will consider the values and professional identity, roles and responsibilities of these professions, the settings in which they work and the challenges and opportunities for working interprofessionally.

It is important to remember the following, which encapsulates the spirit of this book. Inter-professional working is not about fudging the boundaries between the professions and trying to create a generic care worker. It is instead about developing professionals who are confident in their own core skills and expertise, who are fully aware of and confident in the skills and expertise of fellow health and care professionals, and who conduct their own practice in a non-hierarchical and collegiate way with other members of the working team, so as to continuously improve the health of their communities and to meet the real care needs of individual patients and clients.

(Hardy 1999 p 7)

Beveridge – The backdrop for the current welfare state

As the chapters in this book refer to what might be considered branches of the welfare state, in order to set the scene it is important to remind yourself about the Beveridge Report (1942) and the developments that led to the establishment of the welfare state. In the following chapters we will be looking at contemporary areas of policy and service delivery that correspond to themes that informed the Beveridge Report, for example, the themes of education, health, justice, housing and their importance in the context of inequalities and social exclusion.

ACTIVITY **1.6**

Visit the History of Social Work website and discover about the work of William Beveridge, as well as other pioneers from the past. www.historyofsocialwork.org

You will be able to download a range of documents including the first 20 pages of the Beveridge Report, as well as seeing images.

Post-war reconstruction

At the end of the Second World War the Labour government, elected in 1945 with a landslide majority, set about responding to the economic and social conditions that were to lead to the introduction of the welfare state, and the formation of government-delivered education, social security and health services. Principles of collective action, paternalism and pragmatism informed their 'cradle to grave' policies, against the background of what is often described as the 'post war consensus' in relation to economic and welfare policies. The earlier Dawson Report (1920) was an important milestone in the development of health care policies, and was to inform the later NHS Act of 1946. Some of the key recommendations of the Dawson Report included effective domiciliary services, for example general practitioners and midwives; universal provision; and a concern with prevention as well as cure.

The highly significant Beveridge Report (1942) was informed by the changing social and political climate, and consolidated a range of measures that encompassed notions of welfare that had been evident for many years previously. Expressed in the stark language of the time, the measures were intended to address the 'Five Giants' of idleness, want, ignorance, squalor and disease. The responses to these Five Giants are detailed in the table below.

Table 1.1 Beveridge's five giants

Idleness (unemployment)	Labour Exchanges established
Want (poverty)	The Family Allowance Act 1944
	The National Insurance Act 1946
	The National Assistance Act 1948
Ignorance	The Education Act 1944
Squalor (poor housing)	The Town and Country Planning Act 1947
	New Towns Act 1947
	The Housing Act 1949
Disease	The National Health Service Act 1946

Some of the social changes included an increased awareness of, and changing views about, the nature of poverty. The war had led to people from all social classes, who would previously not have come into contact with one another, sharing common experiences both overseas and at home. This included serving in the armed forces, sheltering together from air raids and working to support the war effort. In particular the work of Joseph Rowntree in York and Charles Booth in London raised awareness and brought a greater understanding of impact of economic rather than individual factors. Nye (Aneurin) Bevin, Labour Minister of Health, held views that were left of centre, but Liberal rather than Marxist. He was influenced by the economic philosophy of John Maynard Keynes in which the state takes an active and central role in the regulation of full employment.

Despite some progressive views, issues of the paternalistic and colonial/imperial heritage were embodied in what is often referred to as the 'social contract' for Beveridge's citizen – at the centre was the notion of the white, male, able-bodied breadwinner supporting his family. Women, after working in factories or on the land during the wartime years, came to be redefined as mother, child-rearer, carer and homemaker. Emergency health measures introduced during the Second World War enabled free treatment to be provided initially for servicemen/women and casualties and it was later extended to virtually the whole population, providing a model for the later National Health Service.

ACTIVITY 1.7

To help you make links between the historical and contemporary developments, referring to the table above of Beveridges's Five Giants, make a new table listing the contemporary areas of the welfare state, and legislation and policy documents associated with these areas.

COMMENT

To help you begin to consider the range of professionals that you as a social worker are likely to come into contact with and work collaboratively with, under each of the headings in your table make a list of the professionals that are associated with those services.

As you work through this book you will be able to add to this table.

CHAPTER SUMMARY

This chapter has examined briefly the post-war Beveridge reforms, the New Labour modernisation agenda and the current Coalition government that form a backdrop for interprofessional social work practice. It has also helped you to think about the terminology used and has briefly considered interprofessional education as a scenario for preparing for collaborative working in agency settings. In the next chapter we will be looking more closely at preparing to develop knowledge and skills about interprofessional and inter-agency collaboration, and at the growing evidence base for interprofessional education and collaborative working.

Barrett, G Sellman, D and Thomas, J (2005) (eds) *Interprofessional working in health and social care*. Basingstoke: Palgrave.

This edited text contains chapters written by academics and practitioners from a wide range of professions, including medicine, midwifery, occupational therapy, probation and social work.

Pollard, KC, Thomas, J and Miers M (2010) (eds) *Understanding interprofessional working in health and social care*. Basingstoke: Palgrave.

This edited text is a companion to the above text, and explores some of the theoretical underpinnings to interprofessional working as well as drawing attention to some accounts of interprofessional working.

Morris, K (2008) (ed.) *Social work and multi-agency working: Making a difference*. Bristol: Policy Press

A very useful text on policy, practice and research.

www.caipe.org.uk

The website of the UK Centre for the Advancement of Inter-Professional Education.

A series of multimedia learning resources commissioned by SCIE can be accessed and downloaded free. Of particular relevance are the interprofessional and interagency working series of resources, including the following.

www.scie.org.uk/publications/elearning/index.asp

Whittington, C, Thomas, J and Quinney, A (2008) An introduction to interprofessional and inter-agency collaboration

www.scie.org.uk/publications/elearning/index.asp

Whittington, C, Whittington M, Thomas, J and Quinney, A (2008) Key policy and legislation with implications for interprofessional and inter-agency collaboration (IPIAC): A timeline of examples 1969–2008

pter 2

Preparing to work with other professionals

Introduction

Working collaboratively with other professionals is not a new concept. Over twenty years ago, Bamford (1990 p22), a director of social services, wrote that moves to develop a multi-disciplinary approach to the delivery of services were based on a recognition that *no single profession has a monopoly of skill, knowledge and expertise in dealing with the physical, social and psychological problems* but that it was evident that *goodwill alone would not produce collaboration.*

He identified four main themes, which he called 'structural impediments', that could blight collaborative working (1990, p129). These were:

- policy differences;

- planning and budget differences;

- professional differences;
- cultural differences.

The potential impediments identified by Bamford (1990) would not appear out of place today, and continue to be identified in studies of interprofessional and inter-agency working.

In recent years collaborative practice with other professionals has been widely promoted as a solution for addressing shortcomings and failures in public services, including social work, health, education, youth work and housing sectors. The previous New Labour government's focus on *modern, seamless and personalised* public services (Brindle 2005) sought to meet the increasingly complex needs of service users and carers through a rethinking of the policies, structures and professionals involved. The coalition government has followed this model with the added dimension of greater emphasis on market forces and private sector involvement.

We hope that this chapter will provide you with a greater awareness about yourself as a future social worker and about the other professions you will be working with in order to deliver effective and responsive services.

Messages from recent reviews and inquiries

As you read about in Chapter 1, the restructuring of services for children, young people and their families that arose out of the Laming Report (2003) was a continuation of New Labour's modernisation agenda in relation to public sector reforms and has continued under the Coalition government. The subsequent Laming Report (2009) commissioned after the death of Peter Connolly and the Munro Review (2011) have led to further changes to strengthen and clarify child protection policy and practice. This review recommended that the government revise statutory, multi-agency guidance and focus only on essential rules for effective multi-agency working and on the principles that underpin good practice (para 6). This restructuring has significant importance as it provides far-reaching opportunities for effective interprofessional and inter-agency social work practice, though as we will see throughout the book, the reorganisation of services and the development of new structures do not necessarily result in improved services. The importance of effective interprofessional and inter-agency working is highlighted when children are living with parents experiencing mental health or substance misuse difficulties, with the need for children's services and adult services to work together to assess needs, strengths and risks (see Quinney et al. 2009).

The service user and carer perspective

The QAA Benchmarks for social work tell us that *in providing services, social workers should engage with service users and carers in ways that are characterised by openness, reciprocity, mutual accountability and explicit recognition of the powers of the social worker and the legal context of intervention* (QAA 2008 para 3.9) and work in partnership with service users and carers and other professionals to foster dignity, choice and independence, and effect change (QAA 2008 para 4.6). We will go on to consider how you might go about achieving this.

Underpinning effective interprofessional and inter-agency collaboration should be sound partnerships with service users and carers. Watson and West (2006 p144) point out that this is not to be taken for granted, and warn of the danger of collusion between workers, *to the detriment of the service user's perspective [which] can emerge from an eagerness on the part of the workers to be seen to be sharing a common set of objectives and for relationships to be working well.* In order to avoid this pitfall partnerships must be built on *mutual cooperation, openness and equality* (Beresford et al. 2007 p223). Documenting examples of poor and good practice, they go on to say that partnerships should be about:

- sharing and promoting the idea of service user independence, choice and equality: a social model perspective;

- making working together easier, avoiding misunderstandings, by having planned processes and written agreements;

- providing a framework for negotiating arrangements for individual service users.

(Beresford et al. 2007 p223)

An important parallel is the statement that in order for partnerships to be successful service users need to understand the social worker role, be clear about the boundaries of the role and be clear about what is part of their role and what is not. This applies equally to social workers when working with other professionals and other agencies. It is essential that interprofessional and inter-agency collaboration is undertaken with a focus on partnerships with service users and carers.

Service users and carers were involved in the development of the social work degree in a wide range of capacities, from being involved in stakeholder focus groups (Barnes 2002; Beresford et al. 2007; Sadd 2011) and continue to be involved in the design, delivery and assessment of the social work degree (Wallcroft et al. 2012).

ACTIVITY 2.1

Reflect and make notes on the following questions. You may find it useful to revisit these notes as you prepare for practice learning and discuss them with your practice educator or workplace supervisor.

- *Why is it important to listen to service users and carers?*

- *How might they influence the types and qualities of services available?*

- *What are the possible problems with not taking account of their views?*

- *How might service users and carers develop your awareness of interprofessional and inter-agency working?*

- *How are service users and carers involved in the design, delivery and assessment of the qualifying course you are following? How will this experience help you to seek and take account of service users and carer views as a practitioner?*

A useful source to read to gain better understanding of these issues is a chapter written by service users from the user-led organisation Shaping Our Lives, who had a central role in developing the strategy of service user involvement in the social work degree (see Beresford et al. 2007). They use the social work degree as an example of good practice, in contrast to their reported experiences of poor practice in their interactions with a range of different professionals involved in service delivery. A national forum has been established called SWEP (social work education participation) and a benchmarking study has been undertaken into service user and carer involvement in the social work degree (Wallcroft et al. 2012).

As part of the SCIE initiatives, Sadd (2011) convened a focus group consisting of SWEP group members and service users and carers who acted as visitors in the former GSCC validation processes. The focus groups identified the following benefits for those involved.

- *Giving future social workers a sense of empathy and understanding of how it is to be in receipt of their services.*

- *Promoting an understanding of the power social workers have in their relationships with service users and carers.*

- *Helping to equalise the power imbalance between service users and carers, future service providers and educators.*

- *Increasing confidence and skill levels for future service providers (for example respect, listening, understanding), which may also enhance future career prospects.*

- *Promoting involvement in a wider society.*

- *Providing personal benefits to the health and well-being of the service users and carers involved.*

- *Moving service users away from the role of victim – 'We are more than our story'.*

- *Offering opportunities to identify current issues and gaps in existing social care provision.*

There is a growing body of publications into service user and carer involvement in the social work degree, and the origins and development of service user and carer involvement in social work practice with adults and children are set out clearly by Warren (2007).

Policy-based evidence or evidence-based policy?

It is important to distinguish between policy-based evidence and evidence-based policy. The first is where evidence is used to support or justify a policy retrospectively, the second is where evidence is used as a starting point to inform the development of policy. While government departments may be keen to make positive claims for the growing success of joined-up, integrated ways of working and of structuring and delivering services, it is important to consider this evidence in a more critical way. Government department sources could be accused of using a selective approach to 'evidence' informed by a strong bias in favour of its programme of reforms. It is in its interest to maintain the momentum and demonstrate that outcomes are being met by promoting evidence that supports this centrally led policy. The materials on government websites may not comment critically on the policy, nor offer alternative views or interpretations. These views have to be sought elsewhere. Important additional sources of evidence about interprofessional working are academic texts and articles in peer-reviewed journals and research findings from research bodies that are independent of the government, which offer an independent view about processes and outcomes.

This is a similar situation to the one you read about in Chapter 1 where we referred to the lack of a substantial evidence base for interprofessional education, and the assertion that it is policy driven rather than evidence informed and that the body of knowledge about the processes and outcomes of interprofessional education is in development.

REFLECTION POINT

Research-minded practice

You may wish to reflect on your learning so far on the qualifying social work course you are following about research-minded, or research-informed, practice and how practitioners can access, appraise and apply research findings in their practice to promote ways of working with service users, carers and other professionals that are based on what we know works. The research-mindedness resource hosted by SWAP, the Social Work and Social Policy subject centre (www.resmind.swap.ac.uk) provides materials to help you develop these skills and to support this approach.

Another important source of the growing evidence base for social work includes the materials commissioned and disseminated by the Social Care Institute for Excellence (SCIE) (www.scie.org.uk).

How equipped do you feel to be able to access, appraise and apply findings from research to your practice? How will you go about developing or updating these skills?

The growing evidence base – some snapshots

An evidence base for effective interprofessional working and partnership working with service users and carers is beginning to emerge.

RESEARCH SUMMARY

Several studies have indicated that historical differences in professional status and the organisation of services can lead to territorial attitudes to professional boundaries (Hudson 2002; Lymbery 2006; Townsley et al. 2004). Lymbery (2006) has drawn attention to the importance of social workers being able to challenge other services when older people may be experiencing dehumanising care. Additional time needs to be allowed for the decision-making process with other professionals and for co-ordination of services (Penhale 2007). Care must be taken to include service users and carers in decision-making in interprofesssional contexts (Beresford 2007).

Pessimistic versus optimistic models

Hudson (2002), in his discussion of what he calls 'interprofessionality' in health and social care, describes a 'pessimistic' model of interprofessional working resulting from literature which offers a sceptical view of whether it is possible to have effective collaborative practice between different professional groups. This is found in the literature and offers, as a result of the findings from research undertaken in the north of England, an 'optimistic' view. He is critical of the academic writers who have taken a sceptical or tentative position on interprofessionality and challenges them to undertake research that starts from a positive position.

He reminds us that top-down models of introducing and imposing policies (as with New Labour's 'Third Way' policies at the heart of the modernisation agenda, and those of the coalition government) may not properly take account of influence that frontline staff have on the success of these policies. This is complicated by the reality that the staff who make up the interprofessional teams and organisations operate on an individual, personal level using professional discretion as well as operating as part of an organisation and that these two things can be in conflict. Issues of professional identity, status, discretion and accountability are influential to the effectiveness of collaborative working. While a strong professional identity, for example as a social worker or nurse, might be seen as important, it has also been found that this can create barriers to collaborative working when the different professionals do not share the same beliefs about the contribution that each can bring to the team. This might be expressed as conflicts over beliefs about services being universal or means-tested/targeted, about the lack of clarity about team roles particularly where knowledge and skills overlap, misunderstandings about the relative merits of the medical and social models, polarisations of approaches based on deficits or strengths and concerns about reduced professional discretion and increased accountability.

The 'optimistic' view is based on three reasons.

- Normative reasons – that interprofessionality is a 'good thing' and the need for closer working to develop is a normal feature of organisations especially in a climate of increasing demands and limited resources.

- Policy reasons – the approach is policy-driven in health and social care and associated services, has a growing momentum and further research will help us to understand this way of working better. This reason seems to incorporate a view that interprofessional ways of working are inevitable.

- Academic reasons – given the inevitability of needing to work interprofessionally, academics are challenged to make 'a more constructive' contribution to the policy debates by testing out positive hypotheses.

Simple linear models versus complex and dynamic models

An action research project undertaken by Meads et al. (2003), commissioned by the London regional office of the DoH and undertaken on behalf of the CAIPE (the Centre for the Advancement of Interprofessional Education), looked at the facilitated introduction of partnership working in four primary care settings in London.

Lessons from the project demonstrated that the process of learning to work in partnership across professional boundaries was more complex than had been anticipated and that models to understand this process needed to take account of this complexity.

> *I reflected that a lot of partnership models assume an operational context that is ordered and sequential...not at all how partnership working is experienced in real life.*

(Meads et al. 2003 p 129)

It was also pointed out that differences between professionals can be viewed both as a source of conflict caused by professionals feeling marginalised and behaving in a defensive way, and as a source of creativity, producing opportunities to transform thinking and behaviour.

What helps or hinders?

Barrett and Keeping (2005) identify the following factors as being important in the development of interprofessional working, which provides the opportunity for collaborative social work practice.

- **Knowledge of professional roles**. It is important to be aware of the roles and responsibilities of other professionals as well as having a clear understanding of your own role. The material in the following chapters will help you to have a greater understanding of the professionals that you are likely to work with.

- **Willing participation**. Motivation for and commitment to collaborative practice are important if collaborative practice is to be achieved, along with expectations that are realistic and a positive belief in the potential effectiveness.

- **Confidence**. This refers to both personal confidence and professional confidence achieved through experience, built on a clear professional identity and an understanding of, and belief in, the particular role that social work can play.

- **Open and honest communication**. This includes active listening and constructive feedback that seek to clarify and develop understanding.

- **Trust and mutual respect**. This takes time to develop and is essential for people to feel 'safe' to deal with areas that are challenging or may lead to conflict.

- **Power**. A non-hierarchical structure where power is shared is a preferred model, but responsibility and accountability need to be clear. Power sharing can be difficult to negotiate and is complicated by power being located and experienced at the personal, professional and societal level.

- **Conflict**. Clear ground rules along with a reflective and open approach can help prevent and resolve conflict. Conflict can also produce creativity and energy.

- **Support and commitment at a senior level**. Change and support at all levels is a prerequisite for effective collaborative practice.

- **Professional culture**. Language, traditions and ideologies/perspectives associated with different professional groups may hinder collaborative working but also provide the opportunity for new viewpoints to be considered.

- **Uncertainty**. Uncertainty about roles, boundaries and future developments needs to be acknowledged.

- **Envy**. Tensions can arise from envy and rivalry between individuals and organisations, particularly when competing for resources and power.

- **Defences against anxiety**. Working with people with complex problems and in a complex structure can create anxiety that can become displaced onto other team members.

These have echoes of the barriers outlined by Bamford (1990) and Hudson et al. (1997) that we read about at the beginning of the chapter, but also combine the optimism suggested by Hudson (2002).

Professional identity and interprofessional working

The Munro Review (2011 para 6) recommended that the government *revise statutory, multi-agency guidance to remove unnecessary or unhelpful prescription and focus only on essential rules for effective multi-agency working and on the principles that underpin good practice* and, in order to promote *the exercise of professional judgment, local multi-agency systems will need to be better at monitoring, learning and adapting their practice* (para 18).

We will consider some aspects of good practice and introduce some techniques for effective interprofessional working.

Keeping (2006) considers how to maintain professional identity in an interprofessional and inter-agency setting, from the perspective of social workers in mental health settings and recommends the following.

- Staying integrated in the social work professional community by seeking and maintaining contact with other social workers.

- Staying connected with practice and sense of purpose through supervision and through a reflective approach, reflecting on your values, role and relationships. This might include remembering what it was that motivated you to become a social worker.

- Seeking clarity about the social work role and validation of the distinct social work contribution. This might be through discussions with colleagues and continuous professional development activities.

- Seeking help and guidance from managers, particularly when policies or procedures are having a detrimental effect on practice.

Whittington et al. (2009) set out four areas of assets that social workers can draw on when working with other professionals. These are:

- skills in fostering relationships;

- skills in presenting a case based on expertise in assessment;

- knowledge of resources;

- knowledge about other professions and agencies.

Knowledge about other professionals and the organisations in which they work, which you will develop by reading this book, will assist in enabling you to understand roles, services, structures and priorities in order to hold realistic expectations about each other's involvement in order to respect and value them and to demonstrate your credibility as a social worker. A useful approach is to reflect on differences and similarities and how this aids or hinders practice in an interprofessional or inter-agency context. This might consist of considering what social workers have in common with other professionals, what each professional's distinct contribution is, how roles, skills and resources may be complementary and by identifying the areas of tension and seeking to address them. Building relationships involves awareness of personal and professional attributes.

ACTIVITY **2.2**

Consider and make notes on the potential barriers to effective communication when talking to someone from another profession about a service user you are working with.

COMMENT

The things you have noted down might include some of the following points.

Uncertainty about role and responsibilities.

Differences in professional values.

Differences in priorities and purpose of the agency.

Differences in professional training.

Differences in levels of autonomy.

Different skills and expertise.

Different professional language.

(Adapted from Thomas et al. 2009)

Thinking about situations in which professional language might cause barriers, identify techniques and strategies that you can use to facilitate clear communication. A useful resource is that developed by Lefevre et al. (2008).

Your professional identity as a social worker and your skills in engaging with service users will also be viewed in terms of the organisation and team you are working in. A study by Beresford (2007 p22) pointed out that service users and carers *draw a distinction between individual practitioners working with them, for whom they often have praise and the statutory organisations in which they work, about which they are frequently highly critical.*

From the experiences of running interprofessional courses on psychotherapeutic skills for a wide range of professionals, Hornby and Atkins (2000 p5) tell us that problems affecting effective interprofessional practice include *the divisiveness of language, professional possessiveness, professional identity and the issue of responsibility for initiating contact with other workers* and that solutions should take into account structural and personal issues on an interprofessional, inter-agency and interpersonal level. Hornby and Atkins (2000 p25) also emphasise that *restructuring professions and agencies can never provide the whole answer, and where there are complex problems there will also be a need for highly skilled collaboration between faceworkers* [the individuals who work face to face], and that failures in collaborative working can result from relationships between individual workers as well as factors to do with the organisation or agency.

When working with or consulting other professionals you will need to evaluate the range of perspectives and expertise that others bring to the situation and their knowledge about this particular service user or family and you may give more weight to one person's view over that of others. This might be influenced by many factors including:

- their professional status and expertise;

- the extent of their previous contact or involvement with the service users;

- whether this previous contact was recent;

- your working relationship with them which could influence the way you 'hear' or value the information they provide;

- your level of confidence in working with other professionals.

(Quinney et al. 2009)

Evaluating the range of information about strengths and risk is not straightforward, as indicated by a research review undertaken by Wolstenholme et al. (2008) and it is important to clarify the information in order to guard against misinterpretation or misunderstanding.

Developing trust with social work colleagues, service users and carers, and other professionals is essential, as is being able to challenge constructively. This is explored in detail by Thomas et al. (2009). You might like to undertake the self-assessment exercise in the concluding section to this resource, and discuss your responses with colleagues or with your practice educator. The self-assessment exercise includes questions about constructive negotiation strategies and assertiveness skills, particularly in putting your views across to a more senior colleague from another profession when there is a difference of opinion. Being assertive and confident with other professions is essential for developing effective safe practice.

CHAPTER SUMMARY

In this chapter we have looked at the claims made by the government and by academic researchers and writers about learning for and implementing effective collaborative practice, and emphasised that skills for appraising and using research in practice are important if a critical and balanced approach is to be taken to preparing for the realities of collaborative practice, and that in aiming for collaborative advantage, we should be aware of the pitfalls of collaborative inertia.

Some important messages emerged from the action research project undertaken by Meads et al. (2003) including that *there is no single correct model of interprofessional and interagency learning and development, but that research and experience are available to help; and the people involved are key* (Meads et al. 2003 p132). Given the support provided for the development of partnership working through facilitators in this project to consider one aspect of the reform of public services *it was hard … to escape the conclusion that the delivery of these policies is more fragile than currently acknowledged in central government departments* (p134). However, by being enthusiastic about interprofessional working you will find you are more open to the challenges of liaison, negotiation and co-ordination that this form of working brings.

In the following chapters we will be looking at the different contexts for interprofessional practice and learn about the roles, responsibilities, values and organisational structures of other professional groups that you are likely to work with, in order to break down barriers between professionals through increased understanding. While actively working through these chapters will help to prepare you for interprofessional social work, it is only through experience, in practice learning placement and in working environments on qualification as a social worker, that you will develop the essential face-to-face relationship-based, organisation-based and community-based skills underpinned by social work values in order to become an effective practitioner.

FURTHER READING

Pollard, KC, Thomas, J and Miers, M (eds) (2010) *Understanding interprofessional working in health and social care.* Basingstoke: Palgrave.

This edited text explores some of the theoretical underpinnings to interprofessional working as well as drawing attention to some accounts of interprofessional working.

Morris, K (ed.) (2008) *Social work and multi-agency working: Making a difference.* Bristol: Policy Press

A very useful text on policy, practice and research.

The Journal of Interprofessional Care This international peer-reviewed journal aims to 'promote collaboration within and between education, practice and research in health and social care', including education, health, housing, justice and social services.

WEBSITE

www.scie.org.uk/publications/elearning/communicationskills/index.asp

Trevithick, P, Lefevre, M and Richards, S (2008) *Communication skills.* London: Social Care Institute for Excellence.

www.scie.org.uk/publications/elearning/ipiac/index.asp

Whittington, C, Thomas, J and Quinney, A *Interprofessional and interagency collaboration*. London: Social Care Institute for Excellence.

www.resmind.swap.ac.uk

A website to help you become research-minded in your approach to practice. Case studies addressing themes of mental health, older people, and children and families help students and practitioners apply theory to practice.

Chapter 3
The youth work context

This chapter will help you to develop the following capabilities, to the appropriate level, from the **Professional Capabilities Framework**.

- **Contexts and organisations.** Understand the inter-agency, multi-disciplinary and interprofessional dimensions to practice and demonstrate effective partnership working.
- **Professionalism.** Identify and behave as a professional social worker committed to professional development.
- **Values and ethics.** Apply social work ethical principles and values to guide professional practice.
- **Diversity.** Recognise diversity and apply anti-discriminatory and anti-oppressive principles in practice.
- **Rights, justice and economic well-being.** Advance human rights and promote social justice and economic well-being.
- **Knowledge.** Apply knowledge of social sciences, law and social work practice theory.
- **Judgement.** Use judgement and authority to intervene with individuals, families and communities to promote independence, provide support and prevent harm, neglect and abuse.
- **Critical reflection and analysis.** Apply critical reflection and analysis to inform and provide a rationale for professional decision-making.
- **Contexts and organisations.** Engage with, inform and adapt to changing contexts that shape practice. Operate effectively within your own organisational frameworks and contribute to the development of services and organisations. Operate effectively within multi-agency and interprofessional settings.
- **Professional leadership.** Take responsibility for the professional learning and development of others through supervision, mentoring, assessing, research, teaching, leadership and management.

See Appendix 1 for the Professional Capabilities Framework diagram.

It will also introduce you to the following standards as set out in the 2008 social work subject benchmark statement.

5.1.1 Social work services, service users and carers.
5.1.2 The service delivery context.
5.1.3 Values and ethics.
5.1.5 The nature of social work practice.
5.7 Skills in working with others.

Introduction

According to the National Youth Agency (2012):

> *the main purpose of youth work is the personal and social development of young people and their social inclusion. Youth work helps young people learn about themselves, others and society through non-formal educational activities that combine enjoyment, challenge, learning and achievement.*

Youth workers usually work with young people in the age range of 13–19 but sometimes this is extended to young people up to the age of 24. The National Youth Agency has estimated that in the region of 60% of young people have contact with youth services at some point between the ages of 11 and 25 (NYA 2006 p2).

Professionally qualified youth workers undertake a programme of higher education study, validated by the National Youth Agency, to achieve a recognised degree-level qualification with many similar areas of study to a qualifying social work or teaching course. Professionally qualified youth workers work alongside youth support workers who will have, or be undertaking, a range of vocational qualifications.

According to the QAA benchmarks for Youth and Community Work (2009 para 2.1):

> *Youth and community work is a practice of informal and community education that involves the development of democratic and associational practices, which promote learning and development in the communities or individuals who choose to take part in the programmes that youth and community workers facilitate and support. It is focused on work with adolescents and adults, with groups as well as individuals, and with personal development in the context of the development of wider social networks and collective engagement with issues of social justice.*

The benchmark statements include working with adults, as frequently the professionally qualifying programmes address both youth work and community work. There is an emphasis on participatory methods and both social and personal development. As is the case with social work, there are many types of youth work. Youth work is carried out by a wide range of local authority and voluntary organisations in various forms including centre-based, project-based, activity-based, mobile, detached and outreach work. It has many parallels with social work and with some aspects of teaching but is a distinct activity and profession, and this can be understood more clearly by looking at the history of the youth service. The case study developed in this chapter provides a snapshot of some of the services a local youth advice and information project can offer and illustrates how youth workers can be involved in similar situations to social workers, working with issues that confront young people which social workers will be familiar with.

As in social work:

> *partnership and multi-disciplinary working is a very important contemporary aspect of this field of practice. Students need to understand the specific knowledge, skills, practices and responsibilities associated with their role, and to develop confidence in that role in the context of their contribution to partnerships, integrated teams and multi-professional practice.*

(QAA 2009 para 3.5)

RESEARCH SUMMARY

Around 1 in 10 children and young people are diagnosed with a mental health condition (YoungMinds 2012).

Figures published by the Department for Education for 2012 indicate that 7.3 per cent of 16- to 18-year-olds were not in education, employment or training (NEET). The rates increased with age: 2.3 per cent of 16-year-olds, 6.8 per cent of 17-year-olds and 12.4 per cent of 18-year-olds. The coalition government have described this situation as a ticking time bomb (DfE 2012).

CASE STUDY

Steve and Bob

Steve has reluctantly visited the local youth information and advice drop-in centre, accompanied by Nick who has used the centre. He has been sleeping on the floor of another friend's flat and after a dispute he has been asked to find somewhere else to stay. Steve is unemployed and is estranged from his family. He tells the youth worker that he feels depressed and lonely and is anxious about what is going to happen to him. After a confidential discussion when advice and information on a range of issues, including housing, mental health, employment and courses is provided, Steve is encouraged to stay in the warmth of the centre rather than wander around the town, and Bob the youth worker invites him to a game of pool with him while getting to know him better. The youth worker, Bob, notices that Steve has a rapport with some of the other young people and suggests he comes back the following evening. Nick lives with his parents, who agree to Steve staying overnight.

Some weeks later, having followed up the information and contact numbers provided and supported by Bob, Steve has been offered accommodation in a local housing project for young people, has enrolled for a college computer course and is regularly attending the drop-in sessions. He has offered to help Bob, the youth worker, to develop a website for the project. He is still experiencing feelings of anxiety and depression and has arranged to talk to the nurse who runs the health clinic sessions provided at the drop-in centre. The relationships he had made through coming to the drop-in centre have helped him to feel more positive about the present and the future and he has begun to talk to Bob about the reasons why he is estranged from his family.

A brief history – Philanthropists and early youth organisations

Youth work pioneers, in a similar way to those involved in the organisations that are the forerunners of social work (the Charity Organisation Society and the Settlement movement), were often upper- and middle-class philanthropists targeting working-class young people, with a religious, social and moral zeal (Gilchrist et al. 2001, 2003). Jeffs and Smith

(2002) identified five traditions in the early youth work pioneers, whose ideals inform current practice. These they describe as the Romantics, the Conservatives, the Socialists and Radicals, the Evangelists and the Idealists. You might like to refer back to the book by Nigel Horner (2012) in this series for a discussion of the parallel historical developments in social work and to consider to what extent these five traditions are represented in the development of social work services and the legacy of these origins.

Historical milestones

The outbreak of the Second World War in 1939 also marked the beginnings of the youth service with two key policy documents being issued by the Board of Education which were concerned with organisational issues and with the philosophy and purpose of youth work. In 1939 the first of these, Circular 1486 *The Service of Youth*, provided for 14 voluntary youth organisations, including many which are still in existence today (Boy Scouts Associations, Girls' Friendly Society, National Federation of Young Farmers Clubs, Boys' Brigade, YMCA and YWCA), to be represented on youth committees established to develop local youth provision in the form of after-school and after-work services for young people.

This was important in that it marked an official acceptance of the independent and charitable organisations' remit to work informally with young people outside of their working hours. It recognised that youth organisations were an educational resource, and provided funds for the hire of premises and the training of staff.

The 1940s and 1950s

In 1940 *The Challenge of Youth* (Circular 1516) stated that the general aim that linked all youth organisations and schools was *the building of character: this implies developing the whole personality of the individual boys and girls to enable them to take their place as full members of a free society.* It sought to clarify that the role of the state was *to supplement the resources of existing national organisations without impairing their independence* – to fill the gaps and not replace voluntary activity (Davies 1999a p20).

During the early 1940s the Board of Education saw youth work as a fourth arm of the education service in addition to primary, secondary and adult education. Chapter 4 discusses collaborative working with colleagues from the education services.

The 1944 Education Act established the state's role in relation to the youth service; the local authority had to secure *adequate facilities for leisure time occupation* (s41) and the local authority was to have *regard to the expediency of cooperating with any (appropriate) voluntary bodies or societies* (s53). Significantly, the Act did not refer to the Youth Service – it was a service without a name or title. According to the detailed account by Davies (1999a p26) in 1948 there were approximately 1,800 full-time youth leaders in post. Local Education Authority youth centres saw rapid growth in provision; 900 in 70 local authorities out of 113 were identified in a 1949 inquiry. However, by the end of the 1950s the number of full-time youth leaders had fallen (to 825 by 1953 and 700 by the end of the decade) and there was not yet a nationally recognised structure for training and qualifications.

The Albemarle Report 1960

The Albemarle Report, *Youth Service in England and Wales* (1960), provided radical, innovative and energising proposals for the future of the youth service, including young people as partners in the service, a 10-year development programme, a training college to be established with clear links to social work and teaching, Ministry of Education grants for 'experimental and pioneering work', and the collection and collating of research on young people. Smith (1999, 2002) describes how the report awakened youth workers to the opportunities that could be provided by the large youth club or youth centre. The Albemarle Report (1960) emphasised that *the primary aims of the youth service should be association, training and challenge* and that the youth service should provide *an opportunity for commitment...an opportunity for counsel...an opportunity for self-determination through young people associating in groups* (Smith 1999, 2002 p6). This led to what has been described as a *golden age for youth work in England and Wales* (Infed 2012).

There were claims that the welfare state had led to *a better paid, better fed, better clothed, more comfort loving and gadget using youth* (Longland, in Davies 1999a p40), and Davies reminds us that in a House of Lords debate in 1959 there were concerns expressed about anti-social behaviour and juvenile crime, sexual relationships, alcohol abuse, pressures of the commercial world, and young people unguided by traditional values – concerns that resonate today, particularly in the debate about anti-social behaviour. This was exacerbated in the 1960s with the growth of a definable youth culture which was characterised by a different value base to that of their parents and new-found material wealth.

This was an important and optimistic era for education and consequently in 1963 the Robbins Report on Higher Education was to encourage widening participation in higher education.

1969 – a landmark year

In 1969 the Children and Young Persons Act and the Fairbairn–Milson Report, *Youth and Community Work in the '70s*, were published. The Fairbairn–Milson Report considered not only what sort of youth service do we want but what sort of society. According to Davies (1999a) it was influenced by the work of Etzioni and his concept of communitarianism, which was later to influence New Labour. The report advocated community development as an appropriate method for interacting with young people based on a radical rethinking of the role of young people in society.

The Thatcher years

However, the Labour Party lost the 1970 election and Margaret Thatcher became the Secretary of State for Education in the Conservative government. Youth work began to lose some of its independence and state provision became more prominent, and its location in local authority structures became unclear – belonging sometimes in education, sometimes in leisure and recreation. The targeting of areas of deprivation and the need for accountability and outcomes further compromised the principle of the voluntary nature of young people's involvement. The Thatcherite policies of minimum public expenditure resulted in cutbacks in the youth service and Margaret Thatcher's belief that 'there is no such thing as society' had a profound impact, while the Conservative government policies in general in relation to young people attempted to influence them to take up the values and beliefs of the 'new right'. Employment policies were employer-led, the national curriculum in schools encouraged conformity, Income Support provision was punitive, and child care services were seen as an integral part of law and order services.

The Thompson Report 1982 – important changes

The Thompson Review, which resulted in the Thompson Report 1982 *Experience and Participation; Report of the Review group on the Youth Service in England*, aimed to address the treatment of young offenders, full time schooling, vocational education as well as more central youth work issues. The Thompson Report found that full-time youth worker posts were predominantly held by men but women held the majority of part-time posts, and the number of people from ethnic minority groups was small. Only a quarter held specific youth and community work qualifications and the most common qualification held was a teaching qualification. After 1988 qualified teacher status would no longer offer automatic youth work qualification and the establishing of additional college and university-based education and training courses aimed to fill the gap.

Issues-based youth work

The focus then became one of issues-based work, for example unemployment, poverty, homelessness and law and order, and of offering a critique of the policies of the conservative government by speaking out for young people and the issues that affected them. For example, the Conservative government was very suspicious of community-based approaches and diversionary methods, particularly in relation to young offenders, which was known as Intermediate Treatment.

CASE STUDY

A group of ten young people were identified by their social workers, youth workers and teachers as demonstrating behaviour that placed them at risk of family breakdown, school exclusion or committing offences. Led by a youth worker and social worker supported by trained volunteers from the local community and employing groupwork skills, the group met weekly. The programme consisted of indoor and outdoor activities to build relationships, confidence and self-esteem along with discussion and activities to explore the aspects of their behaviour which were causing concern and to begin to address them. A residential weekend experience in basic accommodation provided an opportunity for sustained and in-depth activity-based work alongside issues-based work.

Intermediate Treatment was later redefined as part of a strategy of custodial provision and at the same time detached work was seen as a way of reducing youth crime. However, without a clear base of evidence-based or research-minded practice, many youth work initiatives lacked focus. The Audit Commission Report *Misspent Youth* (1996) highlighted the potential for youth work and youth workers to have a key role in tackling youth crime. Later initiatives included public health projects related to drug use and abuse.

The role of young women and black and Asian young people continued to be important and later the needs of young people with disabilities and those of gay and lesbian young people provided new focus for youth work services.

By the mid-1990s youth councils and youth forums became a popular vehicle for encouraging participation and consultation in decision making by young people, as did peer education projects.

ACTIVITY 3.1

Undertake a literature search to identify some current examples of participation and consultation with service users in youth projects and in social work projects with young people. Identify the following learning points for your future practice.

- *What are the advantages of user participation?*

- *What are the challenges for the agency and worker to ensure that this is not token involvement?*

- *How can participation by young people be supported?*

COMMENT

Some tips for undertaking a literature search.

This can be done electronically using the internet, but needs to be carried out systematically if you are to access appropriate social work and youth work resources. To practise the skills of electronic searches there is a useful free online tutorial available, the Internet Social Worker (www.vts.rdn.ac.uk/tutorial/social-worker).

If you have electronic access to journals through your library website, this is a useful place to start. In order to read the full text of journal articles you may need to register through your university library for an ATHENS password.

Resources can also be found using databases such as Social Care Online (www.scie-social-careonline.org.uk).

You may come across a report published in 2010 by the Local Government Group and the National Youth Agency entitled Valuing young voices, strengthening democracy: the contribution made by youth engagement *which will help to identify some of the issues involved.*

The impact of New Labour policies

With the advent of New Labour in 1997 there was anticipation that youth work would have a more prominent role. In its early years the government responded to some important youth issues. These included the White Paper *Excellence on Schools* and its concerns with failing and disruptive pupils; the Green Paper *The Learning Age*; the Select Committee report *Disaffected Children*; the New Deal initiative – one of the targets of which was young unemployed people; the Report *Misspent Youth* which would establish youth offending teams; the launch of the Millennium Volunteers; a strategy for tackling drug misuse; and concerns with rough-sleeping, teenage suicides, and the experience of being in care. New Labour's Social Exclusion Unit and the New Deal for Communities also stressed participation and joined-up policy-making and implementation.

The Youth Service became the subject of an audit in 1998, developed from a collaboration between the National Youth Agency, the Local Government Association and the Standing Conference of Principal Youth and Community Workers. One of the key areas considered was the extent to which partnership working and partnership funding was a reality and six key issues were identified. These were:

1. *challenges* to the service;

2. a need for *clarification* of purpose;

3. *coherence*;

4. the *centrality* of young people;

5. the need to embrace *change*;

6. *consistency* of performance.

(Davies 1999b p166)

These features are not dissimilar to the challenges facing social work at the same time and which were central to introduction of the modernisation agenda. However, the hope that the Youth Service would finally become statutory – that local authorities would have mandatory rather than permissive powers to provide a service – was not to be realised, and has not been realised since.

Interprofessional and inter-agency working is an important theme in youth work, as in social work. Partnership and multi-disciplinary working is a very important contemporary aspect of this field of practice. Students need to understand the specific knowledge, skills, practices and responsibilities associated with their role, and to develop confidence in that role in the context of their contribution to partnerships, integrated teams and multi-professional practice (QAA 2009 para 3.5).

Partnership working

An example of partnership working is the Advice and Information Centre where the youth worker Bob is based, who we met earlier in this chapter. It is funded through a partnership of statutory and voluntary organisations, including the county youth service, the district council and a local charity. Health services, including a sexual health clinic, are provided by the local NHS trust, the post-care social worker is able to use the centre to meet with care leavers, young single mothers are supported by the provision of drop in sessions led by a play worker, a social worker from the drug and alcohol team is available for advice and support. Outreach work is provided to offer support to young people who prefer not to visit the drop-in sessions. It is recognised that young people are more likely to access services delivered through this dedicated advice and information centre than by self-referral to a range of agencies. The work undertaken is supported by a team of trained volunteers and young people form part of the management committee.

Transforming Youth Work 2002

In 2002 the Department for Education and Skills published its plans for the Youth Service in England, *Transforming youth work – Resourcing excellent youth services*, a further stage of the 'modernisation' agenda. It set out to promote:

> *the social, moral, cultural, emotional and physical development of young people, involve young people in the governance of relevant services and encourage young people's preparation for the responsibilities, opportunities and expectations of adulthood and citizenship.*

(DfES 2002 p 8)

However, the plans confirm *the movement towards bureaucratization, accreditation and targeting* (Smith 2002 p1) and have *tipped the balance significantly away from the forms of relationship and approach that have been central to the development of youth work.* Smith (2002 pp6–12) identifies fundamental problems under the following headings.

- Centralisation, narrowness and the Connexions agenda.

- Targeting.

- Accreditation.

- Delivery rather than relationship.

- Individualisation.

- Bureaucratisation.

He expresses his concerns that the traditional role of youth work, occupying a middle ground between social work and teaching, will become eroded as youth workers find themselves becoming involved either in assessment and intervention work normally in the social work domain or in delivering curriculum-based services associated with the formal education domain.

The 2005 Green Paper – *Youth Matters*

Youth Matters, the Green Paper for young people that was expected in November 2004, was finally published on 18 July 2005. It was warmly welcomed by the National Youth Agency though a cooler and critical response was published on the Informal Education, infed, website. The Green Paper builds on the Department for Education and Skills (2004) five-year strategy for children and learners, on the report *Transforming youth work: Resourcing excellent youth services* (2001) and importantly on the Green Paper *Every Child Matters* (2003). The National Youth Agency in its review of *Youth Matters* states that it *strikes a good balance between continuity and change; it deals with complex, cross-cutting themes; it finds some welcome warm words for youth work as a form of professional intervention* and places the responsibility of *working in partnership with others* on local authorities. These 'others' include social services, housing, education, and justice aspects of the local authority and also private and voluntary-sector organisations and community groups. The proposals indicate that the Connexions service could remain as a brand but the responsibility for their work will move to local authorities and be divided between schools and colleges on the one hand and Children's Trusts on the other. Central to the vision of the Green Paper is the co-ordination of services through Childrens' Trusts working to ensure the achievement by all young people of the five outcomes set out in *Every Child Matters*, namely:

- being healthy;
- staying safe;
- enjoying and achieving;
- making a positive contribution;
- achieving economic well-being.

There is an emphasis on integrated and co-ordinated services, of partnership working and the importance of young people being involved in decision-making (service user involvement) – themes familiar in social work. Moseley (2005, p31) in her summary of the Green Paper proposals, envisages multi-disciplinary assessment teams to remove *the confusion and duplication young people currently face of having to attend appointment after appointment to repeat their story time and time again* and a system of support for young people which does not depend on their status as care leavers, truants or offenders.

ACTIVITY 3.2

- *Thinking about Bob and Steve who we met earlier, research the services available in your local area and draw up a list of the options available to Steve and the agencies he would need to visit.*

- *What impact would a multi-disciplinary assessment team have on Steve's attempts to secure accommodation, education or training, financial support and health services?*

- *From what professional backgrounds might the staff in the multi-disciplinary team be drawn?*

- *What knowledge, skills and values would you as a social work student be able to contribute to this team?*

COMMENT

The material in Chapters 1 and 2 will be useful for answering these questions.

Smith (2005 p13) described the Green Paper as *fundamentally flawed and deeply problematic* and pointed to five areas of critique.

- Young people are treated not as citizens but as consumers.

- The civil liberties of young people are eroded.

- There is an over emphasis on the school as an organisation.

- There will be increased charging for leisure activities.

- The 'tyranny of joined-up thinking' is evident in the proposals.

(Smith 2005 p19)

This last point is important to an understanding of collaborative practice and a theme introduced in Chapter 1.

What is of particular relevance is that the voluntary and independent sector of youth work has been a key feature throughout and is fundamental to policy and practice. In parallel with this, unlike school education, local authority child welfare and juvenile justice, youth work continued to be based on voluntary involvement. In order to target young people the service needed to maintain its relevance to young people and draw them into 'membership'. Alongside this has been the concern about how to reach and work with 'unattached' young people, those who do not see the relevance of joining clubs or attending centres.

Aiming high for young people: A ten-year strategy for positive activities (2007)

This policy restated much of what was contained in Youth Matters and the Connexions strategy, and while providing some well-needed additional funding for youth work activity it can be seen as fundamentally flawed in not taking account of some of the key principles that underpin youth work, such as a sense of community, developing civil society and social capital.

Nolan (2003 pvii), in his introduction to the Youth and Policy retrospective collection of articles across twenty years of this journal, points out that *Youth work has suffered for many years from being marginalised, underestimated, disparaged, exploited and misrepresented.* This might also be said of social work.

ACTIVITY 3.3

Make notes on how the quotation above from Nolan (2003) might be similar to and different from social work, giving examples of both.

Why might this be the case? For example, what social, political and legislative developments have taken place with a direct impact on social work that might help contextualise this situation?

COMMENT

Looking back across the last decade we can see examples of how social work is portrayed in the media. An article by Hopkins (2001), considering the media image of social work, pointed out that on television, social workers are almost invariably presented in roles that confirm suspicions that they are … incompetent, arrogant, or obstructive *and that while there have been a limited number of documentaries there have been no serials that focus on the work of social workers. While one national newspaper article (Peek 2005) described social workers as* child snatchers, *other articles have attempted to promote a more balanced image, for example the article by Benjamin (2005), which asked key people in social work about their views on the changes to the profession.*

More recently the Social Work Taskforce (2009) and the Social Work Reform Board (2010) have sought to address the poor public image of social work.

The Coalition government is also concerned with the challenges faced by young people but with a different focus.

ACTIVITY 3.4

Visit the website of the Department for Education (www.education.gov.uk) and navigate to the section about young people.

- *What are the distinguishing features of current government policies that impact on young people?*

- *What impact might these policies have on social work with young people?*

- *In what ways have the voices of young people been taken into account?*

- *Returning to the case study where we met Steve and Bob, which agencies might be involved in supporting Steve and what role might Bob have in facilitating this?*

- *Construct a brief critical commentary on the policies you have found out about.*

> **COMMENT**
>
> *It is important to be aware of the inherent bias of government policy documents and to seek out commentaries and critiques of the policies. A useful source of critical commentary is the website infed.org.uk*

Positive for Youth: A new approach to cross-government policy for young people aged 13 to 19 (DfE 2011b)

In December 2011 the ambitious Positive for Youth strategy was launched which aims to bring together all government policies for young people aged 13 to 19, including youth services, education, housing, crime and health. This builds on the earlier document from the Department for Education (2011a), which aimed to address the problem of the large numbers of young people not in education, training or work. The Positive for Youth strategy includes clear statements about the expectations of engagement by a wide range of people and organisations.

* Young people – taking responsibility, making the most of every opportunity available, and speaking up on issues they care about.

* Parents, carers and families – having the primary responsibility and influence to nurture young people through to adulthood.

* Other adults – taking an interest in the lives of their young people and being positive role models.

* The media – taking responsibility for the impact of the images of young people they promote.

* Businesses – building partnerships through which to give time, expertise and money, to projects to support young people.

* Teachers – helping young people aspire and attain, and working in partnership with other services to address early any barriers they face.

* Youth workers – supporting young people's personal and social development and helping them develop strong aspirations.

* Other professionals – providing specialist early help to young people to address issues and stop them escalating and causing harm.

* Local authorities – having the primary responsibility for improving young people's outcomes and commissioning appropriate services.

* Other commissioners – having a responsibility for specific outcomes such as crime and health outcomes for young people.

* Government – promoting new ways of working, facilitating reform, and monitoring overall progress.

(DfE 2011b paras 3.5 to 3.16)

In the foreword to the policy document the minister states that it is *not a knee jerk reaction to the summer 2011 disturbances but a sustainable long term strategy from a Government that is unashamedly positive about our young people* (DfE 2011b foreword). He also emphasises that it is based on genuine partnership and developed in collaboration with young people and a wide range of stakeholders. A range of case studies are included in the policy document, including one on the mental health needs of looked-after children which illustrate the work already being done with young people in a wide range of settings and contexts. However, despite the positive messages there is no funding attached to the policy and it remains to be seen what is possible without financial support.

Debates

We will now move on to consider the parallel debates and contexts in social work and what impact they have on direct work with young people.

Debates in youth work (Davies 1999a) include:

- universal versus selective provision;
- education versus welfare;
- professional versus volunteer;
- voluntary versus state;
- proactive versus reactive;
- purchaser-led versus provider-led services;
- personal versus structural factors.

These debates take place in the context of concerns about changes in the way in which the service is structured and administered, changes in the perceptions about young people, changes in the methods used in the delivery of the service, the resources available (including funding), the changes in education and training qualifications for those involved in delivering the service. Some of these debates may be familiar to you as a social work student or practitioner as they capture the tensions and dilemmas in delivering effective services while adhering to the jointly agreed International Federation of Social Workers and International Association of Schools of Social Work (2000) definition of social work, which seeks to uphold social justice.

The social work profession promotes social change, problem solving in human relationships and the empowerment and liberation of people to enhance well-being. Utilising theories of human behaviour and social systems, social work intervenes at the points where people interact with their environments. Principles of human rights and social justice are fundamental to social work.

The relationship between social work, formal education and youth work

In the development of social work, youth work and education services, youth work contrasted with social work in the following ways.

- A group/collective experience rather than individual experience.

- The club–member rather than client–worker as the central relationship.

- A belief that social and individual change is to be developed through collective, not individual, efforts.

It contrasts with formal education provision in the following ways.

- It is based on voluntary attendance and involvement.

- The programme of social and educational activity is flexible and negotiable.

- It is informed by a liberal education model and not an employment-led model.

(Jeffs and Smith 2002)

The collective v the individual approach

Jeffs and Smith (2002) also raise concerns about the undermining of the fundamental characteristics of youth work, the concern with association and the collective (the gang, the group, the club) and the replacement of this with a focus and emphasis on the individual with individualised interventions such as advice work, mentoring and counselling. They see this as reflecting a *deep pessimism, on the part of this and the previous government, regarding the capacity of social welfare and education to change the behaviour and social mores of what has been termed the 'underclass'* (Jeffs and Smith 2002 p55).

ACTIVITY **3.5** *continued*

- *How do workers reconcile issues of race, sexuality, gender, disability, the disaffected/ hard to reach, rural isolation, etc., in both fields?*

- *What political perspectives might inform social work and youth work with young people?*

- *What methods of intervention are appropriate for working with young people – for example community work, group work, individual work?*

COMMENT

This activity will have helped to highlight the complementary and common (transprofessional) aspects of social work and youth work.

Youth work provision varies enormously and is delivered by a diverse range of agencies, across the statutory and voluntary sectors, some of which may be part of national organisations while reflecting local needs, traditions and agendas, whereas some may be local, independent projects and organisations. The following activity is intended to provide you with a working knowledge of local provision.

ACTIVITY **3.6**

Visit the website of your local authority youth service and that of a voluntary-sector youth group in your area to find out about the services they provide and the values they promote.

For example the Dorset Youth Support (www.dorsetcc.gov.uk) website contains detailed information for young people and youth work staff, including the values informing the service; information about the centres and projects, support groups, and information about participation.

COMMENT

Voluntary-sector provision might include faith-based groups, environmental organisations and international organisations such as the Scouts. The YMCA website (www.ymca.ac.uk) contains information and links to a range of projects, and the publication Inside Youth Work *(Rogers, 2003) can be downloaded, containing many case studies of youth projects and individual young people engaged in youth work.*

Consider the practice learning experiences you have been engaged in or are planning to undertake.

- *How might you promote the involvement of young people in the work undertaken by the agency?*

- *In what ways might youth work provision complement the work you undertake as a social worker?*

- *What knowledge, skills and values will you draw on to enable you to work creatively and effectively with young people?*

The riots of 2011 and the implications for youth work and social work

Smith (2011 p2) has described the riots that took place in England in August 2011 as one of the most serious incidences of civil unrest in a generation, and identifies five different aspects; protest, rioting, looting, damage and spectating, and that *deep-seated economic, social and cultural change combined with flawed policies and approaches concerning young people and marginalised neighbourhoods, and with some initially counter-productive responses, to create an explosive mix.*

RESEARCH SUMMARY

- *41% of suspects who appeared in court in the first week were living in one of the top 10% of most deprived places in the country.*

- *66% of neighbourhoods where the accused live had become poorer between 2007 and 2010. The majority were not in employment, education or training (around 91% of the first 1000 cases).*

- *Youth unemployment and child poverty were significantly higher than the national average and education attainment was significantly lower in almost all the worst affected places where riots took place (Institute of Public Policy Research 2011).*

- *The majority were young men from socially deprived neighbourhoods.*

In his analysis of the riots which explores and critiques the themes of inappropriate policing, inequality and materialism, moral collapse, social breakdown, and policy, Smith (2011 p12) makes four recommendations for youth workers which have relevance for social workers also.

1. *Being clearer about what youth work [or social work] is and offers; to shape their work appropriately; and to tell people about it.*

2. *Working for extended schooling, in particular provision of youth work [or social work] on-site support over the school holidays.*

3. *Developing, and making the case for streetwork – making contact with hard-to-reach young people in their communities.*

4. *Building civil society.*

REFLECTION POINT

How could your social work practice be extended to young people by advocating for responsive and appropriate services along the lines of those recommended by Smith (2011)?

Connexions

The Connexions service was established as a New Labour initiative to address social exclusion in young people (DfE 1999, 2000), but now has a much reduced presence. The service was delivered through an individualised approach, with personal advisors, rather than through a group, club or project and was primarily aimed at supporting young people to engage with education, employment or training. Connexions offices were often located in town centres and styled similar to shop premises to increase accessibility. Drawing on its origins in the New Labour Social Exclusion Unit, the focus was primarily on young people at risk of social exclusion, the unskilled and disaffected, rather than on the provision of a universal service of relevance for and benefit to all young people. An important targeted group were young people not in education, employment or training (NEET).

Personal advisors

At the centre of the Connexions service were personal advisors, whose role involved:

- working with young people to establish their needs and offer information, advice, support and guidance where necessary;

- helping young people face challenges that may affect their capacity to take part in learning and work opportunities;

- working with and supporting schools, colleges, training institutions and employers in designing a range of local courses that will meet the needs of young people;

- working with voluntary, statutory and community agencies and commercial bodies to ensure a co-ordinated approach to overcoming the barriers to learning and employment faced by young people;

- working with parents, carers and families to support young people;

- managing information effectively to facilitate the process of meeting the needs of young people; and

- reviewing and reflecting upon your own professional practice to achieve continuous improvement in performance.

(Connexions 2005)

The value base is founded on similar principles to social work and youth work, in that the welfare of children and young people is paramount, that diversity is respected, that stereotypes should be recognised and challenged and equality promoted at all times, and all work undertaken should be conducted with regard to confidentiality.

While on initial reading there may appear to be common areas with the role and values of a youth worker, the critique offered by Jeffs and Smith (2002) is that this way of working does not sit comfortably with the characteristics of youth work. They go so far as to state that this new emphasis is characterised by the following.

A change in emphasis

- From voluntary participation to coercion/surveillance.
- From association (including group work) to individualised approaches.
- From informal education to case management.
- From informal relationships to bureaucratic relationships.

A shift in resources

- From all young people to those facing multiple problems.
- From universal provision to targeted provision.
- From young women to 'troublesome' young men.

ACTIVITY 3.7

Obtain a copy of the Green Paper (2005) Youth Matters, *from the website of the National Youth Agency (www.nya.org.uk).*

Identify the areas that link to the five outcomes for children and young people proposed in the Green Paper (2003) Every Child Matters.

What are the possible implications for you as a social worker of the proposals relating to collaborative working in both Every Child Matters *and* Youth Matters?

COMMENT

The research publication The contribution of youth work to every child matters outcomes *published by the National Youth Agency (2006) may be helpful and for a critique of* Every Child Matters *in relation to youth work see Hoyle (2008)* Problematizing Every Child Matters, *the encyclopaedia of informal education.* www.infed.org/socialwork/every_child_matters_a_critique.htm.

Social work and youth work – Universal or targeted?

Youth work services can be considered as both universal and targeted. Jeffs and Smith (2002) believe that, in the increasingly managerialist and bureaucratised culture of statutory social work with an emphasis on standardised procedures and targets, the emphasis on the individual, who is often economically disadvantaged, has been detrimental to the social justice values of the profession. Previously the individualised approach was balanced with group work and community work approaches, but this is now less often the case in statutory agencies. However, the journal *Groupwork* emphasises that opportunities for groupwork practice in a range of settings are attracting renewed consideration by academics and practitioners.

ACTIVITY 3.8

Bearing in mind the views of Jeffs and Smith (2002) above, consider the practice learning opportunities that you have experienced as part of the programme on which you are studying.

- *What opportunities are there for engaging in individual, groupwork and community approaches?*

- *Refresh your knowledge and understanding of the social work methods of intervention that you have been introduced to on your course. Which are most suitable for an individual approach, a group approach and a community work/community development approach?*

- *How might the knowledge, skills and values associated with these methods be transferable across a range of settings?*

COMMENT

Students I currently teach have recommended the following texts as being particularly useful for learning about a range of approaches to working with individuals, groups and communities.

Trevithick P (2012) Social work skills and knowledge, a practice handbook. (3rd edn). Maidenhead: Open University Press

Teater B (2011) An introduction to applying social work theories and methods. Maidenhead: Open University Press

CHAPTER SUMMARY

In this chapter we have seen how youth work, which can be seen as occupying a space between social work and formal education, with similarities with and fundamental differences from both, has developed. You have also been introduced to, and been asked to actively consider, some of the common themes which pose challenges to the delivery of effective and meaningful services to young people. A critical stance in relation to current government policy has been encouraged, particularly in considering to what extent these policies enable or compromise the pursuit of social justice. Through a greater understanding of these themes you will be able to develop a sense of your professional identity as a social worker and understand more clearly the knowledge, skills and values that a social worker contributes to working with young people while gaining a clearer understanding of the contribution youth workers can make.

If you are interested in social history the following three books are highly recommended. These edited collections with contributions from academics and practitioners document the diverse history of youth and community work and bring to life the rich social history of this subject area.

Gilchrist, R, Jeffs, T and Spence, J (eds) (2001) *Essays in the history of community and youth work.* Leicester: Youth Work Press.

Gilchrist, R, Jeffs, T and Spence, J (eds) (2003) *Architects of change. Studies in the history of community and youth work.* Leicester: The National Youth Agency.

Gilchrist, R, Jeffs, T, Spence, J and Walker, J (eds) (2009) *Essays in the history of youth and community work: Discovering the past.* Lyme Regis: Russell House Publishing.

Smith, M (1988) *Developing youth work: Informal education, mutual aid and popular practice.* Milton Keynes: Open University Press.

This classic text is also available as an e-text via the archives section of the informal education website. www.infed.org/archives

A useful text that explains groupwork practice in social work but which is equally valuable when working with groups of young people.

Lindsay, T and Orton, S (2011) *Groupwork practice in social work.* 2nd edition. Exeter: Learning Matters

Furlong, A (2012) *Youth studies: An introduction.* London: Routledge.

Youth and policy *The journal of critical analysis.*

Groupwork *An interdisciplinary journal for working with groups.*

www.nya.org.uk

The website of the National Youth Agency. Policy documents can be accessed here, along with commentaries and responses, information about education, training, conferences and publications.

www.infed.org.uk

The Informal Education website containing a wealth of resources. The material on the website provides a critical commentary on areas central to youth work.

Chapter 4
The health context

The policy and service delivery framework

In order to appreciate the diverse roles, responsibilities and value bases of the range of health professionals, we will consider in this chapter the organisation of the National Health Service (NHS), the service delivery structures, and set these in a historical framework. The NHS, as its name implies, is a national centralised organisation. In this sense the structures through which healthcare is delivered have differed in a fundamental way from the traditional structures that determine and support the delivery of social work and social care. However, as we shall see in this chapter, in the last decade incremental changes leading to the restructuring of health service have led to much closer alliances between health and social care towards tackling social problems in a more holistic way. Prior to this, social work was predominantly organised and delivered by local authority, voluntary and independent-sector agencies and organisations that did not share a central overarching common identity with health. While all of these agencies have always had to adhere to the body of legislation and policy guidance that impact on the social work role, following a number of public inquiries and serious case reviews in different areas of social work there has been a subsequent radical reshaping of organisations, commissioning and contracting practice in the NHS. Services have become much more integrated with health, driven by legislation and policy guidance which asserts a more concerted move towards community-based provision. This chapter will provide a background history to developments in health in order to illustrate the significance of these changes in relation to collaborative practice both at an institutional, service and professional practice context starting with the original conception of the UK health service in 1948 up until the passing of the Health and Social Care Act 2012 which paints a very different picture indeed.

A brief history

The creation of the NHS 1948

In 1944 the Ministry of Health explained that the aim of the National Health Service (NHS) was

> *to ensure that everybody in the country – irrespective of means, age, sex and occupation – shall have equal opportunity to benefit from the best and most up-to-date medical and allied services available. To provide, therefore for all who want it, a comprehensive service covering every branch of medicine and allied activity.*

> (Ministry of Health 1944 p 47)

Although introduced by a Labour government, there was cross-party support for the NHS. At the time of its conception, William Beveridge (chair of the Inter-Departmental Committee on Social Insurance and Allied Services that produced the report, known as the Beveridge Report) believed that the NHS would address all health needs and create a healthy population leading to a reduction in the demand for health services. This optimism was partially thwarted when during the year following the introduction of the NHS in 1948, set up to be free and universal, prescription charges were introduced and shortly afterwards charges were introduced for dentistry and optician services, so great had been the unforeseen demand for false teeth and spectacles. You will need to refer back to Chapter 1 to remind yourself of the pivotal role played by Beveridge in the development of the modern welfare state.

The structure of this new NHS, intended to address the 'giant' of disease, was made up of three elements – general practitioners, local government and hospital authorities, a structure which was to last until 1974. See Figure 4.1.

- General practitioners (GPs), dentists, pharmacy and eye care services. Self-employed and funded from central government through executive councils.

- Community services. Focus on health promotion and preventative measures including environmental health, school health services and ambulances.

- Hospital services. Fourteen regional boards were created in England. Each reported to the Minister of Health and contained a medical school. Hospitals for both acute and chronic conditions were created.

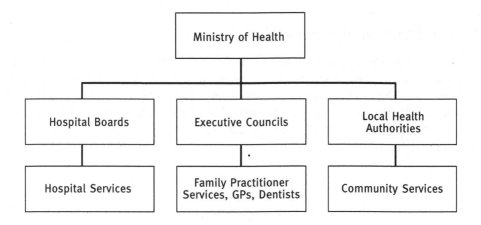

Figure 4.1 The structure of the NHS in 1948

GPs expressed hostility at the time to the plans to create a National Health Service and wielded considerable power in the negotiations. The contract they eventually agreed delayed the introduction of the NHS and this continuing power has been reflected in subsequent contract negotiations. For example, GPs were to remain independent of the local authorities, were able to combine private practice and NHS work, and argued for salary enhancements and for the power to influence at all levels the running of the NHS. GPs have maintained considerable professional autonomy and significant power particularly through their role in the development of Primary Care Trusts (PCTs) which were established to commission primary, community and secondary care from providers as well as to provide services directly through GP-led health centres.

Hospital-based doctors and community-based doctors were to have different contracts and it has been argued that *hospital-based medicine dominated at the expense of prevention, health promotion and community services* (Ranade, 1994, p9). These issues continue to be debated and are reflected in the current growth in interest in the theme of community in relation to health services (Swann and Morgan 2002; Henderson et al. 2004). The replacement of PCTs with GP-led consortia by 2013 for example, will see groups of GP practices coming together to commission services for local populations based on different and diverse models of health care.

In 1982, further changes to the structure and organisation of the NHS were made, with differences between the four UK countries. Alcock (2003 p62) points out that there was a concern amongst some analysts that the radical, anti-public welfare policies of the Thatcher governments would lead to a complete dismantling of the NHS, but this was not to be the case. Instead the NHS became subject to the new managerialist and market-driven culture in the public services and saw the appointment of managers rather than medical professionals to manage the administrative aspects of the NHS and the promotion of private medical insurance and private medical care. Writing in 1990, Bamford, a director of social services at the time, expressed the view that there *is a long history of tension between the health care professions and those services for which local authorities have had responsibility since 1948* (Bamford 1990 p128).

NHS and Community Care Act 1990

As a result of the NHS and Community Care Act 1990, the NHS was once again to be restructured, with an emphasis on market forces and the introduction of the purchaser/provider split. The providers were the NHS Trusts (hospitals, ambulance services and community services) and the purchasers were District Health Authorities. In social work settings, the NHS and Community Care Act 1990 is particularly important in the delivery of adult services. See Figure 4.2.

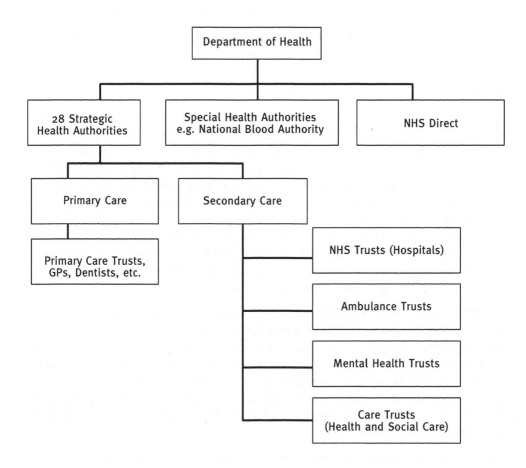

Figure 4.2 The NHS structure which followed the NHS and Community Care Act 1990

Department of Health

The central government department for the NHS is the Department of Health, which also has responsibility for social work and social care. It is headed by the Secretary of State for Health, appointed by the Prime Minister, and a member of the Cabinet, supported by ministers who are elected members of parliament with a wide range of discrete responsibilities for taking forward health and social care policies. Policies and priorities are politically driven but the ministers are advised and supported by other staff in the Department of Health who are civil servants and by staff who represent the professional groups in the NHS, for example nursing and dentistry, known as chief professional officers. Clinical experts have represented the NHS at the Department of Health in the capacity of national clinical directors. Some of their roles, for example in leading the implementation of National Service Frameworks, will be considered later. However, recent changes introduced by the Health and Social Care Act 2012 have reviewed these existing relationships between central government and local structures. In future the Secretary of State will set the strategic direction through a mandate given to an autonomous NHS Commissioning Board. This Board will help develop and support local commissioning groups led by GPs and hold them to account for improving outcomes for patients and getting the best value for money from the public's investment in health services.

Modernisation

As with social work and other public sector services, the NHS became a focus of the New Labour Modernisation Agenda, with the specially constituted Modernisation Agency working alongside the Department of Health which supported initiatives to improve the effectiveness and the quality of health services. An important document with modernisation as a central theme was *The new NHS: Modern and dependable* (DoH 1997), which can be considered to be a parallel document to the White Paper *Modernising Social Services: Promoting independence, improving protection, raising standards* (DoH 1998). Together these documents set out the vision and philosophy for health and social care, including social work, services.

What are health services and who provides them?

The NHS currently employs more people than any other organisation in the world, and in England and Wales employs aroud 1.3 million people.

An article published to mark the 60th anniversary of the NHS makes the following assertions.

- Staff across the NHS are in contact with more than 1.5 million patients and their families every day.
- Approximately 170,000 people go for an eyesight test each week.
- In 2005/06 the NHS helped to deliver around 16,000 babies at home.
- Almost a quarter of all babies born in 2005/06 were delivered by Caesarean section.

- Each month, 23 million people visit their GP surgery or practice nurse.

- In a typical week, 1.4 million people will receive help in their home from the NHS.

- Full-time GPs treat an average of 255 patients a week.

- NHS chiropodists inspect more than 150,000 pairs of feet every week.

- Seventy-five per cent of women aged 53 to 64 in England are screened for breast cancer at least once every three years.

- NHS Direct receives around 20 calls a minute. More than a million people called NHS Direct over the 2007 Christmas period.

- The NHS Ambulance Service received 6.3 million emergency calls in 2005/06, which is roughly 360 an hour.

- Community pharmacies dispensed 745 million prescription items in 2006/07.

- NHS ambulances make over 50,000 emergency journeys each week.

- There are now around 90 NHS walk-in centres, offering convenient access to services, including treatment for minor illnesses and injuries.

(Source: NHS Choices 2008)

The Department of Health is responsible for:

- setting overall direction and leading transformation of the NHS and social care;

- setting national standards to improve quality of services;

- securing resources and making investment decisions to ensure that the NHS and social care are able to deliver services;

- working with its key stakeholders to ensure the overall quality of services.

While the NHS is a UK-wide organisation, there are some differences within how this is organised and relates to other bodies in relation to social work and social care within its four countries. Below we elaborate on some of the parallel organisations within health and social care which have similar objectives and aims, some of which you may already be familiar with.

National Institute for Health and Clinical Excellence (NICE), Social Care Institute for Excellence (SCIE) and the Institute for Research and Innovation in Social Services (IRISS)

No credible health professional would deny that sound evidence about what works best in healthcare interventions should be an integral part of clinical decision-making. Keeping up to date and having involvement in research and generating knowledge have been linked since the 1990s to continuous quality improvement (DoH 2002b). The National Institute for Health and Clinical Excellence (NICE) was established in 1999 to ensure everyone has equal access to medical treatments and high-quality care from the NHS – regardless of where they live in England and Wales. NICE is a *single excellence-in-practice organisation* responsible for providing national guidance on the promotion of good health and the prevention and treatment of ill health (NICE 2008) through its three centres on public health matters, health technologies and clinical practice. NICE aims to take an active role in advising how to improve health and in setting standards for high-quality care through its production of clinical guidelines and public health recommendations (www.nice.org. uk). The work of NICE is not just aimed at the NHS but at local authorities and all those with a remit for improving people's health in the public, private, community and voluntary sectors by tackling a wide range of issues. NICE is advised by a Citizen Council made up entirely of members of the public. Further, *NHS Evidence* was launched in 2009 to manage the synthesis and spread of knowledge in the NHS. Its introduction has ensured that everyone working in health and social care has free access to the quality-assured, best-practice information required to inform evidence-based decision making, quickly and easily (www.evidence.nhs.uk/).

In social care a parallel organisation, SCIE, was established in 2005 to improve the lives of people who use care services by actively gathering and analysing knowledge about what works and to translate that knowledge into practical resources, by its free publication of learning materials and services. SCIE aims to improve the knowledge and skills of those working in care services including managers, frontline staff, commissioners and trainers as well as people who use services. SCIE works across the UK including England, Wales and Northern Ireland. In Scotland, The Institute for Research and Innovation in Social Services (www.iriss.org.uk/) performs a similar role.

Both organisations work closely with related services such as health care and housing, and examples of working together to reflect the importance of evidence-based practice in health and social care around single issues as exemplified in the publication of national guidelines on dementia (NICE and SCIE 2006). Given that the clinical aspects of dementia care are outside the remit of social care, 'guidance' according to Manthorpe and Iliffe (2007) can be seen as authoritative, detailed expectations with the force of regulations and policy documents. However, the guidance on dementia does contain both obligatory and aspirational elements towards achieving more 'person-centredness' in dementia services which demands collaboration at all levels. Manthorpe and Iliffe (2007) for example restate the importance of having a joint publication of the dementia guidelines for social workers in England, partly because support of people with dementia is central to all adult services, and partly because they represent a genuine attempt to combine health and social care provision in a key and growing area of practice.

Registration and regulation of care services for Adults – The role of the Health Care Commission

Since October 2010 following the passing of the Health and Social Care Act 2008, all existing and new English care providers have been required to register and comply with the regulations of the Care Quality Commission (CQC), who are the independent regulator of health and adult social care services in England. Prior to this, there were separate arrangements for health which was provided by the Commission for Health Care Audit and Inspection (CHAI) and the National Care Standards Commission (CSCI) as well as the Mental Health Act Commission. The wholesale separation of services for adults and children in England following Every Child Matters in 2003 and the subsequent structural arrangements for developing children's trusts and trusts for adult care for different user groups has called for more closely aligned arrangements for monitoring and evaluating the quality and performance of these diverse organisations and services. Ofsted is the main registration and regulatory body for children's services in England. In Wales, the Care and Social Services Inspectorate Wales (CSSIW) carries out its functions on behalf of the Welsh Assembly Government and in Scotland, this is done by the Social Care and Social Work Improvement Scotland (SCSWIS) who in turn regulate, inspect and support improvement of care, social work and child protection services. The websites for these different organisations are included in the recommended reading at the end of this chapter to enable you to check on the arrangements in your own country.

Within adult services, whether services are provided by the NHS, local authorities, private companies or voluntary organisations, the CQC has a central role to ensure that people's care meets national standards by driving improvement across health and social care and championing and protecting the rights of individuals using services. Their methodology of registration, inspection and regulation aims to gather and use knowledge and experience to encourage and support good practice as well as taking action to remedy bad practice (CQC 2010). The complete list of activities regulated by the CQC includes the following:

1. Personal care.

2. Primary medical services directly provided by an NHS trust or by organisations, other than an individual GP (from April 2012).

3. Accomodation for people who require nursing or personal care.

4. Accomodation for people who require treatment for substance misuse.

5. Accomodation and nursing or personal care in the further education sector.

6. Treatment of disease, disorder or injury.

7. Assessment or medical treatment for people detained under the Mental Health Act, 1983.

8. Surgical procedures.

9. Diagnostic and screening procedures.

10. Management of supply of blood and blood-derived products.

11. Transport services, triage and medical advice provided remotely.

12. Maternity and midwifery services.

13. Termination of pregnancies.

(CQC 2010 p14)

The CQC also provides an annual report on the State of Care which draws on key external sources of information about the services it registers and takes a broad view about the outcomes emerging for people using care services across the public, private and voluntary-sector providers by drawing on evidence from its regulatory activity and published national statistics. Some of the key findings from its 2010/2011 review are in the Research Summary below.

Key Themes from the CQC 2010–2011 report on the state of health care and adult social care in England

1. Bed capacity in NHS hospitals has continued to reduce and was just over 140,000. This reduction has been attributed in part, to moving treatment out of acute hospital settings to community settings as well as greater use of NHS day services..

2. Changes in adult social care provision have enabled people to live at home longer with a reduction of 10 per cent residential services between 2004–2010 and a corresponding increase of domiciliary care by a third.

3. The most common types of residential provision are for older people with dementia and people with a learning disability. 45 per cent of these are occupied by people funding themselves.

4. In 2011 there has been a slight deterioration in waiting times for hospital admissions whilst outpatient waiting times remain steady.

5. Demand for social care continued to rise with 2.12 million new contacts where 52 per cent resulted in a further assessment or commissioning of ongoing services. Reduction in social care budgets and increased demand has resulted in tightening of eligibility criteria for people to receive state-funded community care.

6. 32 per cent of NHS patients with a planned admission said they had been given a choice of hospital for their first appointment; 52 per cent felt they were 'definitely' involved as much as they wanted to be; 37 per cent said they were involved 'to some extent', and 11 per cent said that they were not involved as much as they wanted to be.

7. A higher percentage of NHS trusts have taken action on all equality strands, except religion and belief, compared to adult social care services, probably due to their increased capacity to undertake equality development work.

8. In relation to quality and safety Outcome 7 says that people can expect to be safeguarded from abuse or the risk of abuse, and their human rights respected and upheld. Independent hospitals and clinics met this outcome most readily, but failures in safeguarding of the most vulnerable remains of utmost priority for providers, commissioners and regulators. In both the NHS and adult social care, failure to comply with was one of the three most common reasons why warning notices were issued.

9. Significant improvements were made to eliminate mixed-sex accommodation in NHS hospitals.

10. There were year-on-year improvements in perceptions of hospital cleanliness and 96 per cent of patients interviewed had seen promotional information asking patients and visitors to wash their hands or use hand-wash gels.

Continued

11. *The 2011 survey of people who use community mental health services was completed by over 17,000 people aged 16 and over showed that overall, 29 per cent of respondents rated the care they had received as excellent, 30 per cent as very good and 20 per cent as good. The vast majority of participants said they were listened to and had trust in their health and social care workers. However, there is room for improvement, in involving people more in some aspects of their care.*

(CQC 2011 p1–7)

ACTIVITY **4.1**

Reflecting on the CQC themes – towards closer integration of health and social care

Based on your reading of the key themes from the CQC report, what do you think are the issues and challenges as health and social care services become more integrated both in the community and within its institutions? Where are further developments needed and are there any relevant to your immediate and current practice environment?

COMMENT

You may have reflected that while the interface between health and social care has improved considerably over the last few years, mounting demands in care budgets may have an adverse influence on progress made with consequences that even fewer people will receive the care and support they need. The CQC have an important role to play in observing the progressive effects of this by reporting on knock-on effects for people needing NHS care, for example in relation to waiting times, patients' experiences and hospital discharge. It is important for social workers to have a good working knowledge of the arrangements for care and how to advise service users, carers and patients in where to look for inspection and reports on the quality of the services you refer them to, particularly for those who may be funding themselves and exercising discretion afforded by individualised budgets and direct payments.

NHS organisational structures

In terms of the co-ordination of healthcare services, the balance of power has moved from the hospital to the community. This section will give a brief overview of how these developments have taken place and the current proposed arrangements in the White Paper *Equity and Excellence: Liberating the NHS* (DoH, 2010a) for delivering health care to communities. Within proposed new structures, social workers will play a far more determining and facilitative role alongside the devolved choice and consumerist approaches being promoted by the government for service users, carers and patients. The White Paper has been said to be the first step towards the coalition government's vision to majorly reform the NHS and as the biggest overhaul in NHS structure since its conception in 1948.

A brief history of the previous structure helps to highlight how these claims have come about. The strategic architecture of the NHS has traditionally been traced through links between the Department of Health and 28 Strategic Health Authorities (SHAs) which were established in April 2002. These bodies took responsibility for ensuring that national strategies and priorities were implemented at the local level through effective performance of local services and planning for health improvement. They also took a developmental role. Healthcare is frequently referred to in terms of primary care and secondary care.

Primary care is the care provided at the first point of contact when health problems are experienced or for routine checkups, for example via visits to the GP, dentist or optician or in contact with telephone services such as NHS direct or more recently, walk-in health centres. The latter two initiatives were developed to divert people away from using more expensive secondary care systems by aiming for better screening and providing people with quicker access to common needs and problems which can be treated easily. Secondary care refers to that care provided when the person is referred to hospital, when more specialist or advanced treatment is provided. These two levels within the healthcare structure have given rise to a number of developments in the organisation of care, particularly in the way market principles have continued to develop and influence provision. These are briefly outlined below.

Primary Care Trusts (PCTs)

These are the organisations responsible at a local level for providing and managing primary services and for commissioning secondary care through their referral and purchasing activity. PCTs control about 80 per cent of the NHS budget and there is more and more emphasis on the role that PCTs and SHAs play in developing preventative and community-based medical services and particularly in meeting the challenge of patient-led care. Policies such as Our Health, Our Care, Our Say (DoH 2006) emphasise the role that local health centres and GP practices play in managing long-term health conditions such as heart disease in the community. They have a particular role in promoting local collaboration through their local boards and membership.

The White Paper (DoH, 2010a) has put forward several proposals aiming to extensively alter the current NHS structure, including the dismantling of the 151 PCTs and 10 SHAs and the distribution of their roles and responsibilities to several new structures. These roles include: holding the majority of the NHS budget and using it to procure health services (particularly from NHS hospitals); public health initiatives; and development of NHS services.

There are a number of other strategic organisations in the NHS referred to as 'trusts'. Achieving trust status encourages overarching organisations to form and bring together a number of stakeholders to tackle a range of financial, quality and governance issues in a particular area or to tackle common issues against core standards. Becoming a trust is thought to enable greater self-governing and has gained popularity in other areas of public services such as in education and crime as well as in the arts, such as in museums. We have outlined here some of the characteristics of Trusts that have emerged in the NHS.

NHS trusts

Also known as acute trusts, these have particular responsibilities for managing hospitals with the task of ensuring that hospital care is of a high standard and are major employers of staff both in the hospital and the community.

Care trusts

These were established by section 45 of the Health and Social Care Act 2001, as part of New Labour's 'modernisation' agenda and provide the organisational structure through which the NHS and local authorities, especially social services, can work in partnership across organisational boundaries to co-ordinate the planning and delivery of services to improve the experience of service users and patients. The powers of the NHS and local authorities are delegated rather than transferred. A range of different models for commissioning and/or providing services are possible as care trusts may focus on a particular service user group, for example mental health services, services for older people or those with learning disabilities. Alternatively they may be concerned with services to all people in a particular geographical area. Key terms used to describe the initiative include partnership, integration, shared responsibility, co-ordination and flexibility. While the organisational structures to support collaborative working have been made possible by the establishment of care trusts, it is the individual and team relationships that will also determine the success of these initiatives and the impact they have on delivering effective services to service users, patients and carers. You may find it helpful here to go back and review the information in Chapter 2 on preparing to work collaboratively.

Foundation trusts

In its White Paper *Equity and excellence: Liberating the NHS* (July 2010) the Government announced that:

> Within three years, we will support all NHS trusts to become foundation trusts. It will not be an option for organisations to decide to remain as an NHS trust rather than become or be part of a foundation trust...

Government policy has encouraged NHS hospitals to run their own affairs and be accountable to local people and patients, as opposed to being subject to top-down direction from the Department of Health. They want hospitals to be tailored to the needs of the local population. Foundation trusts have been given much more financial and operational freedom than other NHS trusts and represent the government's decentralisation of public services. These trusts remain within the NHS and its performance inspection system.

Since 2004, some have sought what is termed as NHS 'foundation trusts' which requires existing NHS trusts to strengthen their governance and financial discipline in order to demonstrate long-term financial viability, and a framework to secure delivery of quality services. The DoH has seen foundation status as a vital step for both acute and specialist hospitals if they are to succeed in an increasingly financially demanding and competitive health service and expects the vast majority of NHS trusts to become foundation trusts by April 2014, through a locally managed process with national support as needed. In

October 2011 there were 139 NHS foundation trusts, and 113 NHS trusts at various stages in the 'pipeline' towards foundation trust status. However, challenges for some trusts who have more deep-seated and long-standing issues about, for example, size and location, have limited their capacity to deliver health services efficiently and effectively (National Audit Office, 2011). They also face the added challenge of achieving 4 per cent efficiency savings per annum if the service is to achieve its target saving of up to £20 billion by the end of 2014–15.

ACTIVITY 4.2

Visit the website of a care trust in the locality where you are have undertaken, or will be undertaking, practice learning to find out about and make notes on the initiatives that are in place for a service user group of your choice and the opportunities for working with a range of other professionals to meet the needs of service users and carers. Look on the website to see how the care trust consults with the local community and see if you can find out how it is governed and it operates. For example, who is on the governing board and which agencies are represented or not?

Ask the local professionals about their views on current developments in the NHS, particularly in relation to the role of GPs in commissioning and how they think this will impact on future provision. Make some notes to discuss with your team and colleagues.

Core principles of the NHS

The NHS, according to its statement of core principles, sets out to provide a universal service for all based on clinical need, not ability to pay. A further core principle of the NHS, set out in the NHS Plan (DoH 2000c), is that it will work together with others to ensure a seamless service for patients, in order to

> develop partnerships and co-operation at all levels of care – between patients, their carers, families and NHS staff; between the health and social care sectors; between different government departments; between the public sector, voluntary organisations and private providers in the provision of NHS services – to ensure a patient-centred service.

The New Labour modernisation agenda introduced some important principles, including the importance of partnership and participation, the closer relationship between health and social care, and the mixed economy of care reflecting choice and market forces, which are evident in this statement. These are themes we will return to later in the chapter.

However, all this was set against a backdrop of services that had been failing to match the expectations and demands of the public, and reports of failures of providers of health care to meet quality assurance standards and targets regularly attract media attention. Specific issues that have attracted media attention have included outbreaks of 'super bugs', lengthy waiting lists, poor standards of cleanliness in some hospitals and challenges to the availability of new drug treatments for cancer.

A significant challenge for the NHS is the balancing of services for preventing ill health and curing illness with the need to manage the budget for expenditure on the NHS when the public's expectations of treatment and service are rising. These are issues that are not dissimilar to some of the dilemmas in social work and social care. One of the philosophies underpinning the Beveridge Report (for more discussion about the Beveridge Report, see Chapter 1), and an assumption explicit in the statements about the new NHS was a belief that the provision of services to improve health would result in a reduced need for these services. Factors having an impact on this include advances in medical diagnosis and treatment and raised awareness of them among the general public, more accessible health services, and demographic trends, in particular the rise in the number and percentage of elderly people.

Radical changes to the NHS – *The Health and Social Care Bill 2011*

The Health and Social Care Bill introduced by the succeeding coalition government of 2010 seeks to introduce radical reforms to the NHS. Reforms were announced as one of the top priorities for the incoming government, who estimate that the NHS budget will rise in real terms from £35 billion in 1997–98 to £110 billion in 2010–11 with spending rising by 4 per cent a year. This has built on reports such as *Healthy lives, healthy people* (DoH 2011b) and aims to complement *A vision for adult social care: Capable communities, active citizens* (DoH 2010b), which asserts that councils, health bodies and providers need to work more collaboratively to personalise and integrate service delivery across health and adult social care; and to make public funding go further. It also recognises the contribution that individuals, families, carers and communities make in providing care and support – both to those who are publicly funded and those who either pay for themselves or rely on family carers.

The government has made commitments to safeguarding the future of the NHS based on a system:

- that is led by frontline professionals;
- where patients and the public have a stronger voice and more control;
- where people's health and social care needs aren't treated separately;
- where local councils have a real say over decisions in the NHS;
- that is focused on the causes of health problems as well as treating them;
- that is judged on the quality of care and results for patients it provides.

(DoH, 2011a)

There had been some previous success by the Labour government in relation to these aims where target-setting which despite unpopularity has reduced waiting times by replacing them with measurement of patient outcomes. However, it is unknown how these outcomes will be measured and whether they are feasible. Reforms will especially target the management structure of the NHS which previously has largely separated clinical practice from the management of the NHS but has produced a large, expensive and overly bureaucratic management structure that oversees clinical practice. One of the major criticisms has been that while making decisions that directly impact on clinical practice, managers actually have little clinical expertise and are therefore not always in a position where they could truly identify benefits and consequences for decisions about health at a practical level. Therefore the reforms in the White Paper aim to delegate clinicians and healthcare workers more managerial responsibility. By stripping a proportion of the current management and bureaucracy away and placing managerial duties on clinicians, it has been speculated that substantial savings can be made in order to achieve the government targets for savings required in an era of austerity and economic downturn. As mentioned earlier in the chapter, some of the main changes involve giving commissioning responsibilities to GP consortia and independent commissioning boards.

The development of GP consortia and independent commissioning boards

The coalition government has encouraged the development of consortia consisting of and being led by GPs with other professionals to bear the responsibility of purchasing health services using NHS funds. In the future, these will act very flexibly and be able to vary and change in size to reflect the local area in which they work. For example, some consortia will be able to coalesce if they need to increase their purchasing power particularly to provide those low-frequency services where it might be uneconomical for individual GPs to provide on their own. Consortia will be supported by independent commissioning boards whose job it is to allocate a budget and fund specialist services such as paediatric intensive care units generally only found in major hospitals. They also have a regulating function in order to guarantee adequate services overall. These moves will give consortia greater freedom from central government influence which has been viewed as restricting the NHS through unnecessary micromanagement. The first groups of 52 GPs' practices from across England, known as pathfinders, have already taken on commissioning responsibilities on behalf of PCTs. These will test the new commissioning arrangements to ensure they are working well before the proposed transfer of statutory commissioning responsibilities to GP consortia from April 2013. The pathfinders are being supported by a national learning network, as well as by regional and local support networks.

The biggest strength of consortia is the huge amount of flexibility incorporated into their design. This, together with their greater financial accountability and consequent ability to fail or thrive, theoretically means that poorly run, inefficient consortia will disappear, to be replaced by successful ones. However, it is hard to see failing consortia not having an impact on the essential services they are responsible for, for example accident and emergency. Despite the commissioning board's role to ensure these services remain unaffected, this may not be enough. This flexibility also gives the consortia the ability to tackle any issue that arises; and to find the right balance to best make the proposals work. The teaming up of consortia is particularly cited as a means of giving them the tools to act with the benefits of both large and small organisations whenever the need arises. However, these proposals have been subject to great criticism. Some of this has been about the lack of defined structure and guidance which could also potentially result in varying methods and design. This may lead to consortia that communicate and work inefficiently and ineffectively with each other, never quite settling into a consistent structure that can be developed and improved, or allows forward planning.

A major focus of the NHS reform and current responsibility of PCTs lies in public health. The Department of Health will have a greater role in public health and be supported by local authorities. Public health is about helping people to stay healthy and avoid getting ill, including work on a whole range of policy areas such as immunisation, nutrition, tobacco and alcohol, drugs recovery, sexual health, pregnancy and children's health. The most controversial aspects of the Health and Social Care Bill (2011) which led to delays and revisions in its passing, is its overemphasis on the market influence on healthcare. For example, private companies are now being encouraged to compete with foundation trusts to provide publically funded healthcare. As we saw earlier, the drive to accelerate the creation of foundation trusts will put them in direct competition with private companies. As a group of lawyers and health academics have asserted, the reforms proposed will abolish England's model of *tax-financed, universal healthcare*, pave the way for a *US-style health system* based on *mixed funding* and fatally undermine *entitlement to equality of healthcare provision* (The Lancet 2012). These changes would further produce inequality in access, uptake and provision and undermine the information systems required to monitor inequalities in health at a local level. Monitor, the board that currently regulates foundation trusts, has stated its intention to move towards a more market-regulating function in which it will issue licences to healthcare providers bidding to sell services to GP consortia. One of its roles is to oversee that fair competition is maintained as well as regulating prices for healthcare. This is a different role to that of the Care Quality Commission (CQC) who will continue to act as quality control by establishing that both NHS foundations and private companies meet assessed criteria in order to provide services.

Boundaries, targets and patient choice

The government asserts that increasing patient choice is at the heart of these new reforms and eliminating the infamous 'postcode lottery' of healthcare distribution. Patients will be allowed to sign up to any GPs in any location. Like social care, patient involvement has evolved substantially over the last decade and a 'Healthwatch' within the local area will help patients decide between services based on users' experiences alongside independent groups made up of members of the community (local inclusion networks, LINKs) who will obtain and then pass on feedback to healthcare providers with the aim of improving services. These proposals have not been received uncritically. For example, in the USA opposition to health reforms have been articulated as erosion of personal freedom by increasing government powers. In the UK, the pro-market reforms of universal services, clearly illustrated above, have been justified for their increase in personal freedom by transferring powers from government to non-government or commercial bodies, which is a far cry from the health service set out by Beveridge described earlier in the chapter. This is said to be necessary to increase personal freedom and choice. However, it also limits the legal duties of government for guaranteeing its citizens' access to healthcare and safeguarding these rights for future generations (The Lancet 2012). The impact of these reforms is yet to be seen.

Find out, by consulting websites, newspapers and other sources from your own profes-sional press, about current national health issues, concerns and priorities and how these are being discussed in the context of the major reforms to the NHS. Within your own agency or area where you live for example, there will be some activity at the local level to prepare and engage with the proposed changes.

COMMENT

You could specifically consider the following.

• What is the role of your agency within the new commissioning context and what arrangements will be made to support local consortia in responding to local healthcare needs?

• Who are the key professionals leading the changes envisaged in the NHS reforms and how are service users and patients being involved?

• What are the views of the main political parties on the themes of the NHS reforms and how have these manifested locally? How would you as a future social worker use this awareness when working with health professionals around the health and social care needs of service users and carers?

Taking the 'national' out of the health service – too much, too fast?

Another of the major criticisms of the changes to the NHS structure is the enormous expenses that could be incurred in achieving the reforms. It is possible that management costs and staffing may even be increased as there will not be the inherent savings of a centralised body. Added to this unpredictability, we have the current economic situation where the NHS is already trying to make huge savings in an unstable financial market.

Further, while the principles of universal free healthcare have been maintained within the reforms to the NHS, there will be a much more mixed approach to provision where a sig-nificant fraction of people will be treated by the private healthcare system and posing risks to the survival of the NHS foundation trusts as they lose the proportion of public funding that private hospitals managed to gain. There may be a knock-on effect on the staff cur-rently working in the NHS and the associated responsibilities for training and benefits and the overall future of the NHS if profit motives are introduced. These emerging patterns of provision may also have implications for health inequalities, which we will now look at in the final part of this chapter.

Health inequalities

The Black Report 1980

While it had been anticipated that the NHS would improve the health of everyone, but in particular the health of the poor who previously had limited access to a limited range of health care services, the Black Report demonstrated that the provisions of the welfare state had apparently failed to address the wide difference in terms of health and life expectancy between the wealthiest and the poorest people, with improvements in standards of health not evenly distributed across the population.

The Conservative government ignored the findings of the report and the publication by Townsend and Davidson (1982) was an attempt to disseminate the findings of the Black Report to a wider audience. When the New Labour government was elected in 1997, the issue of health inequalities was taken up with the commissioning of an independent inquiry, whose findings were published in 1998.

The Acheson Report 1998

According to Alcock (2003 p58), there was evidence that rather than improvements in health there were still significant health inequalities, and in some aspects the inequalities had increased. He states that *the evidence showing a continuing link between poor health and social class was incontrovertible* and that the findings led to health equalities becoming an important focus of government policy, which was to be replaced with a focus on improving health service delivery.

RESEARCH SUMMARY

Health inequalities

- *People in the north of England are 20% more likely to die before they reach 75 than those in the south, and this divide in longevity is likely to worsen in recessions and conditions of economic austerity. Inequalities in all causes of mortality in the north–south divide were severe and persistent over the four decades from 1965 to 2008.*

- *Children in residential care and young men in psychiatric institutions and prisons are at risk of earlier death than other people of comparable age in the general population. (Source: Harding et al. 1999).*

- *People with learning disabilities and mental health problems face serious health inequalities, partly arising from difficulties they encounter in using health services. For example, they often are on benefits and so have fewer financial resources with which to choose and pay for alternative healthcare interventions such as osteopathy or acupuncture. These groups of people also have less money to spend on healthy eating and on opportunities to exercise (Nocon, 2004).*

Continued

- *Looked After Children (LAC) experience significant health inequalities. There is evidence of high levels of unmet needs and poor health outcomes for LAC. The transition from care itself can also adversely affect health and well-being. Research has indicated that systems for managing the transition out of care varies and some young people leaving care find themselves with limited or no support (Scott and Hill 2006).*

As a social worker you must demonstrate a clear commitment to anti-oppressive practice and it is important to be aware of the impact of health inequalities and to develop strategies to challenge practice that perpetuates these inequalities. An approach that focuses on the illness of the individual can be considered as a deficit model, looking at one dimension of the person, whereas a social approach informed by anti-oppressive practice offers the opportunity to understand the service user or patient in relation to the broader circumstances and multiple dimensions that have an impact on life chances. In Chapter 6 we will be exploring the broader notion of social exclusion, and poor health is one of the experiences of people who are socially excluded.

ACTIVITY **4.4**

The information in the research summary above outlines some of the inequalities experienced by some groups of people. Visit the website for government statistics, www. statistics.gov.uk, to find out about health inequalities for minority ethnic groups and older people, by entering these phrases in the search box.

- *How might this information help you to practise more sensitively and effectively?*

- *When working collaboratively with other professions, how might you raise awareness of these issues to challenge discrimination and to promote anti-oppressive practice and social justice?*

COMMENT

McLeod and Bywaters (2000 p1) make a very strong case for social workers to focus on health inequalities based on three reasons.

1. *Socially constructed health inequalities result in suffering.*

2. *Social workers are involved in the system that creates and perpetuates these inequalities.*

3. *Social workers can make a positive contribution.*

   Multiple dimensions of social inequality and discrimination cross-cut health. These result not only in unequal chances of maintaining good health but also in inequalities in accessing treatment, in securing the resources necessary to recovery or to a good quality of life in cases of serious illness, and in receiving high-quality care in terminal illness.

   (McLeod and Bywaters 2000 p3)

Government priorities in relation to health inequalities

During its period in office the New Labour government demonstrated its commitment to tackling 'social exclusion', which encompassed a range of inequalities including those associated with health. It set up the Social Exclusion Unit, apparently having accepted that poverty and ill health are interconnected.

Establishing a Minister of Public Health signalled an understanding of the relationship between health inequalities and poverty. Initiatives such as Health Action Zones (DoH 1997), Health Improvement Programmes (NHS Executive 1998) and the Green Paper *Our Healthier Nation* (DoH, 1998b) underline this, alongside increased expenditure on the NHS.

The government gave a commitment in the NHS Plan to establish national health inequalities targets which would narrow the gap in health status in childhood and throughout life, between socio-economic groups, and between different areas in the country. These were originally announced in February 2001, and then included as part of the regular Spending Review Public Service Agreement (PSA) for the Department of Health.

The Green Paper *Our Healthier Nation* 1998

Building on the earlier White Paper, *The Health of the Nation* (DoH, 1992), the framework for this Green Paper was the setting out of a contract between the government, local communities and individuals, reflecting the government's belief that health was not only a national issue but an area of concern for communities and individuals. One of the key aims was *to improve the health of the worst off in society and to narrow the health gap* (DoH 1998b p5) *by tackling inequality which stems from poverty, poor housing, pollution, low educational standards, joblessness and low pay* (DoH 1998b p12). The Green Paper referred to a new public health force spanning professional boundaries in its response to local need. There is an inherent tension in these approaches between the individual model of responsibility in which people are encouraged to stop smoking, drink less alcohol and take more exercise and the approach which sees the establishment of policies to address some of the social and structural problems that lead to health inequalities.

Social services are seen as pivotal in this vision:

> *high quality social services play a vital role in the health of the people they serve: by protecting the vulnerable, caring for those with problems and supporting people back into independence with dignity, social services have a vital role in fostering better health.*

> (DoH 1998b p 23)

The emphasis was moving away from the individual to the collective with a focus that recognised community development principles. As we discovered in Chapter 3, the youth work and Connexions context, government initiatives such as this can also be seen as an extension of surveillance, with a wider range of everyday behaviours being seen as of interest to government agencies and with individuals being scrutinised by fellow residents in terms of their healthy or unhealthy lifestyles, and in the case of young people in terms of their social activities.

Health Action Zones

Twenty-six Health Action Zones were established in 1998 and 1999 to develop new ways of working in and with communities and across professional boundaries, to address inequalities in health in the poorest areas of the country through local partnerships between social services and health, and focus on regeneration, housing and employment. The intention was to develop approaches and interventions that are more responsive and reflect the needs of the local communities. The strategic objectives of the Health Action Zones included *empowering local communities, developing effective partnerships, multi-agency working and becoming learning organisations – themes familiar in the literature and practice of community work and community development* (Popple and Quinney 2002 p78). This policy for developing local projects employing community development models to tackle the manifestations of poverty and its resultant disadvantage is reminiscent of the Community Development Projects (CDPs) of the 1970s. This time, however, there were clearly prescribed objectives from central government in order to reduce the opportunities for the re-emergence of the radical critique associated with the CDPs, an approach not favoured by the New Labour government. Partnership working in Health Action Zones was an example of a response to an awareness that *complex problems of poverty, social exclusion and poor health require concerted action* (Amery 2000 p29).

Public health and health promotion

With a long history dating back to measures in the mid-nineteenth century to address poor housing and poor sanitation, a concern with public health acknowledges the link between ill health and social conditions.

The Wanless Report, *Securing good health for the whole population*, published in 2004, set out important targets to improve the health of the public and to address health inequalities. In doing so the responsibility of the individual, as well as that of the state, is emphasised:

> *Individuals are ultimately responsible for their own and their children's health and ... need to be supported more actively to make better decisions about their health.*

> (Wanless 2004 p4)

There is a tension between individual responsibility and what is referred to as the social model of health, which takes into account for example the impact of housing conditions and poverty on poor health. McLeod and Bywaters (2000 p12) take a very clear position with their statement that:

> *the unjust human suffering which arises from the impact of social inequalities on health should be a matter of urgent concern to social workers.*

The Health Development Agency – now subsumed into the National Institute for Health and Clinical Excellence (NICE), the parallel organisation to SCIE – has produced a very useful workbook (Henderson et al. 2004) to support the delivery of a community development course to address health inequalities and promote public health. Henderson et al. (2004 p29) explain that the aims of public health are to:

- improve health and well-being in the population;

- prevent disease and minimise its consequences;

- prolong life;

- reduce inequalities in health.

The ACHIEVE project

This local project, established in an area with high indices of poverty and inequalities, supported by joint funding from the health authority and the local university, focused on health improvements using a community development approach involving the local authority, voluntary organisations, health professionals, residents and academics.

Consultation events with local people to ensure their voices and priorities were listened to and acted on identified three themes.

- *Improved access to nutritional meals.*

- *Improved access to information.*

- *Improved access to affordable physical activity.*

Grants enabled a kitchen in a community project to be refurbished and supported by a chef and a health visitor, and a lunch club was formed to enable families to learn how to prepare and cook nutritional low-cost meals and where child health and child development concerns could also be shared in a supportive environment. Strong informal networks developed from this which enabled families to offer and receive peer support for wide-ranging issues.

A 'community shop' was established, staffed by a community development worker assisted by volunteers, which provides an advice and information point for the whole community, including access to financial services such as savings and affordable loans through a credit union located at the 'community shop'. Summer playgroups, exercise classes, parenting groups and a youth drop-in centre were also developed. Education is an important aspect of the work, with the project offering opportunities for residents to develop employment skills and vocational qualifications. A previously socially isolated local resident attending the exercise class, with child care facilities funded by the local authority, was able to access the qualification to become an instructor and went on to lead the class.

The project provided opportunities for social work and nursing students to undertake practice learning placements, experiencing working across professional boundaries and departments. Action research and practice development themes were important to enable a reflective approach to the challenges of this community-led approach to health.

While these local initiatives clearly result in better outcomes for some individuals, short-term funding which undermines sustainability is a real problem and more substantial investment in local regeneration and more redistributive policies are more likely to provide longer-term improvements for those living in poverty.

Popple and Quinney (2002 p83) have commented on the positive benefits of working with local communities with a health improvement focus but have also drawn our attention to some important concerns.

There is real concern that community development is being used to redirect the energies of local people into volunteering and into low-paid, short-term social and community projects ... in order to divert them from critically analysing and challenging New Labour policies for local communities.

The outgoing government had set out a number of targets for reducing health inequalities by 10% before 2010 in relation to infant mortality: reduce inequalities in health outcomes by 10 per cent as measured by infant mortality and life expectancy at birth. This was expected to galvanise a wide range of actions to improve the health of mothers and their children. These include reducing teenage pregnancies, improving access to high-quality ante-natal care, efforts to reduce smoking and improve nutrition during pregnancy and early childhood years, and effective early childhood support.

In detail, these targets included the following.

Reducing the gap in mortality rates between routine and manual groups and the population as a whole.

Reducing by at least 10 per cent the gap between the fifth of areas with the lowest life expectancy at birth and the population as a whole.

International comparisons indicate that there is substantial scope for improvement on both life expectancy and infant mortality. Both targets aim to narrow the gap between those with poor health status and the population as a whole, a gap that is generally widening. Achievement of the targets is not only about saving lives overall, but is about ensuring that a higher proportion of the gains are made by those in poorer circumstances. It focuses attention on the distribution of health benefit, rather than simply on overall health outcomes from the provision of programmes and services. Improvements in life expectancy will be achieved through a very wide range of actions.

In summary, health inequalities may be created and maintained by a variety of factors. These could be environmental, which are generally beyond the individual's immediate control as well as individual lifestyle choices – in particular, varying rates of smoking between different groups. Researchers disagree on which factors are most influential: some emphasise the material conditions in which a person lives, others stress the importance of social and psychological factors and others identify lifestyle choices as the most significant factor (www.kingsfund.org.uk/topics/health_inequalities/).

Fair society, healthy lives: A strategic review of health inequalities in England post-2010

To inform their future strategy on health inequalities after 2010, the previous New Labour government commissioned a major review into health inequalities (Marmot 2010) whose report emphasised the role of a healthy start in life, education, employment, welfare programmes and proactive prevention to address health inequalities and recommended broad-based action on these. The incoming coalition government proposes a new 'health premium' designed to *promote action to improve population-wide health and reduce health inequalities* as part of a ring-fenced public health budget. This involves giving weighting to health inequalities in the formula used by central government for allocating NHS funding. And as we saw earlier in relation to the Health and Social Care Bill (2011), the new arrangements for commissioning healthcare will be required to have regard to the need to reduce health inequalities.

Choice and participation

According to an article in *The Guardian* newspaper (Rankin 2005), while there may be concerns that recent government proposals have led to the subsuming of social care under health services, *with its user-centred model of choice and its tradition of responding to complex needs, social care has much to offer the NHS*. Along with co-ordinated services, issues of choice were enshrined in the National Health Service and Community Care Act 1990. The direct payments system, established by the Community Care (Direct Payments) Act 1996, is an important embodiment of the principles of choice and empowerment, particularly as local authorities and councils now have a duty to make direct payments in some circumstances.

As a result of the Health Care Act 2009 (DoH 2009b), PCTs are already able to offer personal health budgets that do not involve giving money directly to individuals. The Act extended these options by allowing selected PCT sites to pilot direct payments as part of a wider pilot programme to explore personal health budgets guided by *The National Health Service (Direct Payments) Regulations* (HMG 2010). Developments to increase the choice and control people with long-term conditions have over their care have looked to individual budgets, also referred to as personal budgets in healthcare, as one of several mechanisms that could assist in personalising care for people with long-term conditions such as diabetes. This could enable choice over interventions and support for self-care, such as weight management or structured education. However, the complex and unpredictable nature of overall clinical care needs means that this is not straightforward and requires more development, particularly around quality of healthcare. Social workers have a strong role to play in the development of individual budgets which include users' healthcare needs through the support planning process and the availability and provision of high-quality information to support people to make informed choices and decisions about their care.

National Service Frameworks (NSFs)

These are long-term strategies for improving particular areas of health and social care and include initiatives in relation to coronary heart disease, cancer, paediatric intensive care, mental health, older people, diabetes, long-term conditions, renal, and children. A key element in the development of these frameworks is the consultation with service users and carers, health and social care professionals, partner agencies and managers through an external reference group.

While you may initially believe that you are unlikely to be directly involved in many of these frameworks, as social worker students and social workers you are likely to be working within the guidelines of the NSFs in relation to a wide range of service user groups who may be experiencing the impact of a medical condition and not only those that appear to be more relevant to social work – older people, mental health and children. Working in collaboration with other professionals through multi-disciplinary and inter-agency working underpins these frameworks, as does partnership with service users and carers.

Integrated care pathways

Integrated care pathways (ICPs), also known as clinical pathways, clinical care pathways, and care pathways, are another method used in health to promote locally agreed multi-disciplinary and multi-agency practice for specific patient or user groups (Overill 1998). ICPs developed in the late 1990s as a basis for plotting and agreeing pathways of care for particular conditions or procedures using a template. Examples can be seen in mental health or substance misuse and in the care of the dying. Pathways are designed to reduce variation in practice and allow the same quality of care to be delivered to patients across multi-disciplinary and multi-agency teams and in different care settings. Pathways can ensure that the care process is better monitored and evaluated because it learns about the group of people with similar issues and allows people to develop expertise based on experience and knowledge. This experience and knowledge can also be utilised to improve services by setting benchmarks between services and noting trends over time and then use this information to target specific areas in need of improvement. Features of an integrated care pathway include the following.

- Building in indicators both qualitative and quantitative for measuring outcomes and monitoring quality and evaluation as the patient's pathway develops.

- Storing and updating electronic information about patients' progress and status so that everyone, including providers, is able to access it easily and respond as needs develop.

- It facilitates the patient's own view of their pathway and their ability to personally direct it given that it brings together health and social care that is more tailored and personal within the standards set.

- A visual representation of the care plan and course of care which can be useful as an educational tool, particularly for new staff or staff who tend to rotate through different services.

ACTIVITY **4.5**

Find out more detail about either the older people or mental health National Service Frameworks by visiting the Department of Health website (www.doh.gov.uk) or the website of SCIE (www.scie.org.uk). Identify the key standards from these frameworks that you believe are particularly relevant to the aims of collaboration between professionals and agencies and partnership with service users and carers.

- *How might you prepare for collaborative working with this service user group?*

COMMENT

To help you undertake this activity you may also wish to refer to the books by Malcolm Golightly (2008) Social work and mental health *and by Karin Crawford and Janet Walker (2008)* Social work with older people *in this series.*

Challenges at the social work and health interface

Families where alcohol, drug and mental health problems cause concern

Around 90 per cent of people experiencing mental health problems are treated in the community by their GP (Alcock et al. 2000 p204) and a significant proportion are parents with children. Services to support and treat people with mental health problems are provided by Community Mental Health Teams (CMHTs) typically made up of professionals from the health and social work professions, including social workers, psychiatric community nurses and psychiatrists. In families where there are alcohol, drug and mental health problems, a report by Kearney et al. (2003 p3) reminds us that *the present Labour government recognises that the combination of social and medical need in some families can be so substantial that it cannot be met by a single agency, profession or team* and that *in practice, multi-professional working within and between personal social services and health has a long history.* They emphasise the importance of integrated working both across children and families and adult services within Social Services departments, which they refer to as 'interface' working, as well as the importance of working across the 'borders' of health and social work agencies.

RESEARCH SUMMARY

Research suggests that at least a quarter of adults known to adult mental health services are parents, that about one-third of children known to child and adolescent mental health services have a parent with a psychiatric disorder, and that mental illness or substance abuse in a parent is recorded in at least a third of families referred to social services due to child protection concerns.

Falkov (1998), cited in Kearney et al. 2000 p7

In their report Kearney et al. (2000 p12) point out how difficult working across 'borders' and 'interfaces' is in reality, despite clear drives from government and the detailed guidance issued, and point to some of the factors that contribute to the difficulty, particularly in a climate of budget restraints.

- At an organisational level the different values and priorities and different methods of intervention of the organisations and agencies require an investment in time to negotiate, plan, agree and deliver a more joined-up approach.

- At an individual level some professionals may be unwilling to work collaboratively.

An additional factor is that there are of course inevitable areas of tension when the needs of children and adults are in conflict, when interpreting and applying mental health and child care legislation, despite guidance, may be problematic and when issues of civil liberties have to be considered and balanced. Workers in these situations will need to draw on the Department of Health documents *Working together to safeguard children* (1999), and *Framework for the assessment of children in need and their families* (2000a) and the

Department for Education and Skills document *Every Child Matters* (2003). The picture is also complicated by the number of agencies that might be involved in supporting families where there is an alcohol problem (Figure 4.3), with many in the non-statutory sector. Kearney et al. (2000a p21) found that in particular in small non-statutory agencies there is sometimes a *lack of consensus about confidentiality and child welfare paramountcy* and that *knowledge and experience of multi-agency and multiprofessional working is not well developed.*

Building on the findings of their earlier report, Kearney et al. (2003) address the challenges of delivering effective and co-ordinated services across and within organisational boundaries by recommending the development and use of collaborative protocols, detailing the steps involved, and drawing attention to the range of legislation that defines practice in this area.

Figure 4.3 The jigsaw of core legislation for working with families that have alcohol and mental health problems

We are reminded that good practice requires *shared aims, understanding and language. This may mean having to find ways to change habits, attitudes and services* (Kearney et al. 2003 p11). They strongly recommend the development of a 'universal protocol', drawing parallels with the Single Assessment Process of the NSF for Older People and pointing out that these protocols should:

- give instructions and requirements;
- be authoritative;

- be linked to legislation, policy and procedure;

- be easy to use;

- help people think and act differently;

- have a user-led approach.

(Kearney et al. 2003 p12)

They identify the inter-agency child protection policy and guidance protocol drawn up by Bournemouth Borough Council as an example of good practice for working with other professionals and with social work colleagues from adult services and those from children and families services. You can read more about the roles and responsibilities of social workers in a mental health setting in the book in this series by Malcolm Golightly (2011) *Social work and mental health*.

Minority ethnic groups and mental health

The pressure group Mind campaigns for better treatment of people experiencing mental health problems and commissions and disseminates research into mental health. The following information from Mind reminds us that while social workers are required to practice in an antioppressive way and challenge discrimination, there are situations in which their ability to do this appears to be compromised.

A nationwide health census undertaken in 2005 confirmed that disproportionate numbers of black people continue to be sectioned under mental health legislation and reinforced concerns about racist practices.

> *Black people have similar rates of common mental health problems as other ethnic groups – and yet this census shows that they are 44 per cent more likely to be sectioned under the Mental Health Act ... and ... black men are 29 per cent more likely than average to be subjected to control and restraint.*

(Mind 2005a)

Other barriers to good practice in mental health include the racial stereotypes held by professionals. For example, the assumption that older people in the Chinese and Vietnamese communities live with their families was not borne out in research undertaken in Merseyside as it was found that 70 per cent lived alone (Mind 2005b).

Mind (2005c) has also reported that Irish-born people have the highest rates of admission to psychiatric hospitals in the UK, being almost twice as likely to be admitted to hospital for conditions associated with mental distress than other UK residents. As these figures do not include second- and third-generation Irish people the situation is more alarming.

Studies have demonstrated that discrimination within the mental health system is also experienced by lesbians, gay men and bisexual women and men, as service users and carers and as professionals.

RESEARCH SUMMARY

The 2003 Mind/University College London report on the mental health of lesbians, gay men and bisexual people found that up to 36 per cent of gay men, 26 per cent of bisexual men, 42 per cent of lesbians and 61 per cent of bisexual women recounted negative or mixed reactions from mental health professionals when being open about their sexuality (King and McKeown 2003).

Palliative care

In the area of palliative care social workers have an important contribution to make to the care of people with life-limiting conditions. Croft et al. (2005), in a participative research project with service users and carers, found that while service users and carers positively evaluated the contribution made by social workers, there was some reluctance from the health professionals to involve social workers and inconsistency in the way that referrals were made. This was compounded by the service users' and carers' initial misunderstandings and suspicions about the role of social workers; *I thought social work was for the down-and-outs and I was a bit wary of them ... I think we are very influenced by what we read in the press ... thought they might be a bit intrusive into my life.* (Croft et al. 2005 p35). The researchers also highlighted that guidelines issued by the National Institute for Health and Clinical Excellence (NICE) did not include social workers as key members of the team involved in caring for service users in a palliative care setting, seeing their role as optional rather than central.

ACTIVITY *4.6*

Find out more about participative research. You will find information in social work research textbooks and generic research textbooks.

- *Why is this form of research particularly useful in social work?*

- *How does it match with social work values?*

- *How might it help us to understand the experiences of service users and carers?*

- *How might it help social workers and other professionals to learn about the impact and effect of collaborative working?*

Older people

Providing services to support older people and their carers is a further area where you are likely to work collaboratively with health professionals. The numbers of older people in the population are rising, with almost one-fifth of the population being of pensionable age. Women are the most likely to be living alone, as they have a longer life expectancy than men, and approximately four-fifths of people over the age of 85 live in the community, with one-fifth living in care homes or long-stay hospitals. The health needs of older people are illustrated by the findings from national survey information that twice the number of people over the age of 75 attend hospital outpatient or casualty departments than people of all other age groups (Age Concern 2005).

Supporting people to live independently may involve a detailed package of care delivered by a range of professionals and agencies as the following case study illustrates.

CASE STUDY

Mrs Beeston is 78 years old and has been recently widowed. She prefers to be addressed as Mrs Beeston rather than by her first name, although some health and social care staff do not always remember this, which makes her angry. Her only son had been a carer for Mrs Beeston and her husband but he has been offered a senior post by his employer which involves moving to another town.

Mrs Beeston was admitted to hospital for treatment for a degenerative condition. Her medical condition causes her to have speech and swallowing difficulties and treatment has involved the fitting of a tube directly into her stomach for feeding.

The professionals involved in the case conference to plan her discharge from hospital included the consultant, nursing staff, speech therapist, dietician, occupational therapist, physiotherapist, social worker, GP and hospital discharge facilitator.

As part of the plan for her to return home a package of care is arranged in consultation with health and social care providers and co-ordinated by the social worker, consisting of four visits a day by two domiciliary care staff trained in moving and handling techniques, adaptations to the property and aids for daily living.

ACTIVITY 4.7

Having read about Mrs Beeston in the case study above, how would you as the social worker co-ordinating this package try to ensure that both health and social care needs are met?

What might be the priorities and concerns of the health professionals and how might this differ from the social work and social care professionals?

What knowledge, values and skills would you employ to facilitate a seamless service which takes account of Mrs Beeston's needs and wishes?

In what aspects might the values of health and social work professionals be in tension?

How would you aim to ensure that Mrs Beeston is treated with respect and dignity, including being addressed in the way she prefers?

As around one in twenty older people between the ages of 70 and 80 years are diagnosed with dementia, and one in five of those over the age of 80 (Alzheimer's Society 2005), what would be the implications for health, social care and social work professional staff working with Mrs Beeston if she was to develop symptoms of dementia? A useful resource is the website of the Alzheimer's Society which has an area, Real Lives, providing information from the perspective of service users and carers (www. alzheimers.org.uk).

Current challenges to the NHS

The scale of the issues and financial challenges facing the NHS has become even starker, and questions about its sustainability have been reflected in the coalition government's emergency budget, comprehensive spending review and fiscal reduction programme. While health and social care have traditionally worked closely together, there is now a sharper focus on how the inter-dependency of these services in addressing the relentless demands of demography, social change and technological advance can be achieved within the socio-economic and political climate.

Radical proposals to reform the NHS are yet to be realised and include a review of its relationship with local government and exploration of how social care and the NHS would together tackle the challenges brought about by a radically different operating environment. A research report by Harvey et al. (2011) has documented the following issues that will need to be resolved by policy-makers, managers and clinical leaders in order to reduce these.

- Moving beyond short-term cuts and technical efficiencies to longer-term transformational change that will release substantial productivity gains and better outcomes for people and communities. There needs to be a complete rethink of how entire health and social care systems use their combined resources.

- Besides those changes to commissioning, changes to how buildings are used, assessments are streamlined and a re-profiling of the workforce will be required.

- Keeping the focus on patient choice as a driver of change besides the proposed structural arrangements with the role of health and well-being boards performing local leadership.

Health can learn important lessons from the experience of social care who have two decades of experience in managing a mixed economy of care, and where private and third-sector providers are responsible for the majority of services provided including the potential benefits of a more competitive market as well as some of the risks that need to be managed. In your everyday practice, there is plenty of evidence that issues such as delayed transfers from hospital to home and delayed treatments can only emphasise the vital interdependence of these two sectors. It is very challenging to invest in the right types of support which may become low priority when resources are squeezed. Humphries et al. (2010) tell us that it has never been more important for collaboration for a better understanding of the reciprocal relationship between spending in health and social essential to ensure a whole system of care.

┌───┐

CHAPTER SUMMARY

In this chapter we have considered the organisational structures that support health services provided by the National Health Service and have looked at the wide range of professionals employed in delivering health services in the community and in hospital settings. If you have undertaken the activities in this chapter you will have learned about the areas where health and social work professionals are likely to be working collaboratively and be better equipped to practise effectively in your practice learning placements and as a qualified social worker in the future. If you are following a programme where you have the opportunity to be involved in interprofessional education with students from health disciplines you may find it helpful to discuss the activities and case studies with them to more clearly understand different perspectives that can be brought to the same situation.

└───┘

FURTHER READING

Coren, E, Iredale, W, Bywaters, P, Rutter, D, and Robinson, J (2011) *SCIE Research briefing 33: The contribution of social work and social care to the reduction of health inequalities: Four case studies.* London: Social Care Institute for Excellence.

Journal of social work in end-of-life and palliative care published by Taylor and Francis explores issues crucial to caring for terminally ill patients and their families. It contains current research, articles, and continuing features on the 'state of the art' of social work practice, including interdisciplinary interventions, practice innovations, practice evaluations, end-of-life decision-making, grief and bereavement, and ethical and moral issues.

McLeod, E and Bywaters, P (2000) *Social work, health and inequalities.* London: Routledge.

A radical critique of health services in the context of health inequalities.

WEBSITE

www2.warwick.ac.uk/fac/cross_fac/healthatwarwick/research/devgroups/socialwork/swhin/

You could apply to join a Social Work and Health Inequalities Network co-founded by Dr Eileen McLeod (Associate Professor, in the University of Warwick) and Professor Paul Bywaters (Honorary Professor School of Health and Social Studies, University of Warwick), which has approximately 300 members worldwide, in over 25 countries and contains a number of useful resources

www.doh.gov.uk

The website of the Department of Health, the central government department responsible for health and for social work and social care.

www.kingsfund.org.uk

The website of the King's Fund, an independent charitable foundation working for better health especially, though not exclusively, in London. The website contains extensive resource material, providing information on both health and social care issues. The King's Fund carries out research, undertakes policy analysis and supports development activities.

www.caipe.org.uk

The website of the Centre for the Advancement of Interprofessional Education. This organisation aims to promote collaboration and mutual respect between professions through interprofessional learning in health and social work.

Chapter 5
The education context

The policy and service delivery context

The content of this chapter has close links with other chapters of this book, for example Chapter 3, The youth work context, and Chapter 6, The housing and neighbourhood context. Education has a particular role to play in addressing social exclusion and inequalities, a common area where social workers are likely to find themselves working with people who are disadvantaged and marginalised. In this chapter we will be considering collaborative social work practice mainly in the context of formal education provision, with an emphasis on the compulsory education within the school setting, along with Early Years education. Towards the end of the chapter, however, we will also consider some other settings in which education features, for example in relation to community informal education and the concept of lifelong learning in relation to social care. In Chapter 3, the Youth work context, some of the areas referred to as 'informal' education are also addressed. This is because outside of compulsory education, ongoing learning is considered as valuable:

> for its intrinsic value ... it encompasses a huge variety of activities ... made up of a kaleidoscope of part-time, non-vocational learning where the primary purpose isn't to gain a qualification [where] ... people participate for enjoyment and are driven by their desire for personal fulfilment or intellectual, creative and physical stimulation.

(DIUS 2009 p16)

A number of theoretical approaches to lifelong learning in social care (Phillipson 2000; Hafford-Letchfield 2010, 2011) have demonstrated that learning has potential if used within a critical paradigm to promote participation, facilitate transitions in the lifecourse and bring about change.

Within compulsory education, working collaboratively is an expectation of teachers as well as social workers. The guidance produced by the now former Teacher Training Agency (2005a p13) states that *as the importance of effective multi agency working has been emphasised in the government's plans for children*, teachers must be able to establish collaborative working relationships and demonstrate an understanding of the distinct roles and responsibilities of other professionals. Apart from social workers, these relationships may also include educational psychologists, education welfare officers, youth justice workers, Early Years or play workers, school nurses or other health professionals.

In order to appreciate the roles, responsibilities and value base of professionals engaged in the school context, the first half of this chapter will consider the formal provisions and structures of statutory education services and set them in a historical context. We will then go on to explore government policies in relation to education. We will consider the different areas of practice where social workers, teachers and other education professionals may work collaboratively in order to deliver effective services to service users and carers, including informal provision towards the end of the chapter. We will look at any potential obstacles and the strategies for overcoming these.

A brief history of legislation impacting on compulsory education

Education Act, 1944

One of Beveridge's 'five giants' was ignorance. (You can read more about the Beveridge Report in Chapter 1.) To tackle this, the 1944 Education Act established the principle of universal free secondary education, introduced by the efforts of R.A. Butler (known as Rab Butler), Minister for Education at the time. The Act built on the system of free primary education introduced in 1870. It may seem surprising to learn that secondary education had not been free until then. To all intents and purposes secondary education had been the domain of the wealthy, a situation very different to the present day when education up to the age of 18 is free and a significant proportion of young people have gone on to university. Through its policy of widening participation, the Labour government had set a target to increase university attendance to 50 per cent of those in this age group. Alcock et al. (2004 p175) remind us that until the 1944 Act extended educational opportunities:

> For most children the education system generally was a severe disappointment, and the possibility of entering university remote or non-existent.

The Act led to what is known as a tripartite selective system, consisting of grammar schools, technical schools and secondary modern schools which provided for children to be educated up to the age of 15 from 1947. This system was to change with the introduction of comprehensive schools in the mid-1960s.

However, some of this ground has been lost following the independent review of Higher Education (Browne 2010) and its proposals. These were accepted by the coalition government in 2011 and led to the withdrawal of core funding previously given by the government to universities for teaching, with the exception of selective subjects. The future cost of higher education (HE) will be shifted away from government and taxpayers so that more of them are borne by students and/or their parents. While HE will remain free at the point of access, it is difficult to evaluate at the time of writing what impact, if any, higher fees and student loan debt will have on student behaviour, their HE choices, and their perceptions of its affordability. Callender (2010) comments on the difficulties in assessing their effects on HE access and participation, especially for those from low-income backgrounds who are being asked to speculate financially on an imagined but uncertain future.

Education Act, 1962

This Act introduced mandatory grants for students undertaking undergraduate degrees, and some diplomas. It was important also for specifying that parents must ensure their children attend school in order to benefit from education, or have alternative provision (for example home schooling). Legal powers were given to local authorities to enforce this. We will be looking later on in this chapter at the current role of the Education Welfare Officer, part of whose remit is to facilitate school attendance and to initiate formal measures if this fails.

The Robbins Report, 1963

This important report underlined the expansion of higher education provision which was to be supported by the provision of mandatory grants in the Education Act of the previous year.

The Newsom Report, 1963

This report focused on lower-ability secondary school pupils who were not achieving well and recommended measures to improve the quality of teaching.

The Plowden Report, 1967

With the focus on primary school pupils, this report concluded that inequalities were being perpetuated in schools and in the wider community and recommended initiatives to target schools in socially and economically disadvantaged areas in order to improve educational outcomes for children.

Education Reform Act, 1988

A common national curriculum for all children aged 5–16 was established with the controversial testing of primary school pupils at the ages of 7 and 11 years. Measures were introduced to bring market forces into the state school system through a system of local management of schools which removed some power of the local authority and gave head teachers and governors financial control.

Education Act, 1993

This important Act gave parents greater rights in situations where their children had special educational needs, introduced General National Vocational Qualifications and led to the expansion of grant-maintained schools.

Education Act, 1996

This consolidated all previous Education Acts in relation to schools and the National Curriculum, in order to prepare children to play an active part in the economy of the future by ensuring that they have the appropriate range of knowledge which can be extended into further and higher education or into skills for employment. The National Curriculum was broken down into Key Stages and applies to children from the age of three as follows.

Education Stages – National Curriculum

Foundation	age 3–5
Key Stage 1	age 5–7
Key Stage 2	age 7–11
Key Stage 3	age 11–14
Key Stage 4	age 14–16
Post-compulsory education and Further Education	age 16+

In 2011 the Secretary of State for Education for the coalition government announced a review of the National Curriculum in England. As it has developed, the National Curriculum has become more prescriptive and is thus accused of taking up more school time than originally intended when introduced. Both the New Labour and coalition governments have cited the necessity to slim down the National Curriculum. This is so that it properly reflects the body of essential knowledge in key subjects but without absorbing the overwhelming majority of teaching time in schools. Since the National Curriculum was introduced, intense criticism has emerged on its curtailment of teachers' ability to use their professional judgement and freedom to innovate in how they teach and develop new approaches to engage children (Gewirtz and Cribb 2007). While it is intended that English, mathematics, science and physical education continue to be compulsory at all four key stages, further consideration will be given to how other subjects such as art and design, citizenship, design and technology, geography, history, ICT, modern foreign languages, music, should be part of statutory programmes of study. Research by Gewirtz and Cribb (2007) has demonstrated that assessment designed for large-scale statistical comparison of schools is ill suited to the genuine promotion of learning. While the use of testing for accountability purposes has been acknowledged as useful, it is recommended that this should be based more on light sampling techniques rather than on the state-mandated universal system currently in place. New programmes of study are expected to be introduced in late 2012 and you can find out further information about the school curriculum on the Department of Education website www.education.gov.uk/schools/teachingandlearning/curriculum.

Education Act, 2002

A public inquiry into the abuse and death of Lauren Wright in Norfolk in 2000 documented, among others, a catalogue of errors in relation to the school involved, and the role of the education welfare service. It highlighted a lack of appropriate teachers trained in child protection. This was contrary to earlier guidelines set out in Department for Education and Skills (DfES) Circular 10/95 but which did not have any statutory footing. The Education Act 2002 therefore broadened teachers' responsibilities in relation to child protection given that they have day-to-day contact with individual children. Teachers are particularly well placed to observe the outward signs of abuse, or changes in a child's behaviour or development. Local authority education services are under a legal duty to promote and safeguard the welfare of their pupils. There are a number of statutory provisions that have a bearing on this area, either directly or indirectly. The most important are the following.

- Section 17 of the Children Act 1989.

- Section 27 of the Children Act 1989, which requires them to assist in the exercise of functions including those under s17.

- Section 47 of the Children Act 1989 to assist the Local Authority to make child protection enquiries if they have reasonable cause to suspect a child in their school or college is suffering or likely to suffer significant harm.

- Section 175 of the Education Act 2002 referred to in this section which includes proprietors of independent schools (including academies and city technology colleges) to have arrangements to safeguard and promote the welfare of pupils.

- The Non-Maintained Special Schools Regulations 199 requiring governing bodies to make arrangements.

- Sections 10 and 11 of the Children Act 2004 placed a duty on each local authority to make arrangements with relevant agencies to cooperate to improve the well-being of children and ensure their duties are discharged.

- Section 13 of the Children Act 2004 placed a duty on local authorities to establish Local Safeguarding Children Boards. While schools and FE colleges are not statutory board partners, the Board should include representatives of such other relevant bodies as considered fit. The guidance contained in *Working together to safeguard children* (DfES, 2006) makes it clear that they should be involved.

- There is also a range of regulations and guidance under education legislation that requires employers and education institutions engaged with provision of services to children and young people to take steps in their recruitment practices to ensure the suitability of those working in it and to ensure that staff have the skills, means and training necessary to protect and safeguard children. This latter guidance encompasses pupil health and safety, bullying and meeting health needs.

(DfES 2006 pp4–6)

Besides general statutory duties, schools have a pastoral responsibility toward their pupils. According to the DfES 10/95 Circular:

> *every school and college should ... develop a child protection policy which reflects its statutory duties and pastoral responsibilities and refers to the procedures to be followed ...*

> *The key element in ensuring that proper procedures are followed in schools is that the headteacher or another senior member of staff is designated as having responsibility for liaising with the local social services department and other agencies over cases of abuse.*

In all cases where abuse is suspected or a sustainable allegation is made, teachers and other members of staff are required to report the information to the designated teacher. The designated teacher should refer these cases to, or discuss them with, the investigating agencies according to the procedures established by the local Safeguarding Board and, in the case of LA-maintained schools, by the LA. These are important sources of knowledge for social workers investigating and working with children subject to safeguarding procedures.

Education and Inspections Act, 2006

This Act gave local authorities an enhanced strategic role as champion of pupils and parents, with a duty to promote choice, diversity and high standards for every child. As the key commissioner of school places, LAs take all decisions relating the way in which schools are organised in their local area. This Act also enabled all schools to acquire trust status and granted new freedoms seen to promote a stronger voice for parents through parent councils. In general, the Education and Inspections Act 2000 addressed a variety of topics within primary, secondary and further education and training, for example, in relation to food or drink provided on school premises; the establishment of an Office for Standards in Education, Children's Services and Skills; the amendment of references to local education authorities and children's services authorities.

The Education and Inspections Act 2006 also established Ofsted, the regulation and inspection body for children's services. It set out three overriding considerations required for Ofsted to incorporate into everything they do.

- To promote improvement in the services inspected or regulated.

- To ensure that these services focus on the interests of the children, parents, adult learners and employers who use them.

- To see that these services are efficient and effective.

(See Ofsted 2009.)

The Academies Act, 2010

Legislation will be introduced to enable more schools to achieve academy status and give them greater freedoms over the curriculum.

(Queen's Speech 25 May 2010)

The Academies Act is a further step taken by government in line with other moves towards devolving control to local communities. It enables a school to apply for academy status, which in turn grants a number of freedoms and flexibilities and is thought to be associated with a drive to improve standards. The Act's central aim was announced as being necessary to raise standards for all children, while narrowing the gap between the attainment of the most and least advantaged. Its main provisions were as follows.

- Allowing maintained schools to apply to become academies and permit the Secretary of State to issue an Academy Order requiring the local authority to cease to maintain the school.

- Allowing the Secretary of State to require schools that are eligible for intervention to convert into academies.

- Providing for secondary, primary and special schools to become academies.

- Ensuring there is no change of religious character as a result of the conversion process.

- Allowing schools that apply to become academies to keep any surplus financial balance in their budgets.

- Requiring the governing bodies of maintained schools to consult with those persons whom they think appropriate before converting into an academy. These include foundation and voluntary schools with a diocesan board.

- Allowing maintained schools that currently select to continue to do so as an academy.

- Allowing academy trusts to become deemed as charities.

- Allowing the assets of a school converting to an academy to keep and use these for the benefit and use of the pupils of that school.

(Department for Education 2012)

The Education Act, 2011

The Education Act is the second major legislative of the coalition government and was based on the proposals in DoE White Paper (2010) *The importance of teaching*, alongside new funding proposals from the Department for Business, Innovation and Skills (DBIS). Its new themes are:

- targeted free Early Years care for children under compulsory school age;

- changes to school discipline and restrictions on public reporting of allegations against teachers;

- abolition of five quangos: the General Teaching Council for England, the Training and Development Agency for Schools, the School Support Staff Negotiating Body, the Qualifications and Curriculum Development Agency and the Young Person's Learning Agency; the Secretary of State will take over some of their functions;

- removal of some duties of governing bodies, local authorities and further education institutions, including the demise of school improvement partners;

- changes to the arrangements for setting up new schools and academies; amendment of the Academies Act 2010 (already) to make provision for 16 to 19 academies and 'alternative provision' academies;

- a miscellany of measures on admissions, school meals, composition of governing bodies, school inspections, school finance and permitted charges.

Education reform to compulsory education looks set to continue with major reforms for children with special needs following the Green Paper (HMG 2011a), *Support and aspiration: A new approach to special educational needs and disability – a consultation*. This marked the beginning of a process that seeks to make assessment and provision less bureaucratic and less costly. It seeks particularly to address issues in relation to the way in which health and social care is commissioned alongside education which has always been challenging within social work. This will also build on the reforms to the NHS commissioning which we described in Chapter 4 and which has GP commissioning at its core.

Current structures in formal compulsory education

The central government department responsible for education is the Department for Education. In addition, some education initiatives originated from the Social Exclusion Unit located in the cross-cutting Office of the Deputy Prime Minister. The implementation of The Children Act 2004 resulted in a reorganisation of local authority provision to bring all children's services under one umbrella and creating local children's trusts which combined functions previously the responsibility of the distinct social services and education departments of the local authority, headed by a Director of Children's Services. An evaluation of how these arrangements are working can be seen in the research summary below.

RESEARCH SUMMARY

Evaluating the impact of children's trusts arrangements on improving outcomes for children and young people

Based on a small-scale survey of six children's trusts in 2009–2010, Ofsted identified key features of good practice which included the following.

- *A history of strong partnership working at a strategic level and highly effective leadership by directors of children's services and lead members.*

- *Children and young people's plans were clear, focused and designed to have an impact on outcomes.*

- *There was a determined commitment to early intervention and prevention, as well as evidence of services being redesigned around the needs of children and their families.*

- *There was also a range of integrated services in which professionals were clear about the benefits of joint working.*

- *Good relationships and effective co-operation existed between schools, the local authorities' education and social care services, the police, health services and the voluntary sector.*

- *There was evidence of joint commissioning and planning especially in meeting needs of children and families who were at risk of poorer outcomes although this was still at an early stage of development.*

- *Leaders had established an effective framework for co-ordinating the work of partners and were found to be pragmatic in seeking to accommodate differences in ways of working.*

(Ofsted 2010)

The strategic framework for inter-agency co-operation through children's trusts has the following five essential features.

1. **A child-centred, outcome-led vision**: a compelling outcome-led vision for all children and young people, clearly informed by their views and those of their families.

2. **Integrated frontline delivery** organised around the child, young person or family rather than professional boundaries or existing agencies – for example, multi-agency teams, co-located staff in extended schools or children's centres, joint training, and arrangements for identifying a lead professional wherever a child is known to more than one targeted or specialist agency and a co-ordinated response is required.

3. **Integrated processes**: effective joint working sustained by a shared language and shared processes. These include a Common Assessment Framework, effective information sharing arrangements, and the re-engineering of other local processes and procedures to support, joint working.

4. **Integrated strategy** (joint planning and commissioning): joint assessment of local needs; the identification of all available resources; integrated planning to prioritise action and a move towards preventative services; and joint commissioning of services from a range of providers, supported appropriately by shared resources and pooled budgets.

5. **Inter-agency governance**: while each partner is responsible for the exercise of its own functions, robust arrangements for inter-agency co-operation are needed to set the framework of accountability for improving and delivering effective services.

DfES (2004a pp6–7)

ACTIVITY **5.1**

Research the local authority where you live or are studying, or the local authority where you will be undertaking a practice learning placement, to find out about how your local children's trust works in co-ordinating and delivering services for children.

COMMENT

Look specifically at how your local children's trust refers to the five outcomes of Every Child Matters and which agencies or professional disciplines are involved in collaborating and resourcing services to achieve these. You can find information on this area of policy guidance on the DoE website (www.education.gov.uk).

CASE STUDY

The Camden primary schools multi-disciplinary team project

In two primary schools a multi-disciplinary team has been established which delivers preventative work and interventions to support children and families who are identified as causing concern. The team, who are supported by team building and staff development, consists of a wide range of professionals including the headteacher, special educational needs co-ordinator, educational psychologist, social worker, education welfare officer, child psychotherapist, home–school liaison worker and school nurse.

As a result of common assessment and information sharing, a range of interventions are offered including family support, groupwork, counselling and mediation. A SHAPE matrix is used which matches the Every Child Matters priorities (Stay safe, be Healthy, enjoy and Achieve, make a Positive contribution and achieve Economic well-being). An evaluation of the project has demonstrated that positive benefits have been felt by families at risk of social exclusion and that while additional time is needed to work effectively, the multi-disciplinary team approach is positively rated by those working in it.

(Camden Children's Fund 2005)

Department for Education

The Department for Education replaced the previous Department for Education and Skills in May 2010. It sets the priorities for the education workforce and has stated its focus as follows.

- Giving greater autonomy to schools through delegating this to local headteachers and teachers as opposed to bureaucrats and politicians. Emulating education systems in the USA, Canada, Sweden and Finland. This is seen as the means of inspiring pupils and driving school improvement and will be enabled through the government's enabling of schools to acquire academy status.

- Improving parental choice and reforming the admissions system as well as enabling parents, teachers and charities who want to make a difference by making it easier for them to set up and run their own schools.

- Offering more support for disadvantaged children by taking additional money from outside the schools budget. This should ensure those teaching the poorest children get the resources they need to deliver smaller class sizes, more one-to-one or small-group tuition, longer school days and more extra-curricular activities.

- Whole-system improvement by attracting the best people into teaching and further enhancing the prestige and esteem of the teaching profession. This includes tackling pupils' bad behaviour by sharing responsibilities with parents and enabling teachers to exercise discretion and authority.

- Reforming the National Curriculum as outlined earlier in this chapter.

An important concern of the Department is that children and their families receive a seamless service where education, social care, childcare services and support are organised around the needs of children. It supports principles of greater personalisation and choice, more diverse provision, streamlines funding and accountability as reflected in trends within other areas of public services.

Professional standards for teachers

Until March 2012, the professional body for teachers was the General Teaching Council for England which set the standards and regulated the teaching workforce, similar to the General Social Care Council in social work. Both quangos are now abolished and the General Teaching Council was abolished with the passing of the 2011 Education Act. A new set of standards will establish the minimum requirements for teachers' practice and conduct from September 2012. These cover teaching and personal and professional conduct (DoE 2011) and details of the standards are outlined in the box overleaf.

Figure 5.1 Teaching Standards 2012

Part One: Teaching

1. Set high expectations which inspire, motivate and challenge pupils
2. Promote good progress and outcomes by pupils
3. Demonstrate good subject and curriculum knowledge
4. Plan and teach well structured lessons
5. Adapt teaching to respond to the strengths and needs of all pupils
6. Make accurate and productive use of assessment
7. Manage behaviour effectively to ensure a good and safe learning environment
8. Fulfil wider professional responsibilities

Part Two: Personal and professional conduct

A teacher is expected to demonstrate consistently high standards of personal and professional conduct. The following statements define the behaviour and attitudes which set the required standard for conduct throughout a teacher's career.

- Teachers uphold public trust in the profession and maintain high standards of ethics and behaviour, within and outside school, by:

  - treating pupils with dignity, building relationships rooted in mutual respect, and at all times observing proper boundaries appropriate to a teacher's professional position;

  - having regard for the need to safeguard pupils' well-being, in accordance with statutory provisions;

  - showing tolerance of and respect for the rights of others;

  - not undermining fundamental British values, including democracy, the rule of law, individual liberty and mutual respect, and tolerance of those with different faiths and beliefs;

  - ensuring that personal beliefs are not expressed in ways which exploit pupils' vulnerability or might lead them to break the law.

- Teachers must have proper and professional regard for the ethos, policies and practices of the school in which they teach, and maintain high standards in their own attendance and punctuality;

- Teachers must have an understanding of, and always act within, the statutory frameworks which set out their professional duties and responsibilities.

According to its previous body (TDA 2005):

> *Teaching is one of the most influential professions in society. In their day-to-day work, teachers can and do make huge differences to children's lives: directly, through the curriculum they teach, and indirectly, through their behaviour, attitudes, values, relationships with, and interest in pupils.*

There are clear parallels here with social work, particularly in the impact teachers have on the lives of service users and carers through the application of social work values and relationship-based working. Nevertheless, as Miller (2005 p3) reminds us, when writing about the differences and similarities between teachers and youth workers: *Borders and boundaries are inevitably points of interface. They are as much sites of potential conflict and incursions as they are of agreements and resolutions.* As social workers it is important that you focus on the holistic needs of children and their families, whereas teachers are encouraged, by nature of the work undertaken, to concentrate on the processes and outcomes of learning. While teachers need to take into account the wider needs of children and the social and family factors that might impede their learning, in the classroom setting with the demands of the National Curriculum they are not in a position to consider each child in depth, as the social worker would need to do.

The similarities with social workers in teachers responsibilities towards children and young people, are illustrated in the following statements from guidance that accompanied the occupational standards for initial teacher training from the Teacher Training Agency and from the new Teacher Development Agency.

> *The care and education of pupils are often the collective responsibility of a network of professionals and other support staff, who need to work together effectively to ensure that children's needs are met. Teachers need, therefore, to have a good understanding of how other adults, both within the classroom and beyond, can contribute to teaching and learning, and how teachers can use this contribution as a resource. This understanding assumes awareness of other colleagues' roles, and how a teacher's responsibilities relate to and complement those of others. This will include an ability to recognise the limits of their own expertise and authority, and an awareness of when and how to seek help from a colleague.*

(TTA 2005 p 13)

> *Teaching involves more than care, mutual respect and well-placed optimism. It demands knowledge and practical skills, the ability to make informed judgements, and to balance pressures and challenges, practice and creativity, interest and effort, as well as an understanding of how children learn and develop.*

(TTA 2005 p 13)

In the second statement 'social work' could readily be substituted for 'teaching' as the range of personal qualities, knowledge and skills and the integrating of theory and practice will be familiar to you as a student social worker.

Adams and Chakera (2004 p52) state clearly that *teachers are recognised as agents for change working towards greater social equity* and, referring to the former GTC Code of Professional Values and Practices, emphasised the role of the teacher in relation to equal opportunities. However, in contrast to the social work value base and similar to the values of health professionals, the professional values for teaching do not explicitly include the promotion of social justice. Some of these issues will be discussed in the later section on social exclusion and inequalities within education, which emphasises the role of education in providing a key route out of poverty. The recent changes in government policy and direction to the provision of education particularly in relation to higher education have raised many heated debates about these issues which will be discussed in more detail at the end of this chapter.

The role of Ofsted

The Office for Standards in Education, Children's Services and Skills (Ofsted) is the organisation responsible for the regulation and inspection of schools, colleges and teacher training providers. It inspects and regulates all services which care for children and young people and its duties also extend to child care providers, children's services, and youth work. Their remit also includes the dissemination of best practice and the evaluation of government strategies (Ofsted 2005). Ofsted reports directly to Parliament as it is an independent and impartial organisation. In 2010–11, Ofsted undertook over 32,500 inspections in England across the range of services it inspects, costing £183 million (Ofsted 2011). Ofsted publishes its inspection reports on its website (www.ofsted.gov) which should give parents, learners, employers and the public access to information they need to make choices and hold services to account. Ofsted reports that its website receives over seven million 'hits' a month (Ofsted 2011). This may be a site that you may visit if you are working with a local school or looking for a service for a child or young person you are working with. Its inspection workforce is made up of both employed and contracted inspectors with more than 4000 personnel. Its key areas are broad and its programme of work consists of four main areas.

1. *Inspection*
- Children's homes.

- Adoption and fostering agencies.

- Children and Family Court Advisory and Support Service (Cafcass).

- Early Years childcare providers.

- Providers on the Childcare Register.

- Maintained school inspections, those that continue to be 'outstanding' have less inspection during a five-year period whereas other schools are inspected with more frequency.

- Education in independent schools including boarding schools.

- New academies including pre- and post-registration inspections.

- Residential special schools and children's education schools registered by the Ministry of Defence.

- Children's centres.

- Colleges, initial teacher education providers, work-based learning in establishments offering apprenticeships.

- Judicial services including education in prisons, secure training centres, secure children's homes, probation services and immigration removal and detention centres.

- Adult and community learning and training provision for unemployed people, including for disabled people.

- Armed services training establishments which are kept confidential to the Ministry of Defence.

2. *Regulation of childcare and children's social care*

Ofsted registers a range of Early Years and children's social care services, and regulates them by deciding whether people, premises and the services provided are suitable to care for children and potentially vulnerable young people. They carry out checks to ensure those applying to provide these services meet the required standards and, where they do not, take action to prevent them from operating. An important area of work is responding to and investigating complaints.

Ofsted also has powers to investigate complaints about maintained schools, relating to whole-school issues and where the complaints procedure has otherwise been exhausted. They completed 143 of these in 2010–11 compared with 23 in 2009–10. The majority of complaints concerned issues about the leadership and management of a school, the quality of education provided and the contribution made by the school to the well-being of pupils (Ofsted 2011 p14).

3. *Evaluating serious case reviews*

Serious case reviews are local inquiries carried out by local Safeguarding Children Boards into the death or serious injury of a child where abuse or neglect is known or suspected to be a factor. Ofsted took responsibility for evaluating these reviews in 2007, and introduced new procedures for evaluation, including making a graded judgement about their quality. Since this time serious case reviews are now published as a matter of course and open to public and peer scrutiny and Ofsted's role may refocus on assessing progress on the local action and changes stemming from reviews.

4. *In-depth surveys and good practice studies*

Finally, Ofsted draws on the expertise and knowledge of its inspectors to determine, investigate and report on cross-cutting issues facing education, children's services, and in the learning and skills sector. It is in a position to collect evidence about practice and undertake surveys of core topics in education over time and in depth, such as special educational needs and disability arrangements in education and on the different subjects taught in education.

Best practice thematic reviews from Ofsted

We have selected some reports published by Ofsted on their website www.ofsted.gov. Go to the site and using the search facility, search for and download one of the following reports.

Transition through detention and custody: Arrangements for learning and skills for young people in custodial or secure settings, 090115, May 2010.

Local authorities and home education, 090267, June 2010.

Personal, social, health and economic education in schools, 090222, July 2010.

Safeguarding in schools, Best Practice, September 2011.

COMMENT

Make a few notes about the key issues and how these might influence your own practice as a social worker and how you might use the report's findings in your own work with children and young people. Share these with your practice teacher and compare these with the work done in your team and service.

Current issues for compulsory education

One of the most memorable slogans of New Labour, coined by Prime Minister Blair in the run-up to the 1997 election, was 'Education, education, education'. The theme of tackling social exclusion and promoting social justice featured strongly in the former government's education plans as New Labour claimed that education was the most effective route out of poverty and therefore central to concerns with social exclusion. McKnight et al. (2005 p47) remind us that the focus was to be *practical not ideological*. This supports the views of Toynbee and Walker (2001 p47) who have stated that the former government were *extraordinarily pragmatic about how to deliver better schooling* whilst also reminding us that policies were informed by the old Labour principles of *education as emancipation, an antidote to social exclusion, handmaid of social justice* (2001 p44). The standard of education and its institutions has since been the subject of constant legislative reform, as we saw in the beginning of this chapter. Education has been linked to the needs of the economy in the context of globalisation as well as the debates about localism and devolvement of responsibilities for services to local communities. The coalition government has advanced the marketisation agenda within education via the expansion of the academies programme and the introduction of new 'free schools' and 'university technical colleges'. We have summarised some of the most prominent issues impacting on current government policy on education below.

Training of teaching professionals

The training and education of teachers has been subject to much government and public debate. Naidoo and Muschamp (2002 p149) suggest that the professionals involved in the delivery of education have been blamed by the government for poor standards in student achievement.

New core requirements for an initial teacher training course, training for newly qualified teachers, existing teachers and headteachers, and a streamlined procedure for dealing with incompetent teachers made it clear that the teaching profession was responsible for underachievement in schools.

Miller (2005 p6) shares this view, maintaining that the inspection regime has *questioned the integrity of teachers and demoralised the profession* and that, in addition to this, teachers are *constrained by externally imposed curricula and compulsory attendance* (p10). More brazen elitist plans were referred to in the Conservative Manifesto for the 2010 election and in the coalition government's initial teacher training strategy (TDA 2011). There are deliberate moves to drive up standards by offering graduates with first-class degrees in physics, chemistry, maths and modern foreign languages significantly better financial incentives to train as teachers, and requiring all trainees to have high standards of mathematics and English by requiring trainees to pass tougher literacy and numeracy tests before they start teacher training. The government has also allowed and encouraged schools to lead their own high-quality initial teacher training and encouraged more primary specialist teachers to be trained. Further, it has been speculated that the impact of the Comprehensive Spending Review of 2010, which led to job losses, pay freezes and erosion to teachers' pensions, coupled with the introduction of further change policy initiatives, may seriously erode teacher morale (Gewirtz and McGuire 2010). Like social work, the government needs to keep its eye on recruitment and retention issues in teaching and develop workforce initiatives as required, such as the Newly Qualified Social Work (NQSW) status and Assessed and Supported first Year of Practice (ASYE) after qualifying. A report in 2008 showed that only 67 per cent of new teachers remained in the classroom 12 months after training, possibly as a result of 'culture shock', after sampling school life for the first time and being on the receiving end of challenges from poor pupil behaviour and bureaucracy (Paton 2008). It has also been disclosed that a significant number of very young teachers tend to work as supply staff, without a full contract. These may be issues you face when trying to build relationships with your local schools and in achieving continuity for young people you are collaborating together on. Further, figures released by the General Teaching Council for England in 2011 showed that barring failing staff from the profession is at a low rate (around 1 in 30,000 since 2001 and there were only a further 14 teachers suspended over the same period with one teacher struck off in 2010–11). These figures have been interpreted as representing lack of proper attention being given to dealing with weak or failing staff by education managers. As a result the coalition government proposed overhauling the system by introducing clearer capability procedures for schools, lifting a ban on the number of times teachers can be observed by heads and giving headteachers more powers to deal with underperforming staff. The Education Secretary also has direct powers to bar failing teachers from the profession.

Performance of providers

As in other areas of the public sector there has been an emphasis on outcomes and performance measures. Targets were set to improve standards and league tables have continued to be a prominent feature for schools, with the 'naming and shaming' of underperforming schools and the removal from local authority control of 'failing' schools. There was also an emphasis on the responsibilities of parents and the wider community, including the business community. In relation to league tables, concerns have been expressed about the information on which league tables are based. The use of statistics on children in receipt of free school meals as a baseline measures has been criticised as being fundamentally flawed. The continued use of these league tables without a more rigorous and clear use of data has also been said to be *likely to further damage schools and pupils and impede any attempts to raise standards generally* (Plewis and Goldstein 1998). This debate continues. In 2012, the coalition government introduced new performance measures for secondary education which abandon any contextual value-added measures, and thus those that take account of social factors shaping performance. The government asserted that this was *too difficult for the public to understand*. New measures intend to show the actual progress pupils have made including a 'narrowing the gap' measure to compare the exam performance of pupils on free school meals with others taking the same exams. Emphasis will continue on those achieving five or more A*–C grades including maths and English and therefore do not reflect any measures that rewards schools for getting the best out of all pupils, wherever they are on the ability spectrum.

Addressing inequalities in education

Like health, a number of initiatives have been developed to address inequalities, for example, the setting up of Education Action Areas and Fresh Start schools and the Excellence in Cities project for inner-city schools. The latter included measures aimed to tackle truancy and provide facilities for disruptive pupils, supported by an on-site education welfare officer. Education welfare officers are normally qualified social workers and as such they bring the knowledge, skills and values of social work to the education setting by working with headteachers, teachers, and support staff to facilitate children receiving an appropriate education. Concerns were expressed in the 1997 White Paper *Excellence in schools* about the need to address the gaps in achievement between children from different social classes, minority ethnic groups and between genders. Some research (Horgan 2007) has shown that how most children actually experience school is determined by the level of disadvantage they face in that children from poorer families tend to do less well in getting the same quality of schooling, or the same outcomes, as children from better-off families. Some of the contributing factors may include the ability to pay for uniforms, lunches, school trips and out-of-school activities as well as expectations about what education could do for them. Some boys as young as nine were found to be disenchanted with school and starting to disengage. There are differences in the way that boys and girls are socialised as well as difficulties faced by teachers in disadvantaged schools, including environmental, all of which contributed to poorer children's attitudes (Horgan 2007). The active promotion of the 'market' within education has been shown to advantage those families best placed to engage with choice and diversity in provision. It has been demonstrated that children who are socio-economically disadvantaged, particularly those with special needs, are more likely to attend underfunded 'sink' schools, thus narrowing the gap in educational attainment between socio-economic groups (Perry and Francis 2010).

More recent changes to the funding of education services which often support minority groups or those with special educational needs may have a detrimental effect on improving the life chances and national outcomes overall. The ending of the Education Maintenance Allowance (EMA) and the previously ring-fenced ethnic minority achievement award has been replaced by a Pupil Premium (PP) to support the education of disadvantaged children. It was recognised by the Labour government that compared with pupils of similar socio-economic backgrounds, some ethnic minority pupils were underperforming. The ethnic minority achievement award was used to provide support, for example via specially trained teaching assistants working directly with low-achieving ethnic minority pupils and their families. It provided funding for qualified co-ordinators to track pupils' progress, oversee action plans and pass on resources to other staff and professionals.

RESEARCH SUMMARY

Research since the 1950s has demonstrated that:

Children from less advantaged families have lower levels of educational achievement. Such inequalities lead to lifetime inequalities due to the relationship between education, employment and earnings and a range of other adult outcomes such as general health and psychological well-being. Recent evidence suggests that since the 1980s this cycle has strengthened.

(McKnight et al. 2005 p 66)

Evidence suggests that Black, Pakistani and Bangladeshi pupils underachieve, and that Indian and Chinese pupils do better than their white peers and that inequalities between people from different ethnic groups cannot be attributable to inequalities in class and gender.

(Adams and Chakera 2004 p 55)

Currently LA schools work together in groups or 'families' of schools. They are supported by local advisors, who know their schools intimately, facilitate the sharing of best practice and support innovation. Cuts to LAs have resulted in these and other services to schools being threatened, including mental health and language support. Such cuts will make it harder for schools to offer the range of support services to staff, parents and pupils that help to make a difference in disadvantaged settings. Where services are deemed essential, schools will have to look increasingly to private edu-businesses and educational consultancies that are run for profit and not democratically accountable.

(Gewirtz and McGuire 2010 p 40)

ACTIVITY 5.3

- *What other explanations can be put forward to explain these findings?*

- *Suggest three ways in which the inequalities emerging from the above research summaries could be changed – on a policy level, on a school level and on an individual level.*

- *As a social worker how might you challenge racism and promote anti-discriminatory practice when working with education staff and children and young people experiencing disadvantage?*

Access and quality have been two important themes in relation to children from disadvantaged groups (Naidoo and Muschamp 2002). The integration of children with special educational needs (SEN) into mainstream schools has been subject to government policy since 2001 and guidance on this is provided through the Special Educational Needs (SEN) Code of Practice (DfES 2001a). There are approximately 2 million children and young people who require special needs education and the current system remains very complex. This is particularly in relation to identifying funding and protocols to support collaboration around the needs of children and young people that require education and social care and/or healthcare support. In 2011, the coalition government introduced a Green Paper on Special Needs Education (HMG 2011). This aims to introduce radical proposals for a single assessment process through a single Early Years setting-based category and school-based category of SEN. Those with SEN will be eligible for combined education, health and care plans which include parents in the assessment process for the first time and who will be given the legal right to take control of care funding support. More specifically, the Green Paper proposes that:

- *there is early identification and assessment;*

- *local authorities and other services set out a local offer of all services available;*

- *there is an option of a personal budget by 2014 for all families with children with a statement of SEN or a new Education, Health and Care Plan;*

- *parents are given a real choice of school, either a mainstream or special school;*

- *there is greater independence in the assessment of children's needs.*

Much of the detail will be achieved by setting up local pathfinders and the paper also gives parents and community groups the power to set up special free schools as the case study below illustrates.

Extending educational opportunities for people with autism and special educational needs

In 1997, Virginia Bovell, the mother to Danny, her three-year-old son with autism, realised that there were no schools offering the intensive support needed. She got together with four other families and set up a specialist school offering intensive, autism-specific teaching. Fourteen years later the school they created in north London, called Treehouse, is recognised internationally as a model for how children with autism should be taught.

Now that her son is 18 and on the brink of leaving school, a new challenge in finding a suitable place for him to continue his education has emerged as there are so few colleges equipped to accommodate them. About 85% of adults with autism are unemployed. The options are living at home with their parents for the rest of their life, or going to live in a residential community (of which there are very few), or spending time at daycare centres.

CASE STUDY *continued*

This resonates with findings from parents of children with other disabilities, who often find that state support throughout childhood is replaced by a black hole once they reach 16. These are further barriers to their living more independently and gaining employment. This can create large long-term costs to society. The annual cost of supporting people with autism in the UK from social care budgets is estimated to be £27.5bn. Despite even greater recognition that autism, which is a lifelong neurological condition, affects a larger number of people than previously accepted, local authorities have not responded to the growing need.

A national charity, Ambitious about Autism *has since developed plans with a number of FE colleges to support young people with autism to continue their education. The government's Green Paper on SEN proposes that support should be extended for disabled young people up to the age of 25, and* Ambitious about Autism *wants the government to create a legal right to educational support up to the age of 25. Even later in life, when parents die, maybe in their 80s, leaving their child in their 50s or 60s, there can be an emergency resulting in emotional catastrophe and residential care.*

(*Source*: Gentleman, *The Guardian*, 11/10/2011 www.guardian.co.uk/society/2011/oct/11/where-support-autistic-young-people)

Currently for children with SEN there are a range of professionals involved in the planning, delivery and support of education which may include:

- psychology and behaviour support services;
- hearing and vision support services;
- speech and language therapy services;
- occupational therapy and physiotherapy services.

(Source: Bournemouth Borough Council 2005)

Giving children and young people a good start

A number of initiatives have been developed to address inequalities and disadvantage earlier in life which have involved cross-cutting policies that prioritise the needs of young people: identify resources for preventative work and support co-ordinated joined-up working at the highest level (DfES 2001b). During their period in office, New Labour had been concerned with broadening the types of schools and types of learning offered to ensure a range of academic and vocational courses to meet both the needs of schoolchildren and the needs of the economy. For pre-school children the Sure Start centres were strategically situated in areas of high deprivation and were run on community development principles, described by Glass (2005) as *one if its most attractive features*. The overall goal of Sure Start Local Programmes (SSLPs) was to enhance the life chances for young children growing up in disadvantaged neighbourhoods. Children in these communities are perceived as being at risk of doing poorly at school, having trouble with peers and agents of authority and ultimately experiencing compromised life chances in the form of leaving school prematurely, unemployment and limited longevity. These have profound consequences not just for the children but for their families, communities and for society at large. Thus, SSLPs not only aimed to enhance health and well-being during the Early Years, but to increase the chances that children would enter school ready to learn, be academically successful in school, socially successful in their communities and occupationally successful when adult. These intiatives go a long way towards breaking the cycle of intergenerational transmission of poverty, school failure and social exclusion (DoE, 2010b).

As an innovative intervention, SSLPs are area-based with the advantage that services (e.g. childcare, family support) are universally available, thereby limiting any stigma that may accrue from individuals being targeted. In their initial years there was no prescribed 'curriculum' or set of services, but Sure Start had extensive local autonomy over how it fulfilled its mission to improve and create services as needed, without specifying how services were to be changed. During 2005–06, fundamental changes were made to Sure Start as it came under the control of local authorities. Renamed as Children's Centres led to them being more specific about what was on offer. The focus moved from child development, targeted at children in disadvantaged areas, to one more universal in its nature. There was a change of focus to the provision of childcare facilities linked to encouraging parents to work. Children's centres are however a good example of integrated services with local authorities, primary care trusts, education and childcare providers, Jobcentre Plus, social services, community groups and voluntary organisations all working together. These settings also provide an opportunity for collaborative social work practice to ensure that the needs of children and their families are met and that services are delivered in an anti-oppressive framework that promotes social justice. The community development aspect has however been lost as local people and parents are no longer involved in management boards of Sure Start. The important service user and carer involvement has also diminished as the projects moved to local authority control. Overall, they tend to be varied in their implementation, meaning that evaluating their impact remains unique.

The DoE (2010b) defined the national objectives of Sure Start as:

- improving social and emotional development;
- improving health;
- improving the ability to learn;
- strengthening families and communities.

Sure Start has since been extended to children up to the age of 14, and up to age 16 for those with special educational needs and disabilities, bringing together early education, childcare, health and family support services.

Twelve key findings from the national evaluation of Sure Start

Evaluation revealed mixed effects, most being beneficial and a couple being negative in character. The main impacts identified for children were as follows.

- *Children growing up in SSLP areas had lower BMIs than children in non-SSLP areas. This was due to their being less likely to be overweight with no difference for obesity.*

- *Children growing up in SSLP areas had better physical health than children in non-SSLP areas.*

Mothers in SSLP areas reported the following factors.

- *Providing a more stimulating home learning environment for their children.*

- *Providing a less chaotic home environment for their children.*

- *Experiencing greater life satisfaction.*

- *Engaging in less harsh discipline.*

- *Experiencing more depressive symptoms.*

- *Being less likely to visit their child's school for parent/teacher meetings or other arranged visits, although the overall incidence was low generally.*

In terms of change over the time between when children were 3 years and 5 years old in comparison with those in non-SSLP areas, mothers in SSLP areas reported the following advantages.

- *More positive change in life satisfaction.*

- *More improvement in the home learning environment.*

- *A greater decrease in harsh discipline (i.e. greater improvement).*

- *A greater decrease in workless household status (from 9 months to 5 years).*

(Source: The National Evaluation of Sure Start (NESS) Team, DoE 2010b)

Find out about Sure Start initiatives in your area. You can do this by visiting the website of the National Evaluation of Sure Start (NESS) based at Birkbeck, University of London (www.ness.bbk.ac.uk). There are also a range of special interest reports here, for example on the work done with fathers and minority groups through Sure Start.

- *Consider the role that social workers can play in the achievement of the Sure Start objectives.*

Continued

- *Which professionals are they likely to need to work with collaboratively?*
- *How will the learning from this text prepare you for this role?*
- *What sources will you draw on to provide a research-minded base for your practice?*

Extended schools

The Children's Plan (DCES 2007) set out the government's ten-year strategy to improve educational outcomes for children, improve children's health, reduce offending rates among young people and eradicate child poverty by 2020, thereby contributing to the achievement of the five Every Child Matters outcomes. Schools were placed at the epi-centre of this reform, with a target that by 2010, all primary and secondary schools in England would be involved in an extended schools network within their locality (DCES 2007). Parental engagement has been at the heart of government policy, reinforcing the need to involve parents in education in order to secure greater well-being of young people, and also to secure higher achievement. At the core of the Children's Plan is the firm belief that parental engagement makes a significant difference to educational outcomes, and that parents and carers have a key role to play in raising educational standards. Schools are also seen as a focal point for the local community *to foster better relationships between diverse communities* (DCES 2007 p73). The need for a broad, whole-authority approach was reflected in the introduction at the end of 2007 of a cross-government Public Service Agreement (PSA 21) to build more cohesive, empowered and active communities where schools offer integrated services to parents and the local community, including health and social care services; computer and information technology access and training; parenting support; breakfast clubs, after-school clubs; and summer schemes that encourage positive interactions between different groups within their local community (DCES 2007). In relation to promoting equality, a School Linking Network was launched in 2008, with funding, to provide support for schools to develop linking arrangements that would enable greater interaction between children from different cultural backgrounds alongside initiatives that focus on the school curriculum around ethnic, religious and cultural diversity (Ajegbo et al. 2007). Inter-generational learning has also been promoted within extended schools aiming to bring young people together with older people for *mutual gain and the wider benefit of communities* (DIUS 2009).

Parental choice and localism

Schools have been organised in a variety of ways in different authorities, with grammar and comprehensive systems, two- and three-tier structures of primary/secondary and primary/middle/upper school systems, a varied system of post-16 provision, same-sex schools, mixed schools and faith schools. While this may appear to offer choice and variety, it also provides yet another context for inequalities. The ability to choose between state and private-sector provision is an important divide in education but state schools also demonstrate class divisions, particularly in cities where more affluent families can position themselves to take advantage of the better schools. Those without the economic means to increase choice have no option other than to send their children to poorer-performing schools. The British Attitudes Survey (YouGov 2010) found that attitudes towards the 'right to choose' of parents were ambivalent and to some extent contradictory. Parents were shown to want their nearest school to be good enough and to trust professionals with the provision of quality education. The direction of travel, however, in current politics is pro-choice in public services, and for services to be much more responsive to consumers' needs. We have seen throughout this chapter how development of provision, for example, has been directed through the academy programme and through the opportunity to develop independent schools.

Education 'otherwise'

According to Section 7 of the Eduction Act 1996, the parents of every child of compulsory school age must ensure that their child engages in full-time education *suitable to his age, ability and aptitude and to any special educational needs he may have, either by regular attendance at school or otherwise*. The local authority must ensure that this happens. Suitable education might take the form of home tuition for children who are too ill to attend school, and some parents choose to educate their children at home rather than send them to school. With the introduction of supersized primary schools, large class sizes and the squeeze on primary school places, some parents are choosing to educate their children at home for part of the week. However, flaws in home education laws were highlighted following an independent review into the death of 7-year-old Khyra Ishaq in 2010. Khyra starved to death in 2008 at the hands of her mother, while being educated at home. The law's sole focus on parents' rights – rather than their children's – enabled parents to ignore social services and made it impossible for them to intervene. The subsequent review called for changes that ensure that social services speak to children to assess whether home education is in their best interests. The Education (Otherwise) Welfare Team was criticised for not asking to see examples of the kinds of lessons Khyra would be taught and the number of hours education provided. They failed to speak to the children direct. These failures led to a catalogue of missed opportunities to spot neglect and abuse in the home.

Current legislation enables parents to move their children from state education with minimal reasons. This is a particular advantage to parents who may wish to conceal abuse by removing any oversight of a child's welfare or development by professionals. In 2010 before the change of government, a controversial clause to the Education Bill, that would have compelled every parent who home-educates their child to register with their local authority, was dropped. It was one of the concessions made by the then Labour government to push through an education bill before Parliament. However, this was dissolved ahead of the general election and has yet to be resolved.

In summary, whatever approach is used to educate children and young people, there is no doubt that education has an important role to play in strengthening the well-being of families and community cohesion. A systematic review of the research literature (Statham et al. 2010) identified what works in this regard and the key findings are outlined overleaf.

What works in strengthening family well-being and/or community cohesion through the role of schools and extended services?

- *Strengthening family well-being and/or community cohesion requires buy-in and commitment from school leaders and teachers.*

- *Some teachers are unprepared or under-confident in engaging with parents whose cultural or social backgrounds differ from their own, or are unsure how to promote community cohesion through the curriculum. These barriers can be overcome with appropriate support and training.*

- *Family structures and communities are increasingly diverse, and strategies need to take account of different needs, backgrounds and cultural expectations. 'One size fits all' approaches will not work.*

- *There are issues with engagement and take-up for some groups, which may reflect inappropriate forms of support and intervention. Services that are insensitive to families' needs and do not adequately connect with the context of parents' lives and motivations are unlikely to succeed.*

- *Resistance from parents or carers to becoming more involved with the school may be misunderstood as a lack of interest, rather than originating from a lack of time or a lack of confidence.*

- *Developing links with parents and communities and building up trusting relationships takes time, and is difficult to achieve when projects have a limited lifespan or are expected to demonstrate positive outcomes in a short period.*

- *Schools can contribute to strengthening family well-being and community cohesion, but the wide range of external factors that also influence this means that strategies need to operate at multiple levels.*

(Statham et al. 2010 p13)

The role of the Education Welfare Service

The Education Welfare Service provides an extensive network of services to children as the local authority has statutory functions to ensure school attendance and to regulate child employment as well as the licensing of children in entertainment, modelling and paid sporting activities. Education welfare officers, also known as school social workers, will work closely with professionals from a wide range of agencies to carry out these responsibilities and may be involved in:

prosecuting for non-attendance, penalty notices, parenting contracts and parenting orders for attendance, education supervision orders, and truancy sweeps.

(Every Child Matters 2005b)

Education Welfare Officers have traditionally been qualified social workers and the Central Council for the Education and Training of Social Workers, the body previously responsible for the accreditation of social work education courses, issued guidance (CCETSW 1992) on how the practice competencies could be met to support future employment as an Education Welfare Officer.

While qualified social workers and youth workers continue to be employed as Education Welfare Officers, from 2005 specific National Occupational Standards (in Learning Development and Support Services) that relate to this role were developed.

Blyth (2000 p108) states that the aim of education social work is *to ensure that children obtain optimum benefit from a meaningful educational experience* and informs us that other than work carried out which relates to school attendance issues, many of the roles and responsibilities undertaken by an education social worker, or education welfare officer, are similar to duties performed by social workers in other settings. He describes the tasks of education social work as follows.

- Working with disabled children and children with formal statements of special educational need in accordance with statutory provision.

- Child protection.

- Monitoring and regulation of the employment of school children.

- Working with pre-school age children – for example, assisting parents/carers to obtain nursery placements.

- Home–school liaison.

- Inter-agency liaison.

- Preventative programmes on misuse of alcohol, drugs and other substances.

- Working with children exhibiting disruptive behaviour and/or at risk of exclusion from school.

- Securing alternative education provision for persistent non-attenders and children excluded from school.

- Providing individual and/or group work for children with particular difficulties (for example, regarding attendance, behaviour or relationship difficulties) and/or their parents/carers.

- Providing in-service training for other education staff.

- Participating in the juvenile justice system.

- Preparing reports for courts.

- Providing advice/administration concerning welfare benefits.

- Working with pregnant girls and school-age mothers.

- Working with young people who provide care for sick or disabled family members.

- Working with children from traveller families.

Blyth (2000 pp108–9)

A significant challenge is the *punitive, legalistic approach to the management of non-attendance, thus demonstrating the need for the continual assertion of social work values* (Blyth 2000 p109). You may come across an approach from teachers or their managers that interprets truancy and disaffection within school and pathologises the behaviour as *non-productive, dysfunctional and illegitimate* (Miller 2005 p12).

CASE STUDY

Here is a summary of the story of Anita who has experience of working as an Education Welfare Officer and, as a lone practitioner, covered several schools. The main focus of her work was on attendance issues, with parents who often condoned their children's absence from school, or were disinterested. She now works in a behaviour and education support team (BEST) which operates with a collaborative team approach. She and other colleagues in the BEST utilise individual and group work methods to work with pupils and parents, and the team approach enables a preventative as well as reactive approach to be taken, with team members using their expertise to engage with pupils and families, advise on a range of measures including anti-bullying strategies, and encourage a broader understanding of the value of education.

(Source: www.everychildmatters.gov.uk)

ACTIVITY 5.5

Imagine you are involved in the establishment of a BEST. Which other professionals would you hope to include in the team? Justify your choices by explaining the knowledge, skills and values that they will bring and the types of situations these will be applied to. What debates are likely to arise over the issue of truanting/school attendance and challenging behaviour/exclusion from school?

What specific role might a social worker have in the team and what perspective might they bring to the understanding of poor attendance or challenging behaviour?

COMMENT

Useful background readings are the reports on research undertaken for the Joseph Rowntree Foundation by Britton et al. (2002); on the needs of excluded young people in multi-cultural communities, Osler et al. (2002); on girls and social exclusion; and by Vernon and Sinclair (1998) on the role of social services in maintaining children in school. You can find summaries of these research reports on the findings section of the Joseph Rowntree Foundation website (www.jrf.org.uk).

Other factors at play in non-attendance at school issues may include:

- children and young people being overwhelmed by family problems so that they feel unable to attend;

- they are young carers and too tired to attend or worried about leaving their parent who has mental health problems or a physical disability;

- they believe the curriculum is irrelevant and that there are no opportunities open to them when they leave school regardless of their attendance.

It is important to advocate on behalf of children and young people and to mediate between families and the agencies who may want to proceed to a range of measures to enforce attendance. Awareness of the impact of competition and performance measurement in relation to the 'league tables' may also play a contributory role in decision-making in schools as schools are led to compete against one another.

Lifelong learning and informal education

The final section of this chapter refers briefly to post-compulsory education where learning is perceived as a lifelong process and refers to:

all learning activity undertaken throughout life, with the aim of improving knowledge, skills and competences within a personal, civic, social and/or employment-related perspective.

(EC 2000 p 9)

Learning does not often feature as an explicit phenomenon within the activities of social work practice but some have argued that the facilitation of learning opportunities within social care provision can enhance service users' potential for increasing participation, citizenship and social justice (Hafford-Letchfield 2010, 2011). Lifelong learning is both an important feature of human development throughout the lifespan and in itself can contribute to the richness of an individual's life and help to develop social capital in the community. Freire (1972) reminds us that education is never a neutral process and is a major factor in the distribution of power and is therefore an important focus following compulsory education. When working with adults with mental health, physical and learning disabilities, you may wish to find out how service users experienced their compulsory education and whether there were gaps in their basic education that they would like to address as well as identifying aspirational ones.

Aldridge (2009) cites many positive benefits of learning in facilitating physical and emotional health within care settings. She asserts that purposeful learning activities enhance relationships between carers and service users if they are accurate in meeting individual needs. For example, activities where adult service users and carers engage with learning can also provide a means by which service users can reflect on their life experiences and offer protection against cognitive decline, particularly in later life (Withnall 2010). A number of empirical studies (Purdie and Boulton-Lewis, 2003; Hammond, 2004; Jackson, 2006) suggest that participation in learning impacts upon a range of health and social care outcomes such as well-being, recovery from mental ill-health, the capacity to cope with stress-inducing circumstances and the onset and progression of chronic illness and disability. Further, taking on significant caring roles, managing one's own care through direct payments or personalised budgets all require particular skills to take advantage of these developments.

ACTIVITY 5.6

'Co-production' is the policy term used to define the contribution of service users in collaborative relationships with professionals to tackle issues together and accept user expertise in developing appropriate support.

Think about adult service users or carers that you are currently working with. These may include parents and foster carers.

- *What methods might you use in your intervention that capitalises on opportunities for service users and carers to learn and develop their knowledge and skills towards more independence from services and quality of life?*

- *What other professionals or organisations can support the learning and development needs of your service users? These may be informal as well as formal types of learning.*

COMMENT

McClusky (1974) reflects five key areas of need that service users might meet through strategies for learning which Hafford-Letchfield (2010) adapted for social workers to address in their work with older people, but which are relevant to any user group. These mirror the traditional 'ladder' of participation (Arnstein 1969) commonly referred to in social care (Carr 2004) where at the lowest levels, users can expect to have the right to information exchange with professionals, and, at the upper levels achieve delegation of power and control to facilitate citizenship. Other forms of consultation and partnership working fall within these two extremes and it would be useful to consider your own activities in relation to facilitating learning with service users identified in the above activity, against these different levels.

The key areas of learning need refer firstly to the coping needs of service users arising from adjusting to changes in daily life such as physical fitness, economic self-sufficiency and basic education. For example, these might involve the challenges of parenting a disabled child. Secondly, they involve expressive needs such as those related to taking part in activities for their own sake and possibly reflect those social interactions or leisure pursuits that we take for granted but may not be easily accessible to service users. Thirdly, Hafford-Letchfield (2010) cites contributive needs as those where individuals want to continue actively contributing to society and these reflect user participation and involvement activities such as in your own learning and assessment as a student social worker. Fourthly, influence needs occur where service users take a leadership role to achieve social change and are often seen in user-led organisations or campaigning community groups and individuals in social care. A need for transcendence need was McClusky's fifth domain in which service users and carers learn to balance power and demands from society. Learning is thus perceived as a complex social and value-creating activity, both shaping and being shaped by social structure and culture.

Putting people first (HMG 2007) and the Health and Social Care Act (2008) refer to the co-ordination of health, social care, education, housing and other organisations to encourage more innovative and flexible commissioning across a local area. Meeting the learning and educational needs of service users and carers is one of the objectives of integrated services and key to achieving the outcomes of more personalised services. In your own relationships with individual service users, meaningful ways in which to promote social inclusion could be transmitted through learning by encouraging a greater two-way transaction, building on the existing knowledge and experience of service users and carers themselves according to their perceived needs. Given that social work comes from a radical tradition seeking to promote principles of human rights, social justice and the empowerment and liberation of people to enhance well-being (International Federation of Social Work, undated), giving more weight to the quality of partnerships between social workers and service users at the practice level requires recognition in how these are supported within developments at the policy level (DoH 2009c). Opportunities are afforded through maximising learning for people using social care services to promote a more meaningful reality. Different mechanisms of achieving user involvement, participation and strategies for self-directed support might exploit the capacity of adult learners and their contribution to learning communities.

REFLECTION POINT

[Social Work] involves more than care, mutual respect and well-placed optimism. It demands knowledge and practical skills, the ability to make informed judgements, and to balance pressures and challenges, practice and creativity, interest and effort.

Skilled practitioners can make [social work] look easy but they have learned their skills and improved them through training, practice, evaluation and by learning from other colleagues.

(TTA 2005 p 5)

Consider these statements (which were written specifically about teachers but could equally be said of social workers) and reflect on your experience of learning to be a social worker and how you will continue to develop and improve your knowledge, skills and values during the rest of the course, in practice learning placement, by evaluating your practice and by learning from colleagues.

In terms of learning for collaborative social work practice, what knowledge, values and skills have you developed so far and how will you continue to evaluate your learning and your practice? You might find it useful to record this in a reflective diary if you are keeping one or in your personal development portfolio.

CHAPTER SUMMARY

This chapter has introduced you to some important themes and perspectives for working with professionals from an education setting, including Early Years provision, education welfare and adult learning. Education is a complex field and we have considered some of the common areas of knowledge, skills and values and the areas in which different roles diverge. Educational professionals share some similar experiences to social work, and as Miller (2005 p6) reminds us, it is hard *not to see teaching as a beleaguered profession, compromised and ground down by increasing formalisation, inadequately resourced and viewed by successive governments with suspicion and a lack of respect for their professional integrity*. You may find it helpful to review the recent changes in social work that are helping to address the common difficulties that social work has shared with teaching.

FURTHER READING

Horner, N and Krawczyk, S (2009) *Social work in education and children's services* (2nd edition). Exeter: Learning Matters.

Jarvis, P (2009) *Adult education and lifelong learning: Theory and practice* (4th edition). London: Routledge.

For a more detailed explanation of working collaboratively in an education context you may find it helpful to read the text in this series.

Tarr, J (2005) Education. In Barrett, G, Sellman, D and Thomas, J (eds) *Interprofessional working in health and social care*. Basingstoke: Palgrave.

Thompson, J (2010) *The essential guide to understanding special educational needs*. Harlow: Pearson Education.

Blyth, E. (2007) Education social work. In Davies, M (ed.) *The Blackwell dictionary of social work* (3rd edition). Oxford: Blackwell.

A useful summary of the role of the Education Welfare Officer.

WEBSITE

www.teachandlearn.net

A website that supports the continuous professional development of teachers with links to a wealth of resources and information.

www.education.gov.uk/

The Department for Education website for latest news and publications on initiatives on compulsory education and children's services.

www.direct.gov.uk/en/Parents/Preschooldevelopmentand

This is the website of the government's Sure Start initiative.

www.ness.bbk.ac.uk

The website of the National Evaluation of Sure Start, hosted by Birkbeck, London University.

www.ofsted.gov.uk

The website of the inspection body for teaching and Early Years education.

Chapter 6
The housing and neighbourhood context

Why is an understanding of housing and neighbourhood issues important for social workers?

Writing over a decade ago, Stewart and Stewart (1993) reported that social workers found assisting service users with housing problems was one of the most difficult parts of their work and that social workers felt ill-prepared to undertake this work. Housing and accommodation have since been cited as having an important role to play in health, well-being and the delivery of health and social care services particularly as we have moved towards more personalised support. The role of housing becomes pivotal for services to an individual with complex needs and is relevant for service users and carers of all ages. This may include young people being looked after or living apart from their families to accessibility for individuals with disabilities and long-term conditions. It is hoped that this chapter will help to prepare you as a future social worker for undertaking this work by introducing you to some of the important themes and issues relating to housing matters.

While you may have studied issues relating to housing as part of a social policy module, you may not initially have considered housing as an area of study that you would need to learn about in order to be able to work collaboratively. You will find that the impact of housing policies is wide-ranging and Adams (2002 p72) asserts that *social workers have much in common with housing officers*. Other research has suggested that where homelessness and housing support agencies take on primary responsibility for supporting people with multiple and complex needs, workers can often feel isolated and out of their depth (McDonagh 2011). It has been suggested elsewhere that housing support workers are now filling the gap left by the retreat of social workers from direct work with adults. However, while there are common areas of knowledge, skills and values for practice, few social work students have the opportunity to study with housing professionals. This chapter will help you to consider Adams' assertion and to identify what these common areas are.

Coles et al. (2000 p21) draw our attention to how

> *a number of demographic trends and social policies have combined to cluster social and economic disadvantage in particular areas and on social housing estates in particular.*

More recently, in the aftermath of the UK riots in 2011, we saw that most damage was done in communities suffering most from poverty, disadvantage and a depressed environment. Those rioting and looting laid waste to some of the poorest communities in Britain and the victims were among the poorest people. While it is dangerous to connect poverty, bad housing, poor life chances or weak parenting with these events, reflection by the Joseph Rowntree Trust (Low 2011) has drawn on a range of evidence from research findings that illustrate that an environment where there are decaying buildings and abandoned homes can have a severe effect on resident morale. Those affected do not feel they are in control and fear and insecurity are perceived as serious problems. On the positive side Low also notes that neighbourhoods mattered to residents and there can still be a strong sense of community. However, people living in these communities felt they were seen as the 'lowest of the low', and they resented how society seemed to moralise, blame them and attribute their problems to their own behaviour (Pearce and Milne 2010). Earlier work by Page (2000) indicates that *social exclusion, often addressed at the level of individual households, has structural causes and a strong community and neighbourhood dimension* (JRF 2000 p4), and that public services can play a crucial role in preventing social exclusion by:

- keeping vulnerable people connected to mainstream society;

- maintaining a visible physical embodiment of civil society in areas where community safety and mainstream values are breaking down;

- providing vital support to vulnerable families and children at risk (JRF 2000 p1).

There is a strong overlap between experiences of more extreme forms of homelessness and other support needs, with nearly half of service users reporting experience of institutional care, substance misuse, and street activities (such as begging), as well as homelessness (McDonagh 2011).

A recently documented growth in inequality means that the gap in socioeconomic circumstances between children living in social housing and other housing tenures is now wider than for any previous generation (Lupton et al. 2009). Wheeler et al. (2007) drew attention to the notion of 'postcode poverty' whereby the area in which someone lives has a significant impact on life chances, including employment, education and health. Being born under the wrong road sign is a different and perhaps even more intractable problem (Bradshaw 2005). This looks set to be exacerbated in some areas following the coalition government's curbing of housing benefits in its cuts to public expenditure. In an uncontrollable private rental market, this move has been cited as responsible for setting up elite areas juxtaposed with areas of extreme and moderate poverty, thus killing social diversity and putting the nail in the coffin of social mobility leading to stratified communities and reduced social mobility (Brunton 2010). For example, the Chartered Institute of Housing has suggested that such 'social cleansing' will result in almost all (13 out of 14) areas in London becoming unaffordable to welfare recipients by 2020. Further, the proportion of homes which are 'non-decent' is much higher in the more rural areas. This affects around 50% of homes in the most rural areas and villages compared to around 30% in small towns and urban areas in some parts of the country (www.poverty.org.uk/r78/index.shtml?2). In Devon, for example, an integrated approach is being taken to delivering housing and children's services as they have recognised that there are links between an unstable housing history and poor educational and economic outcomes for vulnerable young people (Devon Children's Trust 2004).

Data on the scale of homelessness for young people who are in contact with services indicates that at least 75,000 experienced homelessness in the UK in 2006–07 (Quilgars et al. 2008). More young people were accepted as homeless following the extension of priority need groups in the early 2000s, although numbers have fallen in England and Wales. Young people from disadvantaged socio-economic backgrounds and experiencing disruption or trauma in childhood are at increased risk of homelessness, and a significant minority experience violence in the parental home. Homelessness can also instigate or compound existing mental health and drug misuse problems among young people. Quilgars et al. (2008) found a strong association between homelessness and withdrawing from education, employment or training, with a discord evident between the welfare benefit system and employability initiatives (Quilgars et al. 2008).

Both physical and mental health problems have been linked to poor housing conditions. For example, the greatest risks to health in housing are related to cold and damp (including moulds and fungus) which affect and exacerbate respiratory conditions. People who live alone, disabled people and lone parent households are also particularly at risk of fuel poverty. Living in a cold home or a home that has mould is a predictor of poor physical and mental health, even after taking into account other factors such as a person's financial circumstances. Families with children were much more likely to live in a home with mould. Living in a cold home also contributes to social isolation as tenants may be reluctant to invite others to their home, contributing to their social isolation. This is important, because maintaining a social network is a key predictor of positive mental health (Harris et al. 2010).

CASE STUDY

The Families Project (Hill et al. 2002)

A voluntary-sector agency, supported jointly by the Housing and Social Work Departments of a local authority, works with families facing eviction from their tenancies as a result of their 'anti-social' behaviour (for example, verbal abuse, damaging the property, conflict with neighbours) and takes referrals from social work, housing, health and education professionals. The majority of families are experiencing problems related to poverty and family relationships and frequently have the additional challenge of criminal behaviour, addictions or mental health problems. In the majority of situations there are concerns about care and control of the children, with many families already having experienced a child or children being accommodated by the local authority.

Social workers and housing staff work closely together to help the families bring about change in their behaviour to prevent family break-up and children needing to be accommodated by the local authority.

Comments from the families about the success of the Project included: We would not have had a house and the kids would probably be in care *and,* Now I am getting on better with my children and we have developed a better relationship.

There is a growing awareness that housing plays an important role in the care of older people, particularly as many people continue to live in the community for as long as possible, and attention has been recently drawn to the lack of a robust evidence base which would help us to understand the particular needs of older people with dementia (O'Malley and Croucher 2005). Supporting people to make this transition and to sustain their quality of life is an important part of the work of social workers and care managers.

At the same time, the economic climate for developing homes and services to enable people to continue living independently into old age is changing dramatically, with cuts being made to both capital and revenue budgets.

Local authorities, housing providers and other local place-shapers have been working to address the issues presented by our changing demographics, but progress has not been able to keep pace with the increasing needs of the population (Oxford Economics 2011). The pace of change in demand and need has constantly outstripped the changes in the volume and design of housing and services. Housing providers in the third sector have become increasingly important in the role they play in meeting the needs of older people within their housing and services, but with an increasing older population, the sector needs to continue to plan more strategically and to cater innovatively to their needs. An ageing population brings new opportunities to develop housing and services collaboratively and can also take into account the high levels of owner occupation and housing equity owned by older people to help people capitalise on these in later life. Those with assets will still require trusted providers. Housing providers could also broaden out their services and facilities to the wider community following some examples of what has been done within traditional sheltered housing. These have moved away from providing concentrated support to its tenants towards more hub-and-spoke services which aim to provide outreach services to the wider community. Many housing associations have taken on contracts to deliver extra care support to older people inside sheltered housing and care to those outside across all tenures, in a drive to support the wider community of older people to live independently in their homes. The value of preventative services to maintain housing such as gardening or maintenance work through a handy person's service from the voluntary sector has also been recognised within commissioning. However, funding for these has been difficult to maintain as local authorities increasingly concentrate on their statutory duties in times of financial austerity.

Preventative, independent models of housing and support are widely favoured by older people themselves. A YouGov survey commissioned by the National Housing Federation (NHF 2010) found people aged between 60 and 65 dreaded ending up in a care home or imposing themselves on relatives if they could no longer cope with living on their own, their rating of different accommodation options if they could no longer live independently in their own home resulting in the following:

- 18 per cent had a positive view of living in a care home;
- 10 per cent thought that moving in with their family would be a good idea;
- 80 per cent were positive about downsizing to a smaller, more manageable home;
- 65 per cent liked the idea of living in a self-contained home with support or care available, if required.

Other evidence has suggested (Edwards and Harding 2011) that most older people would prefer to live in a mixed-age community rather than in specialist older-person developments, and that age-segregated housing can be damaging to social interaction and closer integration. Similarly, the development of any specific housing for older people needs to consider the possible provision of some facility for residential or nursing care either on the same site or close by, so that for those who do have to move into a care or nursing setting will not find the move so traumatic.

Personalisation brings new opportunities to more innovative housing solutions for older people and other adults living with disabilities and other social care needs. Taking a more holistic approach to housing-related themes has been echoed in the national dementia strategy (DoH 2009a) as more options in provision will have a clear impact on current housing and support models, as more intensive support is required and, eventually, specialist care as well as early intervention and early provision of support at home.

These developments imply much greater need for collating and sharing information about housing-related issues both at the individual support planning level and in strategic planning at a neighbourhood and national level. Finally the 'localism' agenda offers some significant opportunities, but it also poses real challenges in the provision and management of housing and related services. The coalition government's idea of the Big Society, although regarded by some as a gimmick (Eaton 2011), has highlighted the possibility for communities to be given new rights to run services and own assets where communities, citizens and volunteers play a bigger role in shaping and providing services. There will not be a 'one size fits all' approach to localism, and local authorities, housing organisations and the house-building industry will need to maintain strong relationships with local communities and local people (National Housing Federation 2011).

CASE STUDY

Leonard, aged 81, lives with his wife Ethel, aged 79, in a council-owned, two-storey terraced property. He has become increasingly frail after a long illness and is no longer able to climb the stairs to the bedroom. The property has one small living room and a kitchen downstairs, with a bathroom and two small bedrooms upstairs. At night Leonard sleeps on the settee but this is becoming difficult for Ethel as Leonard is afraid he will fall off the settee in the night and that Ethel will not hear and come to his help. He has also started to wander at night, rattling doors and emptying cupboards and to refer to Ethel as his mother. This is leading to sleepless nights for both, and Ethel has contacted the GP to ask for sleeping pills to help Leonard sleep better.

ACTIVITY 6.1

Imagine you are employed in the community care team in the social services area office which has received a referral from the GP about Leonard and Ethel.

- *What are the housing issues that need to be taken into account when formulating an assessment of the situation? What might be the advantages and disadvantages of remaining in this property?*

- *Which professionals might be involved in the assessment, planning and delivery of care services for Leonard and Ethel?*

- *What services might be arranged to support the couple in this property?*

- *What factors might prevent Leonard and Ethel remaining in their home?*

- *What alternative options involving housing might there be that could meet the needs of Leonard and Ethel?*

- *What facilities and services are there in your local area for supporting older people to remain in their home?*

Strategies for undertaking this activity include looking on the website of your local authority and researching their local housing strategy and social care strategy. Look specifically at how these different strategies talk to each other. Your area should have undertaken a Joint Strategic Needs Assessment (DoH, 2007) in which local agencies assess the needs of the local community and develop a strategic response. You could also look at the websites or information provided by other organisations that are working with the needs of older people, such as Age UK, and consider the types of partnerships they are developing.

A brief history

Early philanthropists

In the nineteenth and early twentieth centuries a number of philanthropic organisations and individuals concerned themselves with housing issues and in effect become the forerunners of the current charitable and independent sector. For example, the Peabody Trust, established in 1862, built blocks of flats in London to house working-class people who would then be bound by strict rules about behaviour and lifestyle, and Octavia Hill, a member of the Charity Organisation Society, established an organisation to manage the letting of properties to 'deserving' poor people, offering a system combining strict advice and inspection in an attempt to improve the behaviour of the poor. Despite the moralistic and authoritarian approach, the work of Octavia Hill was important, particularly as she lobbied Parliament for better housing conditions.

In addition, paternalistic industrialists became concerned for the housing conditions of their workers. For example, Titus Salt in Bradford, who created Saltaire for workers in the textile industry; the Cadbury family, who built housing in the Bourneville area of Birmingham; the Reckitts family in Hull, who are associated with the mustard industry; and the Rowntree family in York began to establish model communities for working-class people.

The work of the Rowntree family was particularly important. Seebohm Rowntree, the son of Joseph Rowntree (1845–1925), the founder of the chocolate industry in York, published a shocking report in 1901 on the working-class people in York, describing the unsanitary and overcrowded housing conditions in which they were living. The report provided new insights into the plight of poor working people and was influential in triggering social reform. An example of the impact of the report was Joseph Rowntree's response, the development of affordable and good quality housing at New Earswick, near York, for his employees and other workers using the model of a 'garden village'. While these rich philanthropists might be criticised for their paternalistic and patronising attitude to the poor and a degree of social engineering to achieve an 'ideal' mix of households, their example of 'model' communities was an important one, demonstrating that good-quality affordable housing could be provided at an economic cost and produce modest profits.

The Joseph Rowntree Foundation continues to be an important social policy research institute which *seeks to better understand the causes of social difficulties and explore ways of overcoming them* (JRF 2005a). The Foundation has a wide-ranging dissemination strategy, with current research themes being housing and neighbourhoods, poverty and disadvantage, practice and research and immigration and inclusion. We will be considering some of the recent research findings from the Joseph Rowntree Foundation later in this chapter.

Beveridge and the emergent welfare state

Housing provision was intended to address 'Squalor', one of William Beveridge's five 'giants' and therefore central to the vision of the emergent welfare state. After the Second World War there was an acute housing crisis causing the post-war government to embark on a large-scale rebuilding programme.

There was an emphasis on the needs of the returning troops, and 'homes for heroes' became a popular slogan, as had been the situation after the First World War. As a result of damage to property sustained during the war, there were considerable regional variations in housing availability and affordability.

The government of the time acknowledged that there was a relationship between housing and health and that other government agencies should be involved in strategic and operational issues. For example, the Housing Manual of 1944 detailed the types of properties that were recommended for building, including guidance for the establishment of new neighbourhoods, the layout of individual properties and the types of fittings that might be installed in them. This was jointly published by the Ministry of Health and the Ministry of Works and its introduction states that the document *has been prepared jointly by the Ministry of Health and the Ministry of Works. The Ministry of Fuel and Power has been consulted ... and the Ministry of Town and Country Planning has advised* (Ministry of Health and Ministry of Works 1944 p7). This is an example of cross-department collaboration, often referred to nowadays as 'joined-up thinking'. In the somewhat paternalistic and optimistic tone of the time, it was recognised that employment, recreational opportunities and shopping facilities were important when planning new housing development as well as *the provision of educational, health and social services* and that attention needed to be paid to *the different classes of people who make up a well balanced residential neighbourhood* (1944 p11). In the rebuilding projects undertaken there was an emphasis on the provision of housing in the public rented sector.

Since this time demographic changes have had an influence on housing demand and availability, including greater geographical mobility, greater life expectancy, an increase in single households and the impact of households dividing as a result of divorce or separation.

The 1980s have been described by Alcock et al. (2004 p219) as

> a decade in which the large-scale provision of state-funded welfare was increasingly questioned and challenged and in the field of housing we witness possibly the most successful attempt to alter radically the pattern of welfare provision.

This was largely as a result of the Conservative government's policy of encouraging private ownership of housing rather than public ownership.

Housing Act, 1980

The landmark 'right to buy' policy introduced by the 1980 Housing Act enabled council tenants to purchase their council house/flat at a discount and with favourable terms. People who had lived in their council house or flat for a minimum of three years were able to buy the property with a substantial discount of 30–50 per cent of the market value. The impact of this was to reduce the overall quality of the council rented housing stock as the most desirable properties were purchased and those in less desirable areas, in a poorer state of repair, and in poorer areas where tenants could not take advantage of discounts and mortgages were not. This contributed to a situation in which local authorities provided what came to be known as 'residual housing'. The Social Security and Housing Benefit Act 1982 transferred the arrangements for paying housing benefit from the Department of Social Security to the local authority, and the purchase of council houses was further made easier by the Housing and Planning Act 1986.

Local authorities now have a role of regulating the housing services provided by a wide range of providers, rather than that of provider of social housing. Alcock et al. (2004 p223) describe the role of the local authority as:

- maintaining standards and regulating rents in the private sector;
- administering housing benefits;
- enforcing environmental health standards;
- providing temporary accommodation for the homeless.

The impact of market forces has contributed to the link between social class and housing, with local authority housing having been seen as the option for those not able to afford to purchase their own homes as a result of unemployment or unstable employment – a last resort rather than a positive choice. New Labour has continued the Conservative ideological commitment to private ownership/owner occupation, individual responsibility and profit rather than emphasising collective responsibility and championing social housing as under previous Labour administrations.

A further move from the collective to the individualised approach is demonstrated in the way in which financial support moved away from the provision of subsidies to local authorities for housing developments to individuals' eligibility to claim housing benefit through means-tested benefits for residents in both private and public sector housing.

Housing Act, 1988

The effect of this Act was to provide tenants with the opportunity to transfer their housing stock to Registered Social Landlords with the agreement of the majority of tenants. Prior to this, local authority housing was popular and waiting lists had been established to allocate the properties. The Act also permitted the creation of Housing Action Trusts to improve council estates that were a cause of concern. As a result of this Act being implemented, the role of housing associations changed from one of shared provision of social housing with the local authority to one of main provider of social housing.

Local Government and Housing Act, 1990

The provisions of this Act led to an increase in rents as local authorities were now not permitted to subsidise rents of council tenants. By the late 1990s local authorities were permitted to transfer the whole social housing stock to what is known as Registered Social Landlords. These are non profit-making and include housing associations, housing trusts, housing cooperatives and companies. They are run by professional staff but have a voluntary management committee. *The privatisation of public rented housing has been viewed by some as an attack on the Welfare State at its weakest link* (Alcock et al. 2004 p220). It effectively brought about a reduction in the number and quality of affordable rental properties.

1995 White Paper, *Our future homes: Opportunity, choice, responsibility*

The government hoped to encourage a balanced mix of households, young and old, low income and better off, home owners and renters living alongside one another to create a 'mixed community' (DoE 1995, cited in Alcock 2003 p107). This is reminiscent of the 1944 Housing Manual that we considered earlier in the chapter.

Housing Act, 1996

This Act is important as it placed a requirement on local authorities to establish whether people applying to be housed were 'intentionally' homeless and restricted eligibility to Housing Benefit payments.

Homes Act, 2001

Local authorities were required not only to monitor homelessness but also to develop preventative measures.

Housing policy in the last decade

The previous Labour government inherited two fundamental ideological assumptions that have driven government policy on housing which has continued to promote the market to deliver and enable the provision of affordable housing. There has also been a growing popularist ideology that home ownership is a desirable basis for citizenship. Following the introduction of council house sales by the Thatcher government which sought to win votes of middle-income and aspirational working-class voters, the idea that housing status conditions people to be dependent and that home ownership would liberate people from dependency has continued to underpin the development of housing policy and provision. The encouragement of shared equity schemes and key worker schemes are examples of the government seeking to increase home ownership to 75 per cent by 2015, a target which according to Bowie (2009) was not based on any assessment of affordability.

Similarly, the provision of new social rented housing has become substantially dependent on private-sector finance and renewal of public-sector stock increasingly dependent on transfer of local authority stock to housing associations or developers, using a mixture of private finance initiative and subsidies. Thus, as Bowie (2009) points out, this has led to reduced security for public tenants and erosion of the key principles of collectively owned and collective publicly accountable management of housing which were fundamental to the welfare state. Whereas the full capital cost of new council housing and housing association housing was mainly funded by government, since the introduction of mixed finance arrangements under the 1984 Housing Act, there have been a number of challenges for communities in building and maintaining sustainable communities alongside housing development. This has to be linked to supporting and funding transport, education, health and leisure as well as the other concepts of what is needed to build a community. Secondly the subsequent 'credit-crunch' period of economic austerity and the linking of house prices to inflation in the economy has led to serious problems in relation to housing provision, for example around homelessness and unemployment.

In 2004, the government published a report called *Delivering Stability: Securing our Future Housing Needs* (Barker 2004) which made a number of recommendations to address the need for a more stable housing market and location of housing supply which supports patterns of economic development. The government wanted to explore how to achieve an adequate supply of publicly funded housing for those who need it alongside a more flexible housing market which reflects the needs of the economy with more equitable distribution of housing wealth. These issues will be reflected upon in more detail in the latter half of this chapter, before which we will turn to how this has informed subsequent policies.

Supplementary guidance on intentional homelessness, 2009

In 2009, the government had to issue supplementary guidance under s.182 of the Housing Act 1996 on homelessness in response to the current economic climate, to help homeowners in financial difficulty. This guided local housing authorities in applying the various statutory criteria, when considering whether applicants who are homeless having lost their home because of difficulties in meeting mortgage commitments are intentionally or unintentionally homeless.

Council housing: The coalition government proposals

In 2010 the government launched a consultation in which they proposed the following:

- Greater flexibility for local authority and registered provider landlords (typically housing associations) to offer different types of tenancies.

- Investment to bring empty homes back into use as affordable housing and providing bonus incentives for local authorities to tackle empty homes as part of their strategy for meeting housing need.

- New legislation to give local authorities back the power to better manage their housing waiting list through removal of constraints in the allocation legislation but by retaining statutory criteria to determine who should have priority for social housing.

- Increasing mobility by introducing a nationwide home swap scheme through national data sharing on a statutory basis.

- Introducing legislation to enable local authorities to fully discharge their duty to secure accommodation by arranging an offer of suitable accommodation in the private rented sector, without requiring the applicant's agreement.

- Ensuring that local authorities become self-financing, by taking on responsibility and accountability for their housing services away from central control and subsidy. This is seen to enable tenants and local taxpayers to hold their landlord to account for the cost and quality of their housing.

- Giving tenants 'stronger tools' to secure better services locally by establishing an independent committee within the Homes and Communities Agency.

- Establishing reforms to tackle overcrowding.

Social exclusion and social justice

Social exclusion has been described as *a shorthand label for what can happen when individuals or areas suffer from a combination of linked problems such as unemployment, poor skills, low incomes, poor housing, high crime environments, bad health and family breakdown* (DSS 1999 p23). We will be considering the impact of housing on individuals, families, carers, groups and communities in order to inform your understanding of some of the complex structural and material factors that influence the life chances of people you are likely to come into contact with as a social worker. This is sometimes referred to as 'postcode poverty' (see Figure 6.1).

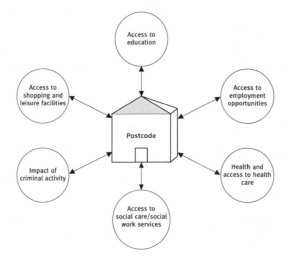

Figure 6.1 Housing and social exclusion – 'postcode poverty'

New Deal for Communities

The New Deal for Communities initiative was launched under New Labour in 1998 under its work programme to promote social inclusion. The Social Exclusion Unit (SEU) was established to work actively across all government departments to address complex social problems aimed at *improving social justice, strengthening communities and support-ing long-term economic growth* (ODPM 2004a). The New Deal programme was one of the most intensive and innovative area-based initiatives ever introduced in England, designed to transform 39 deprived neighbourhoods over 10 years and implementing local regenera-tion schemes each with an average of £50m spend. By levering a further £730m in from other public, private and voluntary-sector sources, the New Deal partnerships developed a range of interventions with partner agencies, such as the police, primary care trusts, schools and employment agencies to support locally developed sustainable strategies that place the community at the heart of the initiative. The outcomes aim to encompass place-related outcomes including crime and community safety, community and housing and the physical environment, and people-related outcome areas of health, education and unemployment. The controversial Community Development Projects of the late 1960s/early 1970s were important forerunners of New Deal projects and had been driven by a radical, emancipatory critique which stressed that structural problems *created an unequal distribution of resources and power throughout society*, rather than at an individual level (Popple, 1995, p18). Some have accused the Labour government of de-politicising the causes of the problems by emphasising the responsibilities of community groups, voluntary sector organisations and individuals in regeneration. This pluralist rather than radical emancipatory approach is based on a belief that power is shared and there is an emphasis on local level change and on consensus. In the radical emancipatory approach there is a clear acknowledgement of the conflict of interest between the different sectors, and that changes to improve the lives of those living in the communities concerned must be on a structural level.

The final evaluation of New Deal for Communities (Batty et al. 2010) explored the degree to which its partnerships achieved its programme-wide objectives between 2002 and 2008 and found relatively greater positive change in relation to its place, rather than people-related outcomes and that there were net positive outcomes in the areas of crime, housing and the physical environment and the community. Some statistically significant effects were demonstrated in relation to improving education and health. The most significant learning from the New Deal evaluation was in relation to partnership working and commu-nity engagement. A summary of the key findings is in the research summary below.

Overall there was considerable positive change in the 39 areas: and in many respects these neighbourhoods were transformed over a period of 10 years. In general NDC areas have narrowed the gaps with the rest of the country.

REFLECTION POINT

Reflect on how you will use an understanding and knowledge of some of the structural factors in relation to living healthily in communities, to help you prepare for practice learning. You may also wish to consider the power relationships between those organi-sations working in local communities. The work of Fook (2002) addresses issues of power and will be helpful here.

Other area-based initiatives promoting social justice

Other area-based New Labour initiatives between 1997 and 2000, described by Lupton and Power (2005 p121) include:

- single regeneration budget projects;

- education action zones;

- health action zones;

- Sure Start;

- excellence in cities;

- employment zones.

Regeneration, renewal, resilience and the Big Society

The concepts of regeneration and renewal have been more recently replaced by the concept of localism where localised, people-based strategies have more to do with Cameron's 'Big Society' than initiating grand projects like those described above. Regeneration tends to be associated with physical change and driven primarily by economic considerations. Renewal is associated with a wider range of people- and place-based interventions, and tends to pay more attention to issues around governance and community participation. We saw the aims of both of these within the aims of the New Deal for Communities earlier and these are interconnected and overlapping in many ways. By 2007, the government switched course to a regeneration-led approach and replaced its National Strategy for Neighbourhood Renewal. Terms used to describe this new approach have included 'resilience' and 're-fitting'. The former is about building the capacity of people and institutions in poor neighbourhoods so they are better able to cope with social, economic and demographic change. Re-fitting, it is suggested (Teasdale 2009) goes a step further, and is *focused on supporting people and institutions to capitalise on those changes, through a rigorous emphasis on skills and social enterprise*. This refers to the development and roll-out of community-led organisations like Tenant Management Organisations, Community Land Trusts, Credit Unions, co-operatives and social enterprises by developing local potential over the long term and releasing existing assets and creating social capital to strengthen local resilience. The key task for public-sector professionals such as social workers would be to localise and mutualise their functions with local community groups as far as possible, in a way that enables them to deliver better local outcomes at lower cost.

Some of these ideas are embedded in the coalition government's initiative Think Local, Act Personal (www.thinklocalactpersonal.org.uk/) aimed specifically at personalisation and community-based support. This initiative brings together 30 national and umbrella organisations aimed at improving practice in six priority areas, as well as advising and influencing government and other bodies. These sorts of task groups and partnerships are essential to being able to work with housing and other community based providers to take a more holistic approach to solving local issues and problems.

Undertake some information-finding research to discover what types of regeneration projects are currently operating in the area where you live or are studying. The website of your local authority is a good starting place, as are national websites such as Think Local, Act Personal (www.thinklocalactpersonal.org.uk).

- *Who are the key professionals involved?*

- *In what ways are they involving service users and carers, groups, families and communities?*

- *What might need to be considered to ensure that services are responsive and appropriate to all sectors of the community and to build community capacity?*

- *What opportunities might these projects provide for meeting the National Capability Framework for Social Work through practice learning?*

Housing tenure

The pattern of ownership and occupancy of different types of accommodation is referred to as tenure (see Figure 6.2). As with different forms of care services, there is also a 'mixed economy' in housing provision, including private, public and independent not-for-profit sectors.

In the early part of the twentieth century local authority 'council' housing was of a high standard, available on a long-term arrangement to better-off working people and their families, while private rented accommodation was often of a lower standard and associated with insecure tenant and landlord agreements.

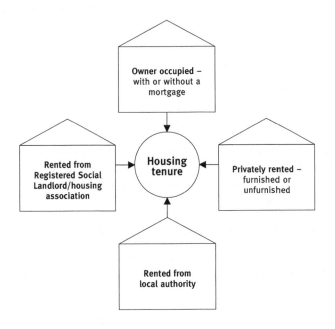

Figure 6.2 Housing tenure types

In addition to acting as landlords for their tenants, local authorities have responsibility for developing strategic plans that match national housing policy.

Housing associations and Registered Social Landlords provide a range of rented accommodation and shared-ownership housing and are able to take advantage of both public and private-sector funding arrangements that are not available to the local authority.

Private rented accommodation varies enormously in standard, including houses of multiple occupancy with a high turnover of occupants. These can be found in once-affluent areas where large houses have been divided into flats of varying quality which are occupied by people with a range of social needs, as in an area of a south coast town described by Popple and Quinney (2002). The private rented sector is typically used by the most affluent and the most economically disadvantaged.

Until recently, council tenants were granted a secure tenancy for life. Housing association tenants had secure tenancy for life after a probationary year. Council tenants had the right to hand the property over to their children, whereas housing association tenants did not. The coalition government has signalled an end to lifetime council tenancies associated with reductions in public expenditure and where fixed terms for all new council and housing association tenancies will last as little as five years. This change has been cited as essential to increase social mobility. Regular reviews of tenancies have been proposed to see if council tenants still need large properties. This will include a review of their income to see if their housing needs can be alternatively met or shifted to the private rented or owner-occupied sector away from subsidised housing by the public sector. It has been asserted that given the costs to taxpayers, the 'tenancy for life' is an inefficient use of scarce resources alongside cuts to housing benefit referred to at the beginning of this chapter. Critics of these reforms say it could disincentivise the unemployed to seek well-paid work as they might lose their tenancy as a result. There are also fears that it would increase the chances of council estates becoming ghettos of the workless poor. Such moves sidestep the fundamental cause of housing crisis which is a lack of affordable housing supply (Wintour 2010).

Earlier in this chapter we looked at the ideology of promoting home ownership and finding different mechanisms to increase the supply of social housing. Back in 1998, the Housing Minister, Hillary Armstrong, commented that:

> *I am agnostic about the ownership of housing – local authorities or housing associations; public or private sector – and want to move away from the ideological baggage that comes with that issue. What is important is not, primarily, who delivers. It is what works that counts.*

Cameron and Clegg have since said that their policies would:

unlock the housing market, get Britain building again, and give many more people the satisfaction and security that comes from stepping over their own threshold.

ACTIVITY **6.3**

Having read the two statements and recapping on how housing policy and strategy have developed, take some time to reflect on the following questions:

- *What is the 'ideological baggage' that Armstrong referred to?*

- *What are the arguments for and against an ideological perspective on housing?*

- *What are the issues on which success might be judged in terms of what works?*

- *How does Armstrong's statement contrast with that of Cameron and Clegg?*

Who should be involved in making such judgements?

RESEARCH SUMMARY

Inequalities in housing

- *Homelessness is a major exclusionary and health-impacting experience whether it is characterised by sleeping rough, in shelters and hostels, precariously avoiding absolute homelessness through the goodwill of friends and relatives, or among the 67,480 households living in temporary accommodation (Shelter 2010).*

- *People sleeping rough and those in hostels who have slept rough for long periods have very poor physical health – higher rates of TB and hepatitis than the general population, poor condition of feet and teeth, respiratory problems, skin diseases, injuries following violence, infections, digestive and dietary problems and rheumatism or arthritis (Shelter 2010).*

- *Mortality rates, particularly for those with mental health problems, are nearly five times higher than for the equivalent age group in the general population (Shelter 2010).*

- *An increasing bank of evidence shows that the physical and mental health of destitute refused asylum seekers deteriorates rapidly (Shelter 2010).*

- *Rising fuel prices may impact further on the problem of poorly insulated and energy-inefficient homes causing more serious fuel poverty and related health impacts. Poor quality private renting is a major problem, but so is concentrated poverty in social housing (Shelter 2010).*

- *The number of owner-occupied households fell from a peak of 14.8 million in 2005 and 2006 to 14.6 million in 2008–09. A third of all working households under the age of 40 cannot afford to buy their own home even at the low end of local housing markets.*

- *The non-take-up rates of Housing Benefit have doubled since 1997 amounting to around half a million people (Communities and Local Government 2010).*

Continued

RESEARCH SUMMARY *continued*

- *A comprehensive review of evidence of the 'housing effect' on children's lives revealed the devastating impact of temporary accommodation and bad housing on children's life chances, including up to 25 per cent higher risk of severe ill-health and disability during childhood and early adulthood (Harker, 2006).*

- *People from minority ethnic groups experience particular disadvantage in relation to housing and neighbourhoods (Chahal 2000) and housing and mental health services are failing to meet the needs of many Asian people with mental health problems (JRF 1996).*

- *Children who live in poverty are almost twice as likely to be in poor housing and are almost twice as likely to leave school without any GCSEs and are more likely to suffer poor health (Communities and Local Government 2010).*

- *A combination of historical factors and cultural aspirations can explain some of the difference in black and minority ethnic groups' tenure patterns. However, recent rises in house prices have turned home ownership into largely unrealisable aspiration for many young households (Markenham et al. 2008).*

- *Fear of racism continues to impact upon the locational choices of non-White households (Markenham et al. 2008).*

ACTIVITY 6.3

Look at the research findings above and undertake the following.

Go to the website of Communities and Local Government (www.communities.gov.uk) and look up the English Housing Survey for 2009–10. Chapter 1 shows the statistics for ethnic minority households by tenure and other cross analysis.

- *What explanations can you think of that might explain these statistics?*

- *In what ways might people from Black and minority ethnic groups experience any disadvantage?*

- *How might you use knowledge of culturally sensitive practice in your future role as a social worker when working with housing professionals?*

Inequalities in housing

As we saw in Chapter 4 back in the 1980s, a government-commissioned report (The Black Report) placed particular emphasis on housing as a health inequality issue and saw decent housing as a prime requisite for health. Similarly, the Acheson Report, Independent inquiry into inequalities in health, specifically recommended that policies should be established to improve insulation and heating systems in new and existing buildings. Campaigning organisations such as Shelter in the UK have continued to research and highlight the growing inequality in housing which *in a country increasingly obsessed with house prices and home improvement ... is marginalising a whole section of society* (St Mungo's et al. 2011, p3). Some of these inequalities are clearly highlighted in the research summary earlier.

The professionals involved

Social workers are likely to come into contact with a wide range of people working in the housing sector.

- People involved with planning and strategy issues.

- People providing housing advice and information.

- People providing individual support to service users and carers.

You may also come into contact with community development workers working in neighbourhoods to increase participation and involvement with individuals and community groups on areas of local policy.

You may find yourself working collaboratively with housing professionals in a wide range of situations, for example:

- when service users are applying for housing, perhaps when leaving residential care or a refuge or seeking asylum;

- people needing adaptations to their homes in order to remain living in the community;

- people whose current housing is inappropriate to their needs, perhaps through overcrowding or poor state of repair contributing to health problems;

- People who require social work support to maintain living in the community, for example people with mental health problems or learning disabilities.

You may also find yourself working with community development workers in a range of situations, including:

- working with asylum-seeker organisations offering support and advice to others seeking asylum;

- working with rural communities to highlight issues that impact on people in rural areas, including lack of transport and lack of facilities for children and young people, and to develop local solutions to these;

- working with a range of community groups, organisations and individuals to capture people's stories in order to contribute to understanding the impact of regeneration projects and to create a social history archive.

Community work has been described by Mayo (2002 p163) as being of benefit to:

encourage self-help and informal caring, compensate for reductions in public service provision within the context of the increasing marketisation of welfare, support strategies to combat poverty and oppression and facilitate community participation and empowerment.

The Community Development Exchange (2005) describes community development as being *about building active and sustainable communities based on social justice and mutual respect* and about *changing power structures to remove the barriers that prevent people from participating in the issues that affect their lives.*

Community development can be seen as a method of intervention in social work and as a discrete activity outside of social work, can be informed by a range of perspectives from the traditional to the transformational, and can be practised by people who are professionally qualified and those who are volunteers, and by local residents with an interest in issues that have an impact on their community or neighbourhood. Professional staff may be employed by a range of organisations, including the local authority, housing organisations, voluntary-sector groups, agencies set up through regeneration projects, and commissioners of health services.

The professional body for housing is the Chartered Institute of Housing (CIH). There will be some big questions for CIH to consider in relation to its role in developing and awarding qualifications to professionals working in housing. There has been a dramatic change in the employment circumstances of those working in housing with a shift from local authorities, housing associations and similar organisations towards more involvement of private-sector organisations who have become directly involved in delivering housing services. Housing organisations are facing a difficult economic climate in the face of government expenditure cuts, housing benefit reform, VAT increases and changes to Supporting People, and need to think how to reduce their expenditure (including spend on staff training) in the context of wider changes in housing policy. These changes will have an influence on future job roles in traditional housing employment. In common with the other professional bodies we have considered in this book, the CIH issues a Code of Professional Conduct, consisting of the following sections: responsibilities of the profession; personal conduct; and terms for self-employed members (who are defined as principals, directors or partners in a practice or firm).

The personal conduct section includes working within the law, respecting confidentiality of information and awareness of diversity issues as demonstrated in the following statements:

2.1 Members must seek to eliminate discrimination and promote equality of opportunity. They must not discriminate against any individual or group on the grounds of origin, nationality, religion, cultural background, sex, domestic circumstances, illness, age or sexual orientation.

2.2 Members must never use language which is likely to offend, such as racist or sexist terms.

(CIH Code of Professional Conduct).

The CIH Professional Qualification Specification framework sets out learning outcomes for housing professionals, which can be achieved at undergraduate or postgraduate level. Mandatory learning themes include managing diversity and professional ethics.

Learning outcomes are grouped under discrete 'Aims', and include the following.

- *A housing professional must understand community regeneration and sustainability, with learning outcomes associated with this being: evaluate the concept of Community and explain the various applications of the term.*

- *A housing professional must engage in partnership, collaboration and joint working, with learning outcomes associated with this being: analyse the policy origins for greater collaboration between groups/organisations/agencies to support communities and critically examine the role of Housing in initiatives led by other agencies such as the police, probation services, health community groups, etc.*

(CIH 2001)

The *Equality and diversity strategy* of the CIH (2004 p2) points out that:

> the population is ageing, becoming more ethnically diverse and more mobile. The growth in asylum seekers and refugees increases the diverse nature and challenging needs of the population as a whole.

The CIH considers race and ethnicity issues to be a high priority, both in the delivery of housing services and in the operation of the organisation itself.

REFLECTION POINT

Reflect on how you might provide evidence for the learning outcomes related to diversity and professional ethics required of housing professionals. This is an outcome for social workers in the Professional Capabilities Framework.

- *How might this sharing of some common elements of knowledge, skills and values help you to collaborate with housing professionals?*

Homelessness

Homelessness is most often associated with people sleeping out or sleeping rough but it is much wider than this. It includes people living in temporary or insecure accommodation and within the legislation is defined as not having the legal right to occupy accommodation or living in unsuitable accommodation such as squats, refuges, or on the sofas of family and friends. Homelessness is also difficult to measure because it involves a transient population and because of the various overlapping ways in which they might present which makes it difficult to capture definitively. Live tables on homelessness can be found on the Department for Communities and Local Government websites, but the main sources of published statistics come from local authorities' data on those sleeping rough, applying to them as homeless or on case of prevention of homelessness. Repossession statistics are another source and in 2011, repossession of mortgaged properties were at their highest since the mid-1990s. A number of charities such as Shelter and St Mungo's also provide statistics about the people they work with. Figures published on 17 February 2011 show a total of 1,768 people were sleeping out across England on any given night and that there are between 310,000 and 380,000 estimated hidden homeless people. This figure includes people in hostels, who are not 'hidden' (Palmer and Parsons 2004). Results from a survey conducted by Shelter in 2010 survey show that:

- 76 per cent of clients were male;

- 24 per cent of clients were female;

- 39 per cent of clients were from BME communities;

- 64 per cent of clients had issues with substance use (drugs and/or alcohol);

- 64 per cent had a physical health condition (medical condition, vision or hearing impaired and/or required regular medication);

- 70 per cent of clients had mental health issues (diagnosed, suspected, depression and/or self-harming);

- 54 per cent of clients had educational needs (learning disabilities, difficulty reading, difficulty with numeracy, managing money and paying bills);

- 8 per cent had been in care;

- 48 per cent of clients were ex-offenders or had been in prison.

In 2010 the Citizens Advice Bureaux across England and Wales dealt with 14% more housing problems compared with the same period the previous year. Rent arrears to private landlords rose by 19% during the same year (St Mungo's et al. 2011).

Homelessness is covered by the 2002 Homelessness Act, which built on previous legislation, The Housing Act 1996, by giving local authorities additional powers to assist homeless people who do not have priority need, including those affected by domestic abuse. Supplementary guidance as we saw earlier in the chapter was issued in 2009 to deal with those at risk from mortgage repossessions.

ACTIVITY **6.4**

Visit the website of the housing charity Shelter (www.shelter.org.uk). Among the wide range of information and resources you will find a section called Real Life Stories, which illustrates the range of situations in which people experience housing difficulties.

You will also find flow charts illustrating Housing Options, Making a homeless application and How the council has to help. Referring to these charts, make notes on the various points at which a social worker might become involved in the process.

- *With which other professionals might you work collaboratively in this situation?*

- *How might you use advocacy skills to represent service users, carers, groups and communities?*

COMMENT

You can find out more about advocacy skills by reading the reports from a study commissioned by the Department of Health and undertaken by researchers from the University of Durham (Barnes et al. 2002). This is available from the University of Durham website and the Department of Health website. While the report focuses on the context of mental health, the skills and principles are transferable to other service user groups. A guide to advocacy is also available from the website of Mind, www.mind.org.uk.

RESEARCH SUMMARY

A national study aimed at teenage girls, conducted by the NSPCC (2005) with 2,000 respondents, found that 33 per cent of teenage girls reported that they had experienced domestic violence or abuse at home, 11 per cent reported seeing their parents physically abusing one another and 25 per cent reported having seen their parents verbally abusing one another, with physical violence more likely to be used by men and verbal abuse more likely by women.

CASE STUDY

Sara made the decision to leave her partner of 10 years after phoning an emergency helpline on the advice of her GP, who she had seen to seek treatment for injuries caused by her partner during an argument that had escalated into physical violence. She was offered a tenancy for herself and her two children, aged seven and three, in a women's refuge run by a national housing organisation. Sara and her partner both misuse drugs and her partner had become increasingly violent towards her after drinking and drug use. She had been reluctant to leave, as she describes her partner as a good parent and as 'a different person' when sober, but the violent incidents had been increasing. Another factor in her reluctance to leave had been her wish to keep the drug use hidden from her wider family, as she believed her family would be shocked and unsympathetic. Sara approached this particular refuge, in a distant part of the UK, as several other family members live in the immediate area and run small businesses. She now hoped that her family would be supportive if she gave up the use of drugs.

In Dorset, women escaping domestic violence (which may consist of physical, sexual, financial or emotional abuse by a partner, ex-partner or family member) may be temporarily accommodated in one of five refuges run by housing associations. Separate accommodation and support services are available for male victims of domestic violence, and there is also an advisory service for lesbian, gay, bisexual and transgender victims of domestic violence. The information leaflet provided by Dorset Police (2005) emphasises that *people are abused from every race, class, religion and culture regardless of age, sexuality, disability or gender*.

The refuges typically offer safe accommodation, 24-hour support and care, advice with legal problems and housing benefits, information about other helping agencies, assistance with securing school and nursery placements, and counselling and support groups. We will be considering issues of domestic violence again in Chapter 7, The justice context.

Referring to the case study described above, imagine that you are a social worker with a remit to work with women and children who have experienced domestic violence. Identify the range of needs, the services that might be available to meet them and the agencies that you are likely to come into contact with in supporting Sara and her children to establish a safe new home.

* *What knowledge will you draw on to enable you to work collaboratively with the staff employed by these agencies?*

* *What possible areas of conflict might arise?*

COMMENT

You will find it helpful to read the other chapters in this book that correspond to the agencies concerned, for example the chapters on health, housing and justice and the chapter on preparing to work collaboratively.

REFLECTION POINT

Reflect on how an understanding of both personal circumstances and structural factors would help you when working with homeless people.

* *Where might you find information about these themes in order to inform your practice and become research minded, and which authors would you associate with these themes?*

The Supporting People strategy

The Supporting People strategy, introduced in 2003, aims to establish clearer partnership working between the many organisations and agencies involved in delivering housing support to a wide range of vulnerable people to enable them to live independently. It is also intended to *prevent problems that can lead to hospitalisation, institutional care or homelessness and can help the smooth transition to independent living for those leaving an institutional environment* (ODPM 2004b p1).

Service user groups include:

* people who have been homeless or rough sleepers;

* ex-offenders and people at risk of offending or imprisonment;

* people with a physical or sensory disability;

* people at risk of domestic violence;

* people with alcohol and drug problems;

* teenage parents;

- elderly people;

- young people at risk;

- people with HIV and AIDS;

- people with learning difficulties;

- travellers;

- homeless families with support needs.

(ODPM 2004b p2)

The strategy is funded through grants to local authorities who work with a range of statutory and non-statutory housing, health, social care and probation service partners to contract and provide services. Support has ranged from benefit advice to live-in full-time support workers. Partnership is of central importance.

> *Supporting People encourages collaborative working between stakeholders of the programme: no single stakeholder can deliver its challenges alone. Partnership is paramount. There is a strong need for multi-agency working to develop and continue the successful delivery of the programme.*

(ODPM 2004b p6)

In 2010, the coalition government reduced funding for Supporting People funding by 11.5 per cent and announced that this would no longer be ring-fenced, leading to concerns that local government will no longer have to account for how its expenditure is supporting more vulnerable people.

CASE STUDY

An example of collaborative practice is the 'floating support' scheme provided by a voluntary-sector housing association to people with mental health problems moving from hostel accommodation to independent living in the community. Floating support workers provide emotional support, information and advice, advocacy and practical help along with facilitating access to other support services, education, training, voluntary work or employment opportunities (Sharples et al. 2002). In this project the support networks involved counsellors, occupational therapists, the probation service, and social work and health professionals from the community mental health team.

Sammi, who has a long history of mental health problems which have sometimes necessitated admission to psychiatric hospital, has recently moved from a hostel for people with mental health problems into a bedsit rented from a private landlord. He is visited by a floating support worker who has supported him with gaining a place at a mental health day centre, registering with a GP, sorting out benefits, and helping him to build a trusting relationship with the social worker from the community mental health team.

The floating support worker attends the team meetings of the community mental health team to provide another perspective to help understand the housing dimension needs of people living in the locality.

Timms and Borrell (2001 p425) have described some of the dilemmas in providing 'assertive outreach' support to homeless people with a mental illness, pointing out that voluntary-sector staff are *increasingly being asked to provide for people with multiple needs that have baffled and frustrated mental health services in the past*. One of these dilemmas is the sharing of information across agency boundaries and with housing support staff who may not be recognised as having a 'professional' status. Unequal power relationships was one of the themes discovered by Sharples et al. (2002 p319) in their evaluation of a 'floating support' project and they pointed out that support workers had *needed to work to establish individual credibility and professionalism for themselves* and were successful in being accepted, despite not being able to draw on the professional knowledge, skills and values of a recognised profession. Nevertheless, their role was sometimes underestimated. The floating support workers in this project worked with a wide range of professionals from a diverse range of services and agencies, including hospital- and community-based mental health teams, a range of day centre providers from both the statutory and independent sectors, providers of home care services, education and training providers and counselling services.

Foyers – housing for young people

The first Foyer opened in the UK in 1992, having originated as a concept in France some 50 years earlier to enable young people living in rural areas to have access to housing to enable them to move to urban areas in search of employment.

According to the Foyer Federation (2005), Foyers provide:

- a stable and secure community in which young people can support one another and achieve independence;

- help with finding appropriate employment, training or education to make this possible;

- training in basic skills and independent living skills;

- help with finding ongoing support when the young person has left the Foyer.

They usually consist of hostel-type accommodation with support available in the form of advice, leisure and education facilities.

CASE STUDY

Here is an extract from the story of Laura, a young person who found accommodation at the Foyer in Scarborough, North Yorkshire. To read the whole story you will need to visit the website of the Foyer Federation (www.foyer.net), where you will find a range of case stories.

Laura, age 15, has been experiencing problems with depression and anger, and her disruptive behaviour and arguments with her parents eventually led to her taking an overdose and being admitted to hospital. She was referred to the Child and Adolescent Community Mental Health team, as in addition to the overdose she had been self-harming through cutting herself. A multi-agency meeting was convened but it was not

Continued

---

possible to reach an agreement between Laura and her parents for her return home on discharge from hospital. A range of options were tried, from temporary bed and breakfast accommodation and a fostering placement but both broke down as a result of Laura's challenging behaviour. A further crisis led to an overdose and after a period in hospital Laura was referred to a Foyer.

ACTIVITY **6.6**

- *Imagine you are Laura's social worker. How might you work with the Foyer staff to support Laura?*

- *What knowledge, skills and values are important in order to work effectively with Laura and other agencies?*

- *What areas of conflict might you have to negotiate in order to secure the best outcome for Laura?*

- *How will you ensure that Laura's own views are listened to and acted on where possible?*

The role of housing in achieving personalisation for people living in care settings

Personalising support for people already living in residential care requires creative thinking about how to offer realistic choices in how and where they want to live. This involves identifying pathfinders and pathways with housing and other providers for people moving out of residential care in a way that existing providers can increase the rights, choices and control of service users from a place of their choosing. This has proved to be one of the more challenging areas for developing partnerships and collaboration with housing and care providers. For example, in recent years there has been a movement away from the use of residential care for people with learning disabilities towards supported housing services that allow individuals to live more independent lives (Strong and Hall 2011). This shift has also made services more person-centric as supported housing often provides more personalised support to service users than residential care. Much of the impetus for this change comes from the provisions of the Mental Capacity Act 2005, which enabled the functions of housing, accommodation and care to be split. The changes introduced have led to more innovative ways of thinking about people in residential care and their options for utilising housing and community support services in different ways. For people with learning disabilities, personalising support for people and the priorities spelt out in *Valuing People Now* (HMG 2011b) have allowed services to tailor provision to the individual, but 30 per cent of people with learning disabilities still live in registered accommodation. Guidance released in 2011 by the personalisation coalition, *Think local, act personal*, builds on the 2005 Act and promotes ways of overcoming difficult and potentially intractable barriers and reducing the number of people in residential care. For this to happen, individuals and their social workers should work closely with commissioners, and the provider organisation should help the person with learning disabilities and their families to build up their support plan. At a strategic level, providers and commissioners have to unpick block contracts and analyse costs for local authorities at the beginning of their journey towards more individualised funding.

A report called 'Feeling settled' (Strong and Hall 2011) set out several good-practice recommendations for how to change residential care to supported living. First, every effort should be made to ensure the service user stays at the heart of the process during all stages and this requires careful planning. Changing from residential care to supported living is likely to involve working with local authorities at two levels by separating out housing provision with support functions towards more flexibility and choice about providers. The provider should put detailed policies and procedures in place to support a change from residential care to supported living and guidance for each stakeholder – including housing providers, care providers, commissioners and social workers. These should be drawn up in advance. Detailed individual step-by-step pathways that set out the activity required by everyone at each step should also be provided.

Given the complexity of some of these processes, different professionals will have to work together to put procedures in place to support decisions in relation to mental capacity and tenancy issues, which include creativity in developing local resources to explain responsibilities and rights that come with tenancies, including advocacy and best-interest decision-making. The Association of Directors of Adult Social Services (ADASS) have developed clear guidance for authorities to encourage them to agree clear protocols in relation to ordinary residence which can sometimes cause a stumbling block. Financial issues also need to be grappled with, given that one aim is to achieve longer term savings on residential care. To ensure change is cost-neutral, councils have to look for opportunities to ring-fence budgets and aggregate resources where some people are living together in the community. This might involve cross-subsidising resources, for example by transferring capital assets using leases, and exploiting opportunities to help individuals gain access to other funding streams. They can also shift costs such as housing and council tax benefits and supporting people grants to reduce direct pressure on social care budgets. Teams around the service users will need to work closely with those responsible for technical issues in relation to planning, building control, design and title issues and managing the expenditure associated with transfer of existing assets. For social workers, this means working closely with occupational therapists.

There are many different levels at which support for people can be transformed and personalised and the government's target for everyone eligible for ongoing social care to have a personal budget by 2013 includes people living in residential care. Strong and Hall (2011) highlighted that every year about 500 people with disabilities get caught up in disputes with local authorities about ordinary residence and this can represent the most significant barrier to progress. Their report makes it clear that personalised services are not just for people who need less support but highlight the need to pay attention through collaborative working that it concerns both the quality and suitability of the support provided. These issues promote bolder thinking around individualised funding with greater transparency in relation to the potential choice in corporate services alongside new partnerships with the local community, services and resources, many of which have been addressed in this chapter. For social workers, you need to be able to advise people properly on their entitlement to benefits as they become tenants and work closely with housing and obtaining any premiums in relation to disability benefits and maximising an individual's natural networks and community resources. Likewise, commissioners and providers need to be bold in responding to the personalisation agenda and imaginative in opportunities for evolving their provision to respond to more individualised needs.

REFLECTION POINT

As we reach the end of this chapter you may like to consider again the statement by Adams (2002 p72) that social workers have much in common with housing officers.

- *What evidence can you offer from this chapter to defend or refute this statement?*

- *What distinguishes a social worker from a housing officer?*

CHAPTER SUMMARY

We have considered a range of situations in which housing and neighbourhood issues will have an impact on the work of a social worker when delivering effective services to individuals, families, groups, and communities.

The theme of social justice is an important thread throughout the chapter, particularly in relation to developing a clearer understanding of the impact of social exclusion and the inequalities that some groups of people face as a result of the housing or neighbourhood in which they live.

It is useful to re-familiarise yourself with the International Federation of Social Workers/International Association of Schools of Social Work definition of social work, which emphasises the social justice theme.

A clear commitment to equality and diversity is essential, along with an awareness and understanding of the role and responsibilities of other professionals whose work will overlap with that of a social worker. By understanding more clearly the roles of other professionals you will be able to develop and maintain a stronger professional identity and be able to deliver to service users and carers a more effective service.

FURTHER READING

Carlton, N and Ritchie, J (2005) Housing. In Barrett, G, Sellman, D and Thomas, J (eds) *Interprofessional working in health and social care*. Basingstoke: Palgrave.

An introduction to the relationship between health and housing and to different forms of housing tenure.

Mayo, M (2002) Community Work. In Adams, A, Dominelli, P and Payne, M (eds) *Social work themes, issues and critical debates*. Basingstoke: Palgrave.

Marj Mayo's chapter in this popular edited collection briefly covers definitions, models and perspectives, issues and dilemmas.

Mullender, A and Humphreys, C (1998) *Domestic violence and child abuse: policy and practice issues for local authorities and other agencies.* London: Local Government Association.

Audrey Mullender has written widely on domestic violence issues. This publication covers issues pertinent to collaborative practice.

Popple, K (2002) Community work. In Adams, A, Dominelli, L and Payne, M (eds) *Critical practice in social work.* Basingstoke: Palgrave.

Keith Popple's chapter in this popular edited collection uses a case study of a housing estate to illustrate the challenges of community work and community development.

Toynbee, P (2003) *Hard work: Life in low-pay Britain.* London: Bloomsbury.

A passionate account of the experiences of a *Guardian* journalist living on a run-down social housing estate in London and seeking employment.

Wheeler, B, Shaw, M, Mitchell, R and Dorling, D (2005) *Life in Britain: Using millennial census data to understand poverty, inequality and place.* Bristol: The Policy Press and Joseph Rowntree Foundation.

A resource pack with photographs, posters and reports which effectively illustrate social exclusion themes through the interpretation of census material, covering health, education, housing, employment and poverty.

WEBSITE

www.jrf.org.uk

The Joseph Rowntree Foundation website provides access to detailed research reports and research summaries, especially in the form of Findings and Foundations – bulletins and summaries of research projects. Information is made available for academics, practitioners, policy makers and the general public, and it is possible to register for research updates to be sent by e-mail.

www.ndti.org.uk/publications/

National Development Team for Inclusion is a not-for-profit organisation which works to promote inclusive lives for people who are most at risk of exclusion and who may need support to lead a full life. They have a number of resources which address collaborative approaches around housing provision to promote inclusion, such as the Feeling Settled report discussed in this chapter (Strong and Hall 2011).

www.shelter.org.uk

This website contains accessible and detailed information with free downloadable guides on a wide range of housing issues, including homelessness, rent arrears, advice for young people including care leavers and asylum seekers, case studies about housing problems and possible solutions, including flow charts about how to seek housing advice.

www.womensaid.org.uk/

Website of Women's aid which provides both audio and visual resources in its 'Survivor's Handbook' on housing issues for women experiencing domestic violence.

Chapter 7
The justice context

Introduction

In this chapter we will be briefly looking at the justice agencies that social workers interact with in their day-to-day practice with service users and carers. As we have seen in the previous chapters, the drive towards partnership working and integrated services that provide the framework for collaborative social work practice involves working with a wide range of services and agencies, in adult services and children's services contexts. This chapter builds on the title in this series by Robert Johns, *Using the law in social work*, and the title *Youth justice and social work* by Pickford and Dugmore (2012) which develops themes relating to youth justice in more depth.

However, the chapter will cover more than criminal justice – the probation and prison services, the police and youth justice – as we will also look at aspects of the family justice system, including the Children and Family Court Advisory and Support Service (Cafcass) and the legal professions.

While some of the professionals involved in this area of work share a common qualification, for example court welfare advisers who are social work qualified, some members of the Youth Offending Team, and probation officers who before 1997 were required to be qualified social workers, many of the professionals you will work with in this context are from a very different professional background. In this area of practice the tensions between care and control, between rights and risks, and between the individual, the family and the public are to the forefront. It is also an area where your knowledge of the law will be tested and will require a clearly articulated and firmly held value base informed by principles of anti-oppressive practice and social justice.

The policy context

Social workers may for example be working with families where a member is in prison or subject to criminal prosecution. They are likely to be working with people experiencing violence or safeguarding issues where intervention requires a working knowledge of the criminal justice system and the specific roles of the professionals involved, including those agencies that provide preventative and support services in the community for victims of crime.

From the 1960s until the early 1990s, governments have had limited but realistic expectations of what the criminal justice system could by itself achieve in reducing crime, reforming offenders and solving social problems. The approach has been one of moderation and restraint in the use of punishment and the criminal law. According to Faulkner (2011), the Criminal Justice Act 1991 which for the first time tried to address issues around how the system could become fairer, and work better and gave less emphasis on the problem of crime itself.

The previous New Labour government had announced its approach as being *Tough on crime, tough on the causes of crime*. According to a comprehensive review (Sylvestri 2011) of government policies during three terms between 1997 and 2010, it has been suggested that the New Labour years saw the incursion of criminal justice into many more areas of life. For example, the criminalisation of 'nuisance' has resulted in catching more and more people (especially children) in the criminal justice system. New Labour's concern with re-establishing social controls and norms of respectability through the criminal justice system was evident from the start with the Crime and Disorder Act 1998, which introduced the concept of Anti-Social Behaviour Orders (ASBOs) resulting in a more punitive and less welfare-oriented focus of crime prevention. Likewise, the introduction of community partnerships such as the Crime and Disorder Reduction Partnerships has meant that welfare agencies, including social work, have become increasingly involved in surveillance (McLaughlin et al. 2001). These have caused tensions alongside discourses about community empowerment. Some of the tough messages about measuring and reporting on crime and its reduction fuelled debates in society about 'illegal immigrants', 'feral youths', benefit 'scroungers' and 'terrorist' religious minorities, to mention but a few. These discourses have gone towards exacerbating a sense of a divided society in conflict with itself which may then end up at the professionals' doorstep.

There have been improvements for example in dealing with hate crime, giving more consideration to victims and making prisons safer and more decent. Faulkner (2011) attributes this to improvements in professionalism as opposed to the services themselves. The era of 'new public management', of targets and performance measures within public and community services has brought some benefits, where setting targets and measurement have sought to increase responsible and accountable practice. However, perverse incentives and unintended consequences have now become evident, and have meant that this approach has neglected a wider range of issues in the justice system which cut across the boundaries of government departments, central and local government, different services and different professional groups. Within criminal justice, you may come across these when working with young adults, women, mental health and youth justice, all of which can be a source of frustration for collaborative working.

Therefore, the incoming coalition government took up office announcing that they would *turn around the lives of the 120,000 most troubled families* and have made the direction clear by being very specific about the way in which public services should be organised and users' needs met. They have spelt out their vision for the role which the state should play in that process. Developing their vision of a 'Big Society' has given emphasis to partnerships, co-working, co-production and other forms of collaboration between government departments, local authorities, statutory services, the private and voluntary sectors and other bodies such as users' groups. Faulkner (2011) describes this as a *rehabilitation revolution*, set in the context of the 'Big Society', with schemes involving the private and voluntary sectors and *payment by results*. For the justice agenda, this is measured in terms of reoffending. Faulkner highlights the gaps made between this and the existing social conditions which are in tension with, or different to the organisational arrangements required for such a revolution to take place. One example he gives is the way in which justice has to deal with the consequences of other areas of government programmes such as in employment, housing and support for families. Austerity, he reminds us, will involve accepting higher levels of risk for some groups of vulnerable people, a greater degree of trust and more tolerance of difference and sometimes failure. These are all issues for social workers to grapple with, in partnership and collaboration with other justice professionals and agencies, some of which we will now consider in the remainder of this chapter.

In England and Wales the law is divided into the areas of criminal law and civil law.

> *Criminal law mostly involves the rules laid down by the state for citizens, while civil law governs the relationships and transactions between citizens.*

> (Department for Constitutional Affairs 2005)

Social workers may find themselves working directly within the frameworks of criminal law as part of a Youth Offending Team or in situations where domestic violence is a feature. Social workers undertaking children and families work may find themselves involved directly with the frameworks of civil law, in particular the family law, when families and relationships break down and their children's welfare becomes the concern of the court. You may also find social workers undertaking collaborative working with justice professions when service users who they are working with, or their family members, are convicted of a criminal act, for example fraud, assault or theft.

Family proceedings are normally held in the Magistrates' Courts and Youth Courts, with some family proceedings being heard in the County Courts, of which there are 218. You can read more about going to court as a social worker in Johns (2011).

The service delivery context

Responsibility for criminal justice issues is shared by three central government departments:

1. **The Home Office**, which is headed by the Home Secretary and five other ministers responsible for immigration; crime prevention and anti-social behaviour reduction; policing and criminal justice; equalities and criminal information; and crime and security. The Home Office in turn works closely with three agencies: the UK Border Agency; the Identity and Passport Service; and the Criminal Records Bureau. These three agencies provide directly managed frontline services from within the Home Office. The Home Office also works with a number of independent services and public bodies.

2. **The Ministry of Justice** (MoJ), which is responsible for criminal law, sentencing, offenders, prisons and probation. It handles relations between the three devolved governments (the Northern Ireland Executive, the Scottish Government and the Welsh Assembly Government) and the UK government. The MoJ holds responsibility for the National Offender Management Service (NOMS), Youth Justice, the Courts and Tribunals Service and the Office for Criminal Justice Reform.

3. **The Office of the Attorney General** (AGO) which provides high-level legal advice and has responsibility for superintending prosecuting departments and a number of independent public interest functions. Some of its functions include making referrals to the Court of Appeal; intervening in the public interest in certain charity and family law cases; appointing advocates to represent the interests of those involved in very sensitive cases; and overseeing the work of the Crown Prosecution Service (CPS), the Revenue and Customs Prosecutions Office (RCPO) and the Serious Fraud Office (SFO).

In 2010, the MoJ set out an overarching framework for bringing agencies together to prioritise work with offenders who cause crime in their locality and are not restricted to statutory or local criminal justice agencies, but involve a wide range of social agencies, including the voluntary sector, who have a role to play in tackling risk factors associated with crime and offending. Under the umbrella term of 'integrated offender management', its members aim to target those offenders of most concern in a more structured and co-ordinated way. They draw on an analysis of local crime and offending problems and look at how they might make the best use of local resources, to ensure that targeted offenders do not fall through gaps and that identified problems are addressed (MoJ 2010).

RESEARCH SUMMARY

Integrated Offender Management Scheme: Key actions and principles

Key actions:

1. *Reduce crime, reoffending and improve public confidence in the criminal justice system.*

2. *Address potential overlaps between existing approaches and programmes to manage offenders and address gaps.*

3. *Align the work of local criminal justice agencies, expanding and improving on partnerships that already exist at the local, area and regional level with wider agendas about social issues.*

4. *Simplify and strengthen governance, and provide greater clarity around respective roles and responsibilities – including leadership, operational decision-making and allocation of resources.*

Key principles:

1. *Tackle offenders together locally including criminal justice and non-criminal justice agencies. Encourage the development of a multi-agency problem-solving approach by focusing on offenders, not offences.*

2. *Deliver a local response to local problems where all relevant partners are involved in strategic planning, decision-making and funding choices.*

3. *Offenders should face their responsibility or the consequences and offenders should be provided with a clear understanding of what is expected of them.*

4. *Make better use of existing resources and use these to increase the benefits for communities and enable partners to provide greater clarity around their respective roles and responsibilities.*

5. *Keep all offenders at high risk of causing serious harm and/or reoffending under review and relate the intensity of management directly to severity of risk, irrespective of position within the criminal justice system or whether statutory or non-statutory.*

(Ministry of Justice 2010 p2)

The research summary above highlights the actions and principles for interdisciplinary working, which provide an important context for collaborative practice.

The family justice council

The Family Justice Council (FJC) was established in 2004 with the aim of stimulating better and quicker outcomes for families and in the family court service. The FJC sits between government and the courts of the family justice system and is supposed to combine the experience of its members, with an understanding of the realities of the system on the ground, The FJC has the benefit of expertise from the legal (judges, barristers, solicitors), medical (a paediatrician and a child psychiatrist) and social care (Cafcass representation and a director of children's services) worlds. It also has authority to appoint sub-committees or working groups to do detailed work where needed.

The Family Justice Council terms of reference are to *facilitate the delivery of better and quicker outcomes for families and children who use the family justice system by*:

- promoting improved inter-disciplinary working across the family justice system through inclusive discussion, communication and co-ordination between all agencies;

- identifying and disseminating best practice throughout the family justice system by facilitating a mutual exchange of information between local committees and the council, including information on local initiatives;

- consulting with government departments on current policy and priorities and securing best value from available resources;

- providing guidance and direction to achieve consistency of practice throughout the family justice system and submitting proposals for new practice directions where appropriate;

- promoting commitment to legislative principles and the objectives of the family justice system by disseminating advice and promoting inter-agency discussion, including by way of seminars and conferences as appropriate;

- promoting the effectiveness of the family justice system by identifying priorities for, and encouraging the conduct of, research;

- providing advice and making recommendations to government on changes to legislation, practice and procedure, which will improve the workings of the family justice system.

(Family Justice Council 2005a)

If you refer to Johns (2011) you will be able to read in more detail about the situations when a social worker will need to attend court. These situations include:

- when young people have been involved in breaking the law;

- when care proceedings are initiated in order to protect children;

- when domestic violence cases are being heard in the County Court.

Who are the professionals involved?

As Lindsay (2005 p143) clearly points out when writing about the probation service in the context of interprofessional working, *effective collaborative working requires professionals to learn about each other's perspectives, priorities, responsibilities and remit.*

ACTIVITY **7.1**

Do some research using any relevant resources in your university library and the websites listed at the end of the chapter to find out more about some of the staff involved in the justice system, choosing from the following list.

- *Police Officers.*
- *Police Community Support Officers.*
- *Crown Prosecution Service Case Workers.*
- *Magistrates' Court Legal Advisers.*
- *Magistrates.*
- *Probation Officers.*
- *Youth Offending Team Social Workers.*
- *Youth Offending Team Volunteers.*
- *Prison Service Officers.*
- *Community Service Supervisors.*
- *Victim Support Volunteers.*
- *Witness Service volunteers.*

COMMENT

The following links might be useful to get you started:

Careers at the Criminal Prosecution Services can be found via their website at www.cps. gov.uk/careers/

The role of probation officers can be found at www.nationalprobationservice.co.uk/page2.html

More about youth justice can be found at www.justice.gov.uk/about/yjb/

A further source is the text editied by Barett et al. (2005), which contains a chapter on the police and on probation.

Pritchard (2008) also offers some interesting chapters about the role of the police in safeguarding practice in her edited book, Good practice in safeguarding adults *(see end of chapter). Once you have completed your research, try to address the following issues.*

- *What are the priorities, responsibilities and remit associated with these roles when working with service users and carers?*
- *What values or codes inform their conduct?*
- *What is their perspective on risk and how might this be similar to or different from that of a social worker?*

Continued

- *In what situations might you come into contact with them or work collaboratively with them?*

- *What are the potential areas of conflict and what might this derive from?*

- *How will you use your social work knowledge, values and skills to work effectively with them to deliver effective services for service users and carers?*

Identify two other professionals that you might come into contact with in civil rather than criminal proceedings, for example in the family court setting, and apply the questions above. For this the website of the Children and Family Court Advisory and Support Service (Cafcass) is a good starting point (www.cafcass.gov.uk).

Cafcass

While Cafcass works in a court context, it is independent of the courts and incorporates services that were previously provided by:

- the Family Court Welfare Service;

- the Guardian ad Litem Services;

- the Children's Division of the Official Solicitor.

Cafcass was established in 2001 in response to the Criminal Justice and Court Services Act 2000 and is concerned with the welfare of children who are the subject of family court proceedings. These may include both public and private law proceedings, for example when children are subject to an application for care or supervision proceedings or subject to an adoption application (public law) or when parents who are separating or divorcing can't agree on arrangements for their children (private law). Professional staff employed by Cafcass to undertake family support work are normally qualified social workers, and as such will share the same value base and adhere to the same professional code of practice as social workers practising in other settings. They work collaboratively with social services and the education and health services and may become involved in the following situations.

- When parents involved in separation and divorce are unable to agree on arrangements for the children.

- When the removal of children from their parents' care is being considered by social services, in order to protect them from significant harm.

- When children are being adopted.

The functions of CAFCASS are to:

- safeguard and promote the welfare of the child;

- give advice to the court about any application made to it in such proceedings;

- make provision for children to be represented in such proceedings;

- provide information, advice and support for children and their families (CAFCASS, 2005).

Cafcass has produced some useful resources for practitioners to use when working directly with children about distressing aspects of their lives and to enhance a child or young person's engagement in the process, which can be accessed through the publications on their website (www.cafcass.gov.uk/publications). Since the highly publicised inquiry into the death of Peter Connolly in England in 2008, Cafcass has experienced an acute rise in demands for their service following applications for public care for children. For example, during 2010–11 there was a 41 per cent increase in care applications following on from a 36 per cent increase the previous year and the highest application for care proceedings ever recorded (Cafcass 2011).

A commissioned report into the operation of Family Courts in England including the impact of Cafcass on court proceedings alongside other proposed changes to legal aid and the role of mediation in resolving matters before they reach court. These recommendations will likely lead to some restructuring of the Family Justice Service and the future role of Cafcass; for example, in a 'Cafcass plus scheme' out-of-court advocacy may bring Guardians into the picture much earlier at the pre-proceedings stage for children identified at risk and of concern. Guardians may be involved to create a better plan for the child and family to either prevent cases going into proceedings or enable them to progress more quickly. In theory, preparing assessment beforehand will reduce the need for independent or specialist assessments, particularly in pre-birth situations and capitalising on the expert knowledge of Guardians.

Other research (Thangham 2011) into the specialist domestic violence risk assessment for safeguarding and family court work, has also recommended that if domestic violence is correctly identified at an early stage by both social workers and Cafcass Guardians, the risks of harm to the children and victim can be reduced. Locally, inter-agency domestic violence risk management now commonly involves a multi-agency risk assessment conference (MARAC) which brings together lead professionals from all relevant agencies to share information about victims at high risk. MARAC uses a common risk identification tool in widespread use in many statutory and voluntary agencies across the country, including social work child protection and Cafcass. Recent evaluation by Debbonaire (2008) of the use of this tool in Cafcass found that its routine use helped to focus attention on key risks and in proposing a plan incorporating these indicators to the safeguarding board and, if necessary, to court.

The probation service

Each year the probation service commences the supervision of some 175,000 offenders. The caseload on any given day is in excess of 200,000. Approximately 90 per cent are male and 10 per cent female. Just over a quarter of offenders serving community sentences are aged 16–20 and just less than three-quarters are aged 21 and over. Approximately 70 per cent of offenders supervised will be on community sentences.

(Home Office 2005)

Probation services are provided by 35 Probation Trusts across England and Wales who receive funding from the National Offender Management Service to which they are accountable for their performance and delivery. Probation trusts are responsible for overseeing offenders released from prison on licence and those on community sentences made by judges and magistrates in the courts.

The probation service has previously had strong links with social work, and the role of probation officers was described as being to 'advise, assist and befriend' offenders. The probation service has experienced considerable 'modernisation' as part of the radical restructuring of public services.

Nowadays, the National Offender Management Service has aligned the probation service with prisons as opposed to social work. As a contracted service, working alongside a mixture of other providers both private and public, the probation service delivers offender services against national outcomes at very local levels and through the trust. Typical roles taken by the probation service will involve them in the following.

- Preparing pre-sentence reports for judges and magistrates in the courts to enable them to choose the most appropriate sentence.

- Working with victims of crimes where the offender has committed a sexual or violent offence and has been given a prison sentence of 12 months or longer.

- Working in approved premises (hostels) for offenders with a residence requirement on their sentences or licences. Probation staff also work in prisons, assessing offenders, preparing them for release and running offending behaviour programmes.

If you have completed Activity 7.1 above, you may have already identified the values of the probation service, which are set out below.

- **Victim awareness and empathy** are central.

- **Protection of the public is paramount**, particularly where there are specific, known victims of violent and sexually violent crime.

- **Law enforcement**, taking positive steps to ensure compliance, but where this fails, acting quickly to instigate breach or recall proceedings.

- **Rehabilitation of offenders**, working positively to ensure their restoration.

- **Empiricism**, basing all offender and victim practice on evidence of what works.

- **Continuous improvement**, always pursuing excellence.

- **Openness and transparency**.

- **Responding to and learning to work with difference** to achieve equality of opportunity for probation staff and service users.

- **Problem solving** as a way of resolving conflict and doing business.

- **Partnership**, using a highly collaborative approach to add value to the capacity of the probation service to achieve its expected outcomes.

- **Better quality services** through contracts which seek to ensure effective system-wide performance (Ministry of Justice 2010).

The offender management model has resulted from emphasis in policy on public protection, law enforcement and victim empathy which came from the last Labour government's intention to be tough on crime and on the causes of crime. Concern with the management of risk is evident in the obligations to work together with other professionals and agencies. The original idea of the National Offender Management Model was to provide a structure within which every sentenced adult offender (18 years +) would be managed either through their custodial or community sentence. The 'manager' is a probation officer who has responsibility for planning and managing both community and custodial sentences and making an assessment of the offender's risk of harm to others and likelihood of reoffending and producing a sentence plan based on this assessment. There have been a number of challenges to the model which are ongoing, for example: a lack of sufficient programmes to address problems faced by offenders such as alcohol misuse, domestic violence and violent behaviour and anger; the lack of a systematic approach to providing education and skills for offenders; poor assessment of mental health and diversity issues and training for staff (Prison Management Offender Inspection 2011). These are all themes that social workers become familiar with when working with families and individuals where there is offending behaviour.

Social workers may also be active in promoting anti-discriminatory practice in work with offenders and their families and networks. Section 95 of the Criminal Justice Act 1991 requires the government to publish statistical data to assess whether any discrimination exists in how the CJS treats people based on their race. This information is used by policy makers, the agencies who comprise the CJS and others to monitor differences between ethnic groups and where practitioners and others may wish to undertake more in-depth analysis and adapt their practice to work with diversity and equality issues, particularly in a local context. The research summary below summarises some of the key findings over the last five years.

RESEARCH SUMMARY

Race and the criminal justice system

Victims

- *The 2010/11 British Crime Survey (BCS) showed that the risk of being a victim of personal crime was higher for adults from a mixed background than for other ethnic groups. It was higher for members of all black and minority ethnic groups than for the white group.*

- *Over the five-year period 2006/07 to 2010/11, there was a statistically significant fall in the risk of being a victim of personal crime for members of the white group of 0.8 per cent. The apparent decrease for those from black and minority ethnic groups was not statistically significant.*

- *Of the 2,007 homicides recorded for the latest three-year period (2007/08 to 2009/10), 75 per cent of victims were white, 12 per cent black and 8 per cent Asian.*

Continued

- *In the majority of homicide cases, victims were suspected of being killed by someone from the same ethnic group, which is consistent with previous trends (88 per cent of white victims, 78 per cent of black victims and 60 per cent of Asian victims).*

Suspects

- *Per 1,000 of the population, black persons were stopped and searched 7.0 times more than white people in 2009/10, compared to 6.0 times more in 2006/07. This data was aggregated from 42 police force areas with different distributions of both ethnic population and use of Stop and Search powers. While the area served by the Metropolitan Police Service accounts for 14 per cent of the England and Wales population, 43 per cent of Stop and Searches are carried out by the Metropolitan Police Service.*

- *Across England and Wales, there was a decrease (3 per cent) in the total number of arrests in 2009/10 compared to 2005/06. While the number of arrests for the white group also decreased during this period, arrests of black persons rose by 5 per cent and arrests of Asian people by 13 per cent.*

- *Overall, there were more arrests per 1,000 population of each black and minority ethnic group (except for Chinese or other) than for people of white ethnicity in 2009/10. Black persons were arrested 3.3 times more than white people, and those from the mixed ethnic group 2.3 times more.*

Defendants

- *Conviction ratios for indictable offences were higher for white persons in 2010 than for those in the black and Asian groups (81 per cent for white, 74 per cent for black, and 77 per cent for Asian).*

- *A higher percentage of those in the BME groups were sentenced to immediate custody for indictable offences than in the white group in 2010 (white 23 per cent, black 27 per cent, Asian 29 per cent and other 42 per cent). This may in part be due to differences in plea between ethnic groups.*

- *In 2010, the highest average custodial sentence length (ACSL) for those given determinate sentences for indictable offences was recorded for the black ethnic group, at 20.8 months, followed by the Asian and other groups with averages of 19.9 months and 19.7 months respectively. The lowest ACSL was recorded for the white group at 14.9 months.*

Offenders

- *On 30 June 2010, the total prison population in England and Wales was 85,002. Of these, 21,878 prisoners (just under 26 per cent) were from BME groups, a number which has remained consistent.*

- *The vast majority (88 per cent) of self-inflicted deaths involved prisoners of white ethnicity. Over 80 per cent of self-harm incidents in 2010 also involved white prisoners.*

Staff and practitioners

- The CPS and Probation Service appeared to have the highest proportion of black and minority ethnic staff, with 14 per cent of staff in each from a BME background.

- The police and the judiciary appeared to have the lowest proportions (fewer than 5 per cent). High proportions of staff with unknown ethnicity for both the CPS and the judiciary mean that these findings should be treated with caution.

(Source: Ministry of Justice 2010a)

Youth justice

As with other areas of welfare provision, youth justice has undergone a substantial over-haul. The Youth Justice Board established through the Crime and Disorder Act of 1998 oversees the youth justice system in England and Wales and works to prevent offending and reoffending by children and young people under the age of 18. In 2009, the National Standards for Youth Justice Services outlined the minimum standards for youth offend-ing team (YOT) managers, YOT practitioners and other relevant partners delivering youth justice services within the youth justice system. These standards primarily focus on youth justice services in the community and the interface between YOTs and secure accommoda-tion and to prevent offending by children and young people by ensuring that:

- there is effective governance, planning and performance management within YOTs to support the delivery of youth justice services;

- all children and young people entering the youth justice system benefit from a structured needs assessment to identify risk and protective factors associated with offending behaviour to inform effective intervention;

- court orders are managed in such a way that they support the primary aim of the youth justice system, which is to prevent offending, and that they have regard to the welfare of the child or young person;

- reports prepared by the YOT for courts and youth offender panels are effective and of a high quality;

- the needs and risks of young people sentenced to custodial orders (including long-term custodial orders) are addressed effectively to enable effective resettlement and management of risk ;

- those receiving youth justice services are treated fairly, regardless of race, language, gender, religion, sexual orientation, disability or any other factor, and actions are put in place to address unfairness where it is identified;

- strategies and services are in place locally to prevent children and young people from becoming involved in crime or anti-social behaviour;

- out-of-court disposals deliver targeted interventions for those at risk of further offending;

- comprehensive bail and remand management services are in place locally;

- restorative justice approaches are used, where appropriate, with victims of crime and that restorative justice is central to work undertaken with young people who offend.

- all relevant information is captured and recorded accurately on the YOT case management information system.

(Youth Justice Board 2010)

In setting these standards it is recognised that children and young people within the youth justice system have complex risks and needs. Research suggests that young people coming to the attention of the youth justice system may have low educational attainment, communication difficulties, mental health problems and learning disabilities and learning difficulties. Therefore this is an area which requires sophisticated and effective strategies to respond to youth crime and anti-social behaviour which involves both YOTs and a range of partner agencies delivering universal and specialist services. In 2009/10, for example, 240,000 (17 per cent) of 1.4 million people arrested for notifiable offences were aged 10–17 years. Within certain areas of the UK, there has been a growing and ongoing concern with gangs which, while recognised since the late 1980s, have become a common stereotype of young people in society. These developments have been linked to gun and knife violence problems, drug trading and associated with high levels of social exclusion.

Muncie (1999 p59) has pointed out that the rhetoric of *'prevention' and 'risk management' is quite capable of being used to justify any number of repressive and retrograde means of dealing with young people*. This is a reflection of how the system for working with adult and young offenders has moved from a welfare-based model to one based on punishment, from one informed by liberal and humanitarian values to an authoritarian and managerial approach. This appears to be more concerned with protection of the public than with concerns for the circumstances of the offender and their social and personal circumstances, and how these might be addressed to enable them to be rehabilitated.

Recent developments

- The Children and Young People's Plans in 2006 (CYYPs) have made joined-up services including youth offending a statutory requirement. YOT managers, for example, have to demonstrate how and where prevention and early intervention services integrate with existing local children, young people and family services.

- The Youth Rehabilitation Order as part of the Criminal Justice and Immigration Act 2008 introduced a new sentencing framework using the Scaled Approach, which determines the level of supervision required for each young person. Enforcing curfews and electronic monitoring are also features of YOT work.

- YOT team members have to formally assess all children and young people using the YJB approved assessment tool (currently Onset) within four weeks of initial referral to identify the risks and needs associated with potential offending and anti-social behaviour. They also contribute to the Common Assessment Framework (CAF) assessments used by social workers and have to target youth support services as appropriate. YOT data would record and analyse the breakdown of looked-after children, by ethnicity and other key criteria, for example via Asset.

- YOT use a central information sharing index – databases of information about children – and use a common Youth Justice Board approved assessment tool (currently Onset) to record and manage information, in particular to establish evidence-based and outcome-focused interventions, and review progress against clear timelines.

- Local authority staff have a duty to ensure that a young offender's status as a looked-after child is recognised and to put in place any formal arrangements in agreement with the YOT regarding its duties towards young people

Inter-agency working is a strong feature of youth justice work, and this is normally organised through Youth Offending Teams (YOTs). Membership of these teams includes professionals from social work, probation, health, education and police services including, where appropriate, staff from voluntary and independent sector agencies. As Johns (2011) points out, *the local authority social services department has a key role in youth justice, co-ordinating and managing multi-disciplinary teams of workers*. There is also an important role for education staff to play in these teams, as links have been reported between poor school attendance and juvenile crime. For example, the DfES (2005b p1) tells us that *those who self-report truancy and exclusion are twice as likely to self-report offending and the majority of children on supervision orders are out of education or training* and advocates that in order to tackle disaffection with school *it is essential to take a multi-agency approach*.

While the new justice policies understandably have their critics, Smith (2002) reminds us that there has been a growing track record of research-informed practice in this area with initiatives being evaluated. The creation of YOTs was a demonstration of a commitment to more integrated and joined-up policy and practice clearly recognising the part that professionals from health, education, social work, police and probation could bring to interventions with young offenders. An example of innovation, the drug treatment and testing order, *suggested a more holistic understanding of the problem of young people's offending than is implied by a simply punitive response* (Smith 2002 p316).

ACTIVITY 7.2

Visit the Youth Justice Board website and search for the publications on either parenting or mentoring and identify the roles that other services and agencies can play in youth justice. You may also wish to look at the reports which document research on risk and protective factors associated with youth crime, and effective interventions to prevent it. What role can social workers play in this? Identify two or three key areas in which other areas of social work practice influence the life chances of young people who end up in the youth justice system.

The legal profession

A further group of professionals that you may have contact with in a legal context are solicitors and barristers. The professional and regulatory body for solicitors is the Law Society; for barristers it is the Bar Council. These bodies, as with professional bodies in other areas that we have covered in this book, have the responsibility of ensuring the public receive a service that is ethical and accountable. The role of solicitors and barristers is to represent individuals or local authorities in the courts and to advocate on their behalf. While solicitors are consulted by members of the public for a wide range of legal problems, barristers have more specialist knowledge and are not consulted directly but by referral from a solicitor. As explained by Johns (2011), judges are normally experienced barristers and they hear the serious complex criminal and family proceedings cases.

Social workers may be called upon to write welfare reports for court in private cases, particularly where they have been involved with a family and if the court requests such a report, and the social worker is under a duty to provide it. Following the Family Procedure Rules 2010 which were implemented in April 2011, new rules also came in governing the writing of these reports. The author should get to know the child in his/her own home and observe their relationship with any relevant adults. Interviews with the child and parents in an office environment will tend to be insufficient. Burman (2011) offers the following tips for writing a report in cases involving children, alongside the welfare checklist outlined in the Children Act 1989.

- Make all necessary investigations including contacting and interviewing the parties and obtaining whatever professional assistance they or the court has deemed necessary.

- Notify the child of the contents of the report, bearing in mind their age and level of understanding, and explain the contents of the report to them in an age-appropriate manner.

- Attend hearings as directed by the court.

- Advise the court of the child's wishes and feelings.

- Advise the court if they feel joining someone as a party to proceedings would safeguard the child's welfare.

- Consider whether the child should be made a party to proceedings (and notify the court if so).

- File the report and serve a copy of it on the parties. It is good practice for the report to be disclosed to each party, giving them enough time to discuss it with their legal advisers.

Once the report has been written, that document is confidential. Social workers can be questioned by the parties about their report. They can also be cross-examined in court, and judges have power under the Family Procedure Rules to limit the issues on which social workers can be questioned.

The police

You may work closely with the police in safeguarding work, in domestic violence situations, when adults and youths have committed crimes, including working with mentally ill offenders. You may also come across police officers in their community liaison role in neighbourhoods and as representatives to partnership working meetings.

Kennison and Fletcher (2005) explain that the role of the police is wide-ranging. They play an important role in preventative work in communities and are an important agency in information-sharing networks and partnerships that are an important tool in crime reduction, including that associated with anti-social behaviour.

CASE STUDY

The local police became involved when neighbours began to make complaints about a family with school-age children whose behaviour was becoming increasingly difficult to tolerate. The police were called to incidents involving damage to neighbours' property, including cars, shouting abuse, playing loud music and using verbal abuse and threats of violence to people who tried to intervene.

The police liaised with a range of services, including a local project run by a national children's charity which provides intense support for families at risk of eviction and with education, social services and housing professionals to find a solution to the problem. Close working and information sharing have enabled the agencies involved to look holistically at the problem and not intervene independently to address single aspects such as criminal behaviour and child protection concerns.

While the above approach was successful, as Kennison and Fletcher (2005 p125) point out, partnership working is not easily achieved as:

> There are problems of culture and power relations where some agencies assume
> control and influence by exerting their own group norms, beliefs, socialisation,
> understandings and goals on others to the detriment of the partnership.

As with other areas of public services, there are sometimes serious shortcomings in the way in which responsibilities are carried out. In Chapter 1 we considered the findings of serious case reviews and inquiries and saw that the police are one of the agencies implicated, along with social services and education and health services. Some of the difficulties in the relationships between agencies may be attributed to stereotyped attitudes and established working cultures which lead to an unwillingness to challenge the views of other professionals.

There have been enormous improvements in the working relationships between the police and social work both strategically and operationally. While the main functions of the police are to prevent, detect and investigate crime, they also provide a number of community-based services and can exercise some discretion in situations, which prevents automatic escalation, particularly in youth justice, so that professionals can have more freedom to determine the most appropriate response, depending on the severity of the offence and the circumstances (Pickford and Dugmore 2012). At the opposite end of the scale there has been some criticism of the police in their reluctance to take action in some crimes against vulnerable user groups. For example, research has shown (Voice UK 2001) that of 284 suspected cases of alleged sexual abuse against people with learning difficulties, only 63 (less than a quarter) were investigated by police and only two of these went to court with one conviction. The Youth Justice and Criminal Evidence Act 1999 and guidance such as *Achieving best evidence* (2000) have recognised that with proper support vulnerable people can make good witnesses both for themselves and for crimes against others. However, there have been resource issues in fully implementing the changes and, in some areas, commitment is not sufficient to effect changes. Joint training with the police and those working with victims is crucial, particularly that which involves service users in the training programme as participants and trainers.

Within domestic violence, the Multi-Agency Risk Assessment Conference (known as MARAC) is a model of intervention in which risk assessment and a multi-agency approach are combined to help very high-risk victims of domestic abuse. This originated from Wales where 16 agencies, including police, probation, local authority, health, housing, refuge and the Women's Safety Unit, were brought together and the outcomes extensively evaluated and researched (Robinson 2004). It followed from a review of 47 domestic homicides investigated by the South Wales Police, research, and input from partner agencies and a risk assessment tool was reviewed and approved by service users in domestic violence. The tool gathers information on past physical abuse, escalation of abuse, use of weapons, unemployment or financial problems, substance abuse, pregnancy, jealous or controlling behaviour, impending or ongoing relationship separation, threats, sexual abuse and suicidal thoughts. These risk factors also feature in forms used by agencies in other jurisdictions. Outcomes indicated that the meetings yielded substantial improvements both to the practice of professionals and to the safety of victims and their children. This model was then disseminated and adopted widely in the UK.

The goal of these conferences is to provide a forum for sharing information and taking action to reduce future harm to very high-risk victims of domestic abuse and their children. The police play an important role in identifying very high-risk victims who are then placed at the heart of the system. Interviews with practitioners showed confidence that such approaches could achieve many key objectives, including information-sharing between agencies, contributing to victims' safety (Robinson 2004). Pickles (2007) has published a case study which demonstrates how MARAC might work in practice.

CASE STUDY

MARAC

Jean, a 38-year-old mother of three children aged 13, 9 and 4, was pregnant again, although separated from her partner. At a routine ante-natal visit where she was asked about domestic abuse, Jean disclosed ongoing harassment by her ex-partner. She was referred to the Women's Safety Unit and a MARAC by her midwife.

At the MARAC it was agreed that agencies would support Jean to collect evidence for a civil or criminal case, that the children would be offered support in school, Jean's home would be made more secure and a regular police drive-by would start. Information about the perpetrator's level of threat was shared across agencies. All actions were co-ordinated by the advocate at the Women's Safety Unit who was Jean's primary contact. Jean felt reassured that agencies were taking her concerns seriously and she no longer felt alone. She chose to go down the civil justice route as she thought this would warn him off as he was working and worried about losing his job. Jean and her children are still safe nine months after the MARAC.

(Pickles 2007)

REFLECTION POINT

Breakdowns in effective working can be attributed to individual, organisational and cultural factors. How will you maintain a reflective approach that acknowledges, takes account of and addresses these factors?

CHAPTER SUMMARY

Justice is a complex and challenging area of practice for social workers as it raises far-reaching questions about care and control, about rights and risks, and about working with other professionals who may have very different views about the term 'justice'. These challenges can begin to be overcome through developing clarity of purpose about the role and professional values of social work, a greater understanding of the moral dilemmas involved and an appreciation of the perspectives of other professional groups. It is an area where sudden changes in policy are likely to take place as a result of politically expedient decisions that play to the public's fear of crime (Smith 2002).

An important issue for social workers and their concern with social justice is pointed out by Charman and Savage (2002 p227) in their evaluation of New Labour's record on criminal justice, in their conclusion that what matters are *the social and cultural forces that cause crime, not finding out more and more severe ways to punish the small percentage of offenders who are actually detected and convicted.*

Faulkner (2011) has expressed an expectation that the programme of reduction in public expenditure and reform of the criminal justice system by the coalition government and other public services will be made with proper regard for their effects on partnerships and shared services, including the voluntary and

Continued

CHAPTER SUMMARY

community sector and the small and often local schemes which the 'Big Society' is intended to promote and support around the justice arena. Criminal justice is also affected by the loss or lack of attention to the small and often unseen and uncounted relationships and 'civilities' which can make all the difference to the life of a vulnerable young person or to someone's chances of rehabilitation. Faulkner reminds us that differences of power, influence, professional culture and capacity have to be reconciled to create a sense of shared ownership of the challenges ahead. Partnership activities such as commissioning, localisation, the use of evidence and expert advice, the management of risk, the encouragement of innovation and the role of the voluntary sector will all need to be re-examined. He goes on to evaluate the limitations of command models based on authority and top-down communication which do not work in settings which involve disadvantaged and vulnerable people and their families as referred to in earlier chapters of this book. New ways of working have to be found which are based on consultation and mutual confidence and respect. Several statutory and voluntary agencies may need to be engaged – health, social services, housing, education, as well as those that are part of the criminal justice system. For social workers, engaging with a range of people with different personal qualities and skills is needed in order to get something done rather than to protect positions and avoid risks.

It is this wider perspective based on an understanding of inequalities that social workers can contribute to these often complex situations in which collaborative practice may be more difficult to achieve but where achieving it should make a significant impact on the lives of service users and carers.

FURTHER READING

Johns, R (2011) *Using the law in social work*. 5th edition. London: Learning Matters at Sage.

This well-established book looks at how the law in England and Wales interacts with key aspects of practice such as human rights, mental health, youth justice and community care.

Pickford, J and Dugmore, P (2012) *Youth justice and social work*. 2nd edition. London: Learning Matters at Sage.

A detailed text on the complexities and debates about the youth justice system enables the reader to follow complex and often difficult legislation and law and the roles of different professionals within the system.

Pritchard, J (2008) *Good practice in safeguarding adults: Working effectively in adult protection*. London: Jessica Kingsley.

This comprehensive text has separate chapters on the different professionals' contributions to safeguarding adults.

WEBSITE

www.cafcass.gov.uk/ Cafcass.

The website of the Children and Family Court Advisory and Support Service

www.justice.gov.uk/ Justice.

Website of the Ministry of Justice

www.scie.org.uk/assets/elearning/law/law05/resource/html/object5/index.htm

Social Care Institute for Excellence: Courtroom skills: an e-learning resource provided by the Social Care Institute for Excellence. This consists of a series of video extracts designed to enable students to feel more confident and effective when consulting and working with others, and more competent when exercising social worker powers and responsibilities.

Appendix 1 Professional Capabilities Framework

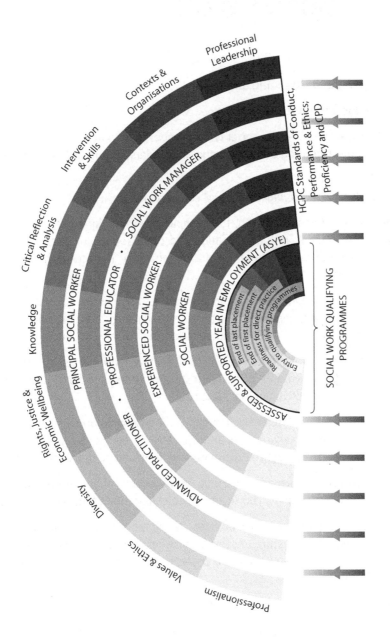

Professional Capabilities Framework diagram reproduced with permission of The College of Social Work.

Appendix 2 Subject Benchmark for Social Work

Subject knowledge, understanding and skills

Subject knowledge and understanding

5.1 During their degree studies in social work, honours graduates should acquire, critically evaluate, apply and integrate knowledge and understanding in the following core areas of study.

5.1.1 Social work services, service users and carers, which include:

- the social processes (associated with, for example, poverty, migration, unemployment, poor health, disablement, lack of education and other sources of disadvantage) that lead to marginalisation, isolation and exclusion, and their impact on the demand for social work services;

- explanations of the links between definitional processes contributing to social differences (for example, social class, gender, ethnic differences, age, sexuality and religious belief) to the problems of inequality and differential need faced by service users;

- the nature of social work services in a diverse society (with particular reference to concepts such as prejudice, interpersonal, institutional and structural discrimination, empowerment and anti-discriminatory practices);

- the nature and validity of different definitions of, and explanations for, the characteristics and circumstances of service users and the services required by them, drawing on knowledge from research, practice experience, and from service users and carers;

- the focus on outcomes, such as promoting the well-being of young people and their families, and promoting dignity, choice and independence for adults receiving services;

- the relationship between agency policies, legal requirements and professional boundaries in shaping the nature of services provided in interdisciplinary contexts and the issues associated with working across professional boundaries and within different disciplinary groups.

5.1.2 The service delivery context, which include:

- the location of contemporary social work within historical, comparative and global perspectives, including European and international contexts;

- the changing demography and cultures of communities in which social workers will be practising;

- the complex relationships between public, social and political philosophies, policies and priorities and the organisation and practice of social work, including the contested nature of these;

- the issues and trends in modern public and social policy and their relationship to contemporary practice and service delivery in social work;

- the significance of legislative and legal frameworks and service delivery standards (including the nature of legal authority, the application of legislation in practice, statutory accountability and tensions between statute, policy and practice);

- the current range and appropriateness of statutory, voluntary and private agencies providing community-based, day-care, residential and other services and the organisational systems inherent within these;

- the significance of interrelationships with other related services, including housing, health, income maintenance and criminal justice (where not an integral social service);

- the contribution of different approaches to management, leadership and quality in public and independent human services;

- the development of personalised services, individual budgets and direct payments

- the implications of modern information and communications technology (ICT) for both the provision and receipt of services.

5.1.3 Values and ethics, which include:

- the nature, historical evolution and application of social work values;

- the moral concepts of rights, responsibility, freedom, authority and power inherent in the practice of social workers as moral and statutory agents;

- the complex relationships between justice, care and control in social welfare and the practical and ethical implications of these, including roles as statutory agents and in upholding the law in respect of discrimination;

- aspects of philosophical ethics relevant to the understanding and resolution of value dilemmas and conflicts in both interpersonal and professional contexts;

- the conceptual links between codes defining ethical practice, the regulation of professional conduct and the management of potential conflicts generated by the codes held by different professional groups.

5.1.5 The nature of social work practice, which include:

- the characteristics of practice in a range of community-based and organisational settings within statutory, voluntary and private sectors, and the factors influencing changes and developments in practice within these contexts;

- the nature and characteristics of skills associated with effective practice, both direct and indirect, with a range of service-users and in a variety of settings;

- the processes that facilitate and support service user choice and independence;

- the factors and processes that facilitate effective interdisciplinary, interprofessional and interagency collaboration and partnership;

- the place of theoretical perspectives and evidence from international research in assessment and decision-making processes in social work practice;

- the integration of theoretical perspectives and evidence from international research into the design and implementation of effective social work intervention, with a wide range of service users, carers and others;

- the processes of reflection and evaluation, including familiarity with the range of approaches for evaluating service and welfare outcomes, and their significance for the development of practice and the practitioner.

Skills in working with others

5.7 Honours graduates in social work should be able to work effectively with others, ie to:

- involve users of social work services in ways that increase their resources, capacity and power to influence factors affecting their lives;

- consult actively with others, including service users and carers, who hold relevant information or expertise;

- act cooperatively with others, liaising and negotiating across differences such as organisational and professional boundaries and differences of identity or language;

- develop effective helping relationships and partnerships with other individuals, groups and organisations that facilitate change;

- act with others to increase social justice by identifying and responding to prejudice, institutional discrimination and structural inequality;

- act within a framework of multiple accountability (for example, to agencies, the public, service users, carers and others;

- challenge others when necessary, in ways that are most likely to produce positive outcomes.

References

Adams, C and Chakera, S (2004) *Tackling black and minority ethnic underachievement*. Viewpoint 4. London: General Teaching Council. Available at www.gtce.org.uk

Adams, R (2002) *Social policy for social work*. Basingstoke: Palgrave.

Ajegbo, K, Kiwan, D and Sharma, S (2007) *Curriculum review: Diversity and citizenship*. London: DfES.

Albemarle Report (1960) *Youth service in England and Wales*. London: HMSO.

Alcock, P (2003) *Social policy in Britain*. 2nd edn. Basingstoke: Palgrave Macmillan.

Alcock, C, Payne, S and Sullivan, M (2002) *Introducing social policy*. Harlow: Prentice Hall.

Aldridge, F (2009) *Enhancing informal adult learning for older people in care settings: Interim report and consultation document*. Leicester: National Institute for Continuing Education.

Amery, J (2000) Interprofessional working in Health Action Zones: How can this be fostered and sustained? *Journal of Interprofessional Care*. 14.1: 27–30.

Arnstein, Sherry R (1969) A ladder of citizen participation. *Journal of American Institute of Planners*, 35(04): 216–24.

Association of Directors of Social Services (2011) *ADASS position on ordinary residence*. Available at www.adass. org.uk

Bamford, T (1990) *The future of social work*. Basingstoke: Macmillan.

Banks, S (2006) *Ethics and values in social work*. Basingstoke: Palgrave.

Barker, K (2004) *Review of housing supply, delivering stability: Securing our housing needs final report – Recommendations*. London: HMSO.

Barnes, D, Brandon, T with Webb, T (2002) *Independent specialist advocacy in England and Wales: Recommendations for good practice*. University of Durham/Department of Health.

Barnes, J (2002) *Focus on the future: Key messages from focus groups about the future of social work training*. London: Department of Health.

Barr, H (2002) *Inter-professional education: Today, yesterday and tomorrow. Occasional Paper No. 1*. London: Health Sciences and Practice LTSN/CAIPE.

Barr, H and Ross, F (2006) Mainstreaming interprofessional education in the United Kingdom: a position paper. *Journal of Interprofessional Care*, 20(2): 96–104.

Barrett G and Keeping C (2005) The processes required for effective interprofessional working. In Barrett, G, Sellman, D and Thomas, J (eds) (2005) *Interprofessional working in health and social care*. Basingstoke: Palgrave.

Barrett, G, Greenwood, R and Ross, K (2003) Integrating interprofessional education into 10 health and social care programmes. *Journal of Interprofessional Care*, 17: 293–301.

Barrett, G, Sellman, D and Thomas, J (eds) (2005) *Interprofessional working in health and social care*. Basingstoke: Palgrave.

Batty, E, Beatty, C, Foden, M, Lawless, P, Pearson, S and Wilson, I (2010) *The new deal for communities evaluation: Final report – Volume 7*. Centre for Regional Economic and Social Research, Sheffield Hallam University: Department for Communities and Local Government.

Benjamin, A (2005) Soul searching. *The Guardian*, Wednesday 14 September.

Beresford, P (2007) *The changing roles and tasks of social work from service users' perspectives: A literature informed discussion paper*. Shaping Our Lives.

Beresford, P, Branfield, F, Maslem, B, Sartori, A and Jenny, M and M (2007) *Partnership working. Service users and social workers learning together*. In Lymbery, M and Postle, K (eds) *Social work: A companion to learning*. London: Sage.

Bevan, M (2002) *Housing and disabled children: The art of the possible*. Bristol: Policy Press.

Beveridge, Sir W (1942) *Report on social insurance and allied services*. Cmnd 6404. London: HMSO.

Blair, T (2004) *Fabian Lecture on education at the Institute of Education*. Wed July 7. Available at www.suttontrust.com

Blackman, T and Harvey, J (2001) Housing renewal and mental health: A case study. *Journal of Mental Health*, 10(5): 571–83.

Blyth, E. (2000) Education social work. In Davies, M (ed.) *The Blackwell dictionary of social work*. Oxford: Blackwell.

Bournemouth Borough Council (2005) *Children's Information Service*. Available at www.bournemouth.gov.uk

Bowie, D (2010) *Government and property market failure: The political and ideological origins of the housing market downturn in England and the need for a new funding model*. Paper presented at International Sociological Association (ISA) Housing Conference, Glasgow, 1–4 September 2009. Available at www.londonmet.ac.uk

Bradshaw, S (2005) *The postcode trap. How the postcode on your address can affect your opportunities and what it means for children like Kurt*. Available at news.bbc.co.uk

Brindle, D (2005) New realities: Integrated partnerships across health, social care and housing. *The Guardian*, 02/03/05.

Britton, L, Chatrick, B, Coles, B, Craig, G, Hylton, C and Mumtaz, S (2002) *Missing ConneXions; The career dynamics and welfare needs of black and minority ethnic young people at the margins*. Bristol: Policy Press.

Browne, J (2010) *Securing a sustainable future for higher education*. Available at www.bis.gov.uk

Brunton, A (2010) Housing benefit. In Yeates, N, Hawkes, T, Jawad, R and Majella Kilky (eds) *In defence of welfare: The impacts of the spending review*. Social Policy Association. Available at www.social-policy.org.uk

Burman, M (2011) How to prepare a welfare report. *Community Care*, 27/10/2011.

Cafcass (2011) *Cafcass care demand – Latest figures for August 2011*. London: Cafcass.

Callender (2010) Higher education. In Yeates, N, Hawkes, T, Jawad, R and Majella Kelley (eds) *In defence of welfare: The impacts of the spending review*. Social Policy Association. Available at www.social-policy.org.uk

Camden Children's Fund (2005) *Schools based multi-disciplinary team*. Available at www.everychildmatters.gov.uk

Care Quality Commission (2010) *A new system of registration: The scope for registration*. Newcastle-upon-Tyne: CQC.

Carpenter, J and Dickenson, H (2008) *Interprofessional education and training*. Bristol: Policy Press.

Carpenter, J, Schneider, J, Brandon, T and Woof, T (2003) Working in multi-disciplinary community mental health teams: The impact on social workers and health professionals of integrated mental health care. *British Journal of Social Work*, 33(8): 1081–103.

Carr, S (2004) Has service user participation made a difference to social care services? *Position Paper no. 3.* London: Social Care Institute for Excellence.

Central Council for Education and Training in Social Work (1989) *Multidisciplinary teamwork. Models of good practice.* London: CCETSW.

Central Council for Education and Training in Social Work (1992) *Preparing for work in the education welfare service.* London: CCETSW.

Centre of the Advancement of Interprofessional Education (1997) *Interprofessional education – A definition.* CAIPE Bulletin No. 13. London: CAIPE.

Chahal, K (2000) Ethnic diversity, neighbourhoods and housing. *Foundations.* Ref 110. JRF. Available at www.jrf.org.uk

Chartered Institute of Housing (2000) *Code of professional conduct.* Available at www.cih.org

Chartered Institute of Housing (2001) *Professional qualifications specification 2001.* Coventry: CIH.

Chartered Institute of Housing (2004) *Open to all, closed to prejudice. Equality and diversity strategy.* Coventry: CIH.

Children and Family Court Advisory and Support Service (2005) *About Cafcass.* Available at www.cafcass.gov.uk

Clark, C (2000) *Social work ethics: Politics, principles and practice.* Basingstoke: Palgrave.

Coles, B, Britton L and Hicks, L (2004) *Building better connexions: Interagency work and the Connexions service.* Bristol: Policy Press.

Coles B, England, J, and Rugg, J (2000) Spaced out? Young people on social housing estates: Social exclusion and multi-agency work. *Journal of Youth Studies,* 3(1): 21–33.

Community Development Exchange (2005) *What is community development?* www.cdx.org.uk

Connexions (2005) *The role and qualities of a personal advisor.* www.connexions.gov.uk

Criminal Justice System (2005) Aims and objectives. Available at www.cjsonline.gov.uk

Crawford, K and Walker, J (2004) *Social work with older people.* Exeter: Learning Matters.

Davies, B (1999a) *From voluntaryism to welfare state. A history of the youth service in England. Vol. 1 1939–1979.* Leicester: Youth Work Press.

Davies, B (1999b) *From Thatcher to New Labour. A history of the youth service in England. Vol. 2 1979–1999.* Leicester: Youth Work Press.

Debbonaire, T (2008) *Evaluation of the use of a risk identification tool in Cafcass, Relate and Respect projects.* London: Cafcass/Relate/Respect.

Department for Children, Education and Skills (DCES) (2006) *Working together to safeguard children: A guide to inter-agency working to safeguard and promote the welfare of children.* Norwich: The Stationery Office.

Department for Children, Education and Skills (DCES) (2007) *The children's plan: Building brighter futures.* Norwich: The Stationery Office.

Department for Constitutional Affairs (2005) *The legal system.* Available at www.dca.gov.uk

Department for Education (2010a) *The importance of teaching – The schools White Paper 2010.* London: DoE.

Department for Education (2010b) *National evaluation of Sure Start local programmes: An economic perspective.* London: DoE.

Department for Education (2011a) *Building engagement, building futures: Our strategy to maximise the participation of 16–24 year olds in education, training and work.* London: DoE.

Department for Education (2011b) *Positive for youth: A new approach to cross-government policy for young people aged 13 to 19*. Available at www.education.gov.co.uk

Department for Education (2011c) *Teachers' standards effective from 1 September 2012*. London: DoE.

Department for Education (2012a) *General article 'About academies'*. Available at www.education.gov.uk

Department for Education (2012b) *16- to 18-year olds not in education, employment or training (NEET)*. Available at www.education.gov.uk

Department for Education and Employment (2000) *Connexions: The best start in life for every young person*. London: DfEE.

Department for Education and Skills (2001) *SEN code of practice*. London: DfES.

Department for Education and Skills (2002) *Transforming youth work – Resourcing excellent youth services*. London: DfES.

Department for Education and Skills (2003) *Every Child Matters: Change for children*. Cm 5860. London: HMSO.

Department for Education and Skills (2004a) *Every Child Matters: Change for children in social care*. London: DfES.

Department for Education and Skills (2004b) *Putting people at the heart of public services: Five year strategy for children and learning*. Cm 6272. London: DfES. Available at www.dfes.gov.uk

Department for Education and Skills (2005) *Multi-agency working*. Available at www.everychildmatters.gov.uk

DfES Circular 10/95. *Protecting children from abuse: The role of the education service*.

Department of Health (1992) *The health of the nation*. Cmnd. 1986. London: HMSO.

Department of the Environment (1995) *Our future home: Opportunity, choice, responsibility*. Cmnd 2901. London: HMSO.

Department of Health (1997) *The new NHS: Modern and dependable*. London: DoH.

Department of Health (1998a) *Modernising social services: Promoting independence, improving protection, raising standards*. Cm. 4169. London: HMSO.

Department of Health (1998b) *Our healthier nation: A contract for health*. London: The Stationery Office.

Department of Health (1998c) *Partnerships in action: New opportunities for joint working between health and social services*. London: Department of Health.

Department of Health (1999) *Working together to safeguard children. A guide to inter-agency working to safeguard children and promote the welfare of children*. London: The Stationery Office.

Department of Health (2000a) *No secrets: Guidance on developing and implementing multi-agency policies and procedures to protect vulnerable adults from abuse*. London: Department of Health.

Department of Health (2000b) *The NHS Plan: A plan for investment, a plan for reform*. Cmnd 4818. Available at www.nhs.uk

Department of Health (2000c) *Framework for the assessment of children in need and their families*. London: Department of Health.

Department of Health (2002) *Quality in social care. The national institutional framework*. London: The Stationery Office.

Department of Health (2006) *Our health, our care, our say: A new direction for community services*. London: DoH.

Department of Health (2007) *Guidance on joint strategic needs assessment*. London: DoH.

Department of Health (2009a) *Living well with dementia: A national dementia strategy*. London: DoH.

Department of Health (2009b) *Health Act 2009*. Available at www.legislation.gov.uk

Department of Health (2009c) *Working to put people first: The strategy for the adult social care workforce in England social care*. Leeds: DoH.

Department of Health (2010a) *Equity and excellence: Liberating the NHS*. Available at www.dh.gov.uk

Department of Health (2010b) *A vision for adult social care: Capable communities and active citizens*. Crown Copyright.

Department of Health (2011a) *Safeguarding the NHS. Press release*. Available at www.dh.gov.uk

Department of Health (2011b) *Healthy lives, healthy people. Update and the way forward*. Crown Copyright.

Devon Children's Trust (2004) *Case study: An integrated housing and children's services strategy*. Available at www.everychildmatters.gov.uk

Dickenson, H (2008) *Evaluating outcomes in health and social care*. Bristol: Policy Press.

DIUS, Department for Innovation, Universities and Skills (2009) *The learning revolution*. DIUS: Crown Copyright.

Dominelli, L (2002) *Anti-oppressive social work theory and practice*. Basingstoke: Palgrave.

Dorset Police (2005) *Domestic violence*. Leaflet produced by the Dorset Domestic Violence Co-ordinator. Bournemouth.

Dyson, A, Farrell P, Hutcheson, G and Polat, F (2004) *Inclusion and pupil achievement*. London: DfES

Eaton, G (2011) Cameron's 'big society' relaunch repeats old errors. *New Statesman*, 14/2/2011.

Edwards, M and Harding (2011) Building our futures: Meeting the housing needs of an ageing population. In Sylvestri (ed.) *Lessons for the coalition: An end of term report on New Labour and criminal justice*. The Hadley Trust. London: Centre for Crime and Justice Studies.

European Commission (EC) (2000) *Memorandum on lifelong learning*. Commission Staff Working Paper. Brussels: Commission of the European Community.

Every Child Matters (2005) *Education welfare officers*. Available at www.everychildmatters.gov.uk

Family Justice Council (2005) http://www.family-justice-council.org.uk

Faulkner, D (2011) Criminal justice reform at a time of austerity: What needs to be done? In Sylvestri (ed.) *Lessons for the coalition: An end of term report on New Labour and criminal justice*. The Hadley Trust. London: Centre for Crime and Justice Studies.

Fook, J (2012) *Social work: A critical approach to practice*. London: Sage.

Foyer Federation (2005) *What is a Foyer?* Available at www.foyer.net

Freire, P (1972) *Pedagogy of the oppressed*. Harmondsworth: Penguin.

Gewirtz, S and Cribb, A (2007) *Supporting teacher professionalism: Recent research and policy starting points*. London: King's College London.

Gewirtz, S and McGuire, M (2010) Compulsory education. In Yeates, N, Hawkes, T, Jawad, R and Majella Kelley (eds) *In defence of welfare: The impacts of the spending review*. Social Policy Association. Available at www.social-policy.org.uk

Glasby, J and Dickenson, H (2008) *Partnership working in health and social care.* Bristol: Policy Press.

Glass, N (2005) Surely some mistake? *The Guardian,* 05/01/05.

Golightly, M (2004) *Social work and mental health.* Exeter: Learning Matters.

Hafford-Letchfield, T (2010) The age of opportunity? Revisiting assumptions about the lifelong learning needs of older people using social care services. *British Journal of Social Work,* 2: 496 – 512.

Hafford-Letchfield, T (2011) Grey matter really matters: A study of the learning opportunities and learning experiences of older people using social care services. *International Journal of Education and Ageing,* 2(1): 23 – 40.

Hammond, C (2004) Impacts of lifelong learning upon emotional resistance, psychological and mental health: Fieldwork evidence. *Oxford Review of Education,* 30(4): 551 – 68.

Harding, S, Brown, J, Rosato, M and Hattersley, L (1999) *Socio-economic differentials in health: Illustrations from the Office for National Statistics longitudinal study.* London: Office for National Statistics.

Hardy J (ed.) (1999) *Achieving health and social care improvements through interprofessional education.* Conference Proceedings. Institute of Health and Community Studies: Bournemouth University.

Harris, J, Hall, J, Meltzer, H, Jenkins, R, Oreszczyn and McManus, S (2010) *Health, mental health and housing conditions in England.* London: National Centre for Social Research.

Harrison, L and Heywood, F (2000) *Health begins at home: Planning at the health-housing interface for older people.* Bristol: Policy Press.

Harvey, S, McMahon, L and Humphries, R (2011) *Routes for social health care: A simulation exercise.* London: The King's Fund.

Henderson, P, Summer, S and Raj, T (2004) *Developing healthier communities.* London: Health Development Agency.

Her Majesty's Government (2004) *Every child matters: Change for children.* London: HMG.

Her Majesty's Government (2006) *Working together to safeguard children: A guide to inter-agency working to safeguard and promote the welfare of children.* London: HMG.

Her Majesty's Government (2007) *Putting people first: A shared vision and commitment to the transformation of adult social care.* London: HMG.

Her Majesty's Government (2010) *The National Health Service (Direct Payments) Regulations.* Crown Copyright.

Her Majesty's Government (2011a) *Support and aspiration: A new approach to special educational needs and disability – A consultation.* London: HMG.

Her Majesty's Government (2011b) *Valuing people now: The delivery plan 2010-2011.* London: HMG.

Hill, M, Dillane J, Bannister, J and Scott, S (2002) Everybody needs good neighbours: An evaluation of an intensive project for families facing eviction. *Child and Family Social Work,* 7: 79 – 89.

Hodgson, J (2005) Working together – A multi-disciplinary concern. In Parker, J (ed.) *Aspects of social work and palliative care.* Quay Books/MA Healthcare Limited.

Hopkins, G. (2001) Screened Out. *Community Care,* 31 January: 31.

Horgan, G (2007) *The impact of poverty on young children's experience of school.* York: Joseph Rowntree Foundation.

Hornby S and Atkins J (2000) *Collaborative care: Interprofessional, interagency and interpersonal.* 2nd edn. Oxford: Blackwell Science.

Horner (2012) *What is social work?* 4th edn. Exeter: Learning Matters.

Hudson, B (2002) Interprofessionality in health and social care: The Achilles' heel of partnership. *Journal of Interprofessional Care*, 16(1): 7–17.

Hudson, B, Hardy, B, Henwood, M and Wistow, G (1997) *Inter-agency collaboration: Final report*. Leeds: Nuffield Institute for Health.

Humphries, R, Forder, J and Fernandez, J L (2010) *Securing good care for more people: A long-term approach*. London: The King's Fund.

Infed (2012) *Youth work – An introduction*. www.infed.org

Institute of Public Policy Research (IPPR) (2011) Exploring the relationship between riot areas and deprivation – An IPPR analysis. www.ipp5r.org

International Federation of Social Work and International Association of Schools of Social Work (2000) *Definition of social work*. IFSW/IASSW.

Jackson, S (2006) Learning to live: The relationship between lifelong learning and lifelong illness. *International Journal of Lifelong Education*, 25(1): 51–73.

Jeffs, T and Smith, M K (2002) Individualisation and youth work. *Youth and Policy*, 76: 39–65.

Johns, R (2011) *Using the law in social work*. Exeter: Learning Matters.

Jordan, B (2004) The personal social services. In Ellison, N, Baud, L and Powell, M (eds) *Social Policy Review 16: Analysis and debate in social policy 2004*. Bristol: Policy Press/Social Policy Association.

Joseph Rowntree Foundation (1996) *Housing and mental health needs of Asian people*. Social Care Research Findings No. 79. York: JRF.

Joseph Rowntree Foundation. (2000) *The reality of social exclusion on housing estates*. Findings No. 120. York: JRF.

Joseph Rowntree Foundation (2005) *Introduction to the Joseph Rowntree Foundation*. Available at www.jrf.org.uk

Kearney, P, Levin, E and Rosen, G (2000) *Alcohol, drug and mental health problems: Working with families*. London: Social Care Institute for Excellence.

Kearney, P, Levin, E, Rosen, G and Sainsbury, M (2003) *Families that have alcohol and mental health problems: A template for partnership working*. London: SCIE, 83–4.

Keeping, C (2006) *Emotional aspects of the professional identity of social workers working with Avon and Wiltshire Mental Health Partnership NHS Trust*. Bristol: University of West of England.

Kennison, P and Fletcher, R (2005) The police. In Barrett, G, Sellman, D and Thomas, J (eds) *Interprofessional working in health and social care*. Basingstoke: Palgrave.

Laming Report (2003) *The Victoria Climbié Inquiry: Report of an inquiry by Lord Laming*. London: The Stationery Office.

Laming Report (2009) *The protection of children in England: A progress report*. London: The Stationery Office.

The Lancet (2012) *How the Health and Social Care Bill would end entitlement to comprehensive health care in England*. Available at www.allysonpollock.co.uk

Lefevre, M, Richards, S and Trevithick, P (2008) *Communication skills*. London: Social Care Institute for Excellence. Available at www.scie.org.uk

Lindsay, J (2005) Probation. In Barrett, G, Sellman, D and Thomas, J (eds) *Interprofessional working in health and social care*. Basingstoke: Palgrave.

Low, J (2011) *The riots: What are the lessons from JRF's work in communities?* York: Joseph Rowntree Foundation.

Lupton, R and Power, A (2005) Disadvantaged by where you live? New Labour and neighbourhood renewal. In Hills, J and Stewart, K (eds) *A more equal society? New Labour, poverty, inequality and exclusion.* Bristol: Policy Press.

Lupton, R, Heath, N and Salter, E (2009) Education: New Labour's top priority. In Hills, T, Sefton, T and Stewart, K (eds) *Towards a more equal society: Poverty, inequality and policy since 1997.* Bristol: Policy Press.

McClusky, H Y (1974) Education for ageing: The scope of the field and perspectives for the future. In Grabowski, S and Mason, W D (eds) *Learning for ageing.* Washington, DC: Adult Education Association of the USA.

McDonagh, T (2001) *Tackling homelessness and exclusion: Understanding complex lives (round-up).* York: Joseph Rowntree Foundation.

McKnight, A, Glennester, H and Lupton, R (2005) Education, education, education…: An assessment of Labour's success in tackling education inequalities In Hills, J and Stewart, K (eds) *A more equal society? New Labour, poverty and exclusion.* Bristol: Policy Press.

McLaughlin, E, Muncie, J and Hughes, G (2001) The permanent revolution: New Labour, new public management and the modernization of criminal justice. *Criminology and Criminal Justice,* 1(3): 301–18.

McLeod, E, and Bywaters, P (2000) *Social work, health and inequality.* London: Routledge.

Manthorpe, J and Iliffe, S (2007) Dementia: New guidelines from NICE and SCIE. *Community Care,* 25/1/2007. Available at www.communitycare.co.uk

Manthorpe, J, Moriarty, J, Rapoport, J, Clough, R, Cornes, M, Bright,,L, Iliffe, S and OPRSI (2007) There are wonderful social workers but it's a lottery: Older people's views about social workers. *British Journal of Social Work.*

Marmot, M (2010) *Fair society, healthy lives: A strategic review of health inequalities in England post-2010.* The Marmot Review. Available at www.marmotreview.org

Miller, T (2005) *Across the great divide: Creating partnerships in education. The encyclopedia of informal education.* Available at www.infed.org

Ministry of Health (1944) *A National Health Service.* Cmnd 6502. London: HMSO.

Ministry of Justice (2010) *Integrated offender management: Key principles.* London: MoJ.

Morris, K (2008) *Social work and multi-agency working: Making a difference.* Bristol: Policy Press.

Moseley, J (2005) They need to be involved. *Community Care,* 4-10 August.

Muncie, J (1999) *Youth and crime: A critical introduction.* London: Sage.

Munroe, E (2011) *The Munro review of child protection: Final report. A child-centred system.* London: The Stationery Office.

Naidoo, R and Muschamp, Y (2002) A decent education for all? In Powell, M (ed.) *Evaluating New Labour's welfare reforms.* Bristol: Policy Press.

National Audit Office (2011) *Achievement of foundation trust status by NHS hospital trusts.* London: The Stationery Office.

NHS Executive (1998) *Planning for better health and better health care.* York: National Health Executive HSC: 169.

National Housing Federation (2010) *Public support house-building drive to tackle the country's housing crisis.* Available at www.housing.org.uk

National Institute for Health and Clinical Excellence (2008) *NICE guidance for health promotion.* London: NICE.

National Institute for Health and Clinical Excellence and Social Care Institute for Excellence (2006) Dementia: Supporting people with dementia and their carers in health and social care. *Nice Clinical Guideline 42.* London: The National Collaborating Centre for Mental Health.

National Youth Agency (2006) *The contribution of youth work to Every Child Matters outcomes.* Leicester: NYA.

National Youth Agency (2010) *Valuing youth work.* Leicester: NYA.

National Youth Agency (2011) *Raising the participation age: Developing an engaging offer to young people. Emerging findings.* Leicester: NYA. http://nya.org.uk

Nocon, A (2004) *Background evidence for the DRC's formal investigation into health inequalities experienced by people with learning difficulties or mental health problems.* London: Disability Rights Commission.

Nolan, P C (ed.) (2003) *20 years of youth and policy. A retrospective.* Leicester: The National Youth Agency.

NSPCC (2005) *Teen abuse survey of Great Britain 2005.* Available at www.nspcc.org.uk

ODPM (Office of the Deputy Prime Minister) (2004) *What is supporting people?* London: ODPM Available at www.spkweb.org.uk

ODPM (Office of the Deputy Prime Minister) (2005) *Lessons from the past, challenges for the future.* Housing Research Summary number 214. Available at www.odpm.gov.uk

Ofsted (2005) *What we do.* Available at www.ofsted.gov.uk

Ofsted (2009) *Raising standards, improving lives: Key contacts for local authorities.* Manchester: Ofsted.

Ofsted (2011) *Office for Standards in Education, Children's Services and Skills. Annual report and accounts 2010–11 (for the year ended 31 March 2011).* London: HMSO.

O'Malley, L and Croucher, K (2005) Housing and dementia care – A scoping review of the literature. *Health and Social Care in the Community,* 13(6): 570–77.

Osler, A, Street, C, Lall, M and Vincent, K (2002) *Not a problem? Girls and social exclusion.* London: National Children's Bureau.

Overill, S (1998) A practical guide to care pathways. *Journal of Integrated Care,* 2: 93–8.

Oxford Economics (2011) *Housing market analysis July 2011.* Oxford: Oxford Economics for the Housing Federation.

Palmer, G and Parsons, N (2004) *A review of government policies that have an impact on the single homes.* New Policy Institute.

Parrott, L (2007) *Values and ethics in social work practice.* Exeter: Learning Matters.

Paton, G (2008) Trainee teachers quitting classroom after less than a year. *The Telegraph,* 18/9/2008.

Payne, M (2000) *Teamwork in multi-professional care.* Basingstoke: Palgrave.

Payne, M (2006) *What is professional social work?* Bristol: Policy Press.

Payne, M (2007) *Partnership working: The interdisciplinary agenda.* In Lymbery, M and Postle, K (eds) *Social work: A companion to learning.* London: Sage.

Pearce, J and Milne, E J (2010) *Participation and community on Bradford's traditionally white estates.* York: Joseph Rowntree Foundation.

Peek, L. (2005) Why did no-one act to curb child-snatchers? *Daily Mail,* Friday 26 August, page 23.

Perry, E and Francis, B (2010) *The social class gap for educational achievement: A review of the literature*. London: RSA.

Phillipson, C (2000) Critical and educational gerontology: Relationships and future developments. In Glendenning, F (ed.) *Teaching and learning in later life*. Hampshire: Ashgate.

Pickford, J and Dugmore, P (2012) *Youth justice and social work*. 2nd edn. London: Sage.

Pickles, J (2007) Risk assessment and domestic violence: The multi-agency Marac model of intervention. *Community Care*, 19/4/2007.

Plewis, I and Godstein, H (1998) The 1997 Education White Paper – A failure of standards. *British Journal of Curriculum and Assessment* 8:17–20.

Pollard, K C and Miers, M E (2008) From student to professionals: Results of a longitudinal study of attitudes to pre-qualifying collaborative learning and working in health and social care in the United Kingdom. *Journal of Interprofessional Care* 22(4): 399–416.

Pollard, K C, Thomas, J and Miers, M (eds) (2010) *Understanding interprofessional working in health and social care*. Basingstoke: Palgrave.

Popple, K and Quinney, A (2002) Theory and practice of community development: A case study from the UK. In *Journal of the Community Development Society*, 33(1): 71–85.

Power, A and Willmot, H (2005) Bringing up families in poor neighbourhoods under New Labour. In Hills, J and Stewart, K (eds) *A more equal society*. Bristol: Policy Press.

Prison Management Offender Inspection (2011) *A joined-up sentence? Offender management in prisons in 2009/2010*. Joint Offender Management Service: HMSO.

Pritchard (2008) *Good practice in safeguarding adults: Working effectively in adult protection*. London: Jessica Kingsley.

Purdie, N and Boulton-Lewis, G (2003) The learning needs of older adults. *Educational Gerontology*, 29(2): 129–49.

Quality Assurance Agency (2008) *Benchmarks for social work*. Gloucester: QAA.

Quality Assurance Agency (2009) *Benchmarks for youth and community work*. Gloucester: QAA.

Quilgars, D, Johnsen, S and Pleace, N (2008) *Youth homelessness in the UK: A decade of progress?* York: Joseph Rowntree Foundation.

Quinney, A, Hutchings, M and Scammell, J (2008) Staff and student experiences of using a virtual community, Wessex Bay, to support interprofessional learning: Messages for collaborative practice. *Social Work Education* 27(6): 658–64.

Quinney, A, Thomas, J and Whittington, C (2009) *Working together to assess needs, strengths and risks*. London: Social Care Institute for Excellence. Available at www.scie.org.uk

Ranade, W (1994) *A future for the NHS? Health care in the 1990s*. London: Longman.

Rankin, J (2005) Choice matters. *The Guardian*, 21 September.

Robinson, A L (2004) *Domestic violence MARACs for very high-risk victims in Cardiff: A process and outcome evaluation*. Cardiff University.

Robinson, K and Webber, M (2011) Models and effectiveness of service user and carer involvement in social work education: A literature review. *British Journal of Social Work* (2012): 120.

Rogers, A (2003) *Inside youth work*. London: YMCA George Williams College.

Sadd, J (2011) *'We are more than our story': Service user and carer participation in social work education*. London: Social Care Institute for Excellence.

Scammell, J, Hutchings, M and Quinney, (2008) *A virtual practice community for student learning and staff development in health and social work interprofessional education: Changing practice through collaboration.* HEA Health Sciences and Practice.

Scott, J and Hill, M (2006) *The health of looked after and accommodated children and young people in Scotland: Messages from research.* Edinburgh: Social Work Inspection Agency.

Sharples, A, Gibson, S and Galvin, K (2002) 'Floating support': Implications for interprofessional working. *Journal of Interprofessional Care,* 16(4): 311–22.

Shelter (2010) *Response – Marmot Review of health inequalities in England post 2010.* London: Shelter.

Smith, M K (1999, 2002) Youth work: An introduction. *The encyclopaedia of informal education.* Available from: www.infed.org

Smith, M K (2002) *Transforming youth work – Resourcing excellent youth services. A critique.* The informal education homepage. Available at www.indef.org.uk/

Smith, M K (2005) *Youth matters – The Green paper for Youth 2005.* The encyclopaedia of informal education. www.infed.org

Smith, M K (2011) *Young people and the 2011 'riots' in England – Experiences, explanations and implications for youth work.* www.infed.org

Social Work Reform Board (2010) *Building a safe and confident future: One year on.* London: SWRB.

Social Work Taskforce (2009) *Building a safe and confident future. The final report of the Social Work Taskforce.* London: SWT.

Statham, J, Harris, A and Glenn, M (2010) *Strengthening family wellbeing and community cohesion through the role of schools and extended services.* London: Centre for Excellence and Outcomes in Children and Young People's Services.

Stewart, G and Stewart, J (1993) *Social work and housing.* Basingstoke: Macmillan

Strong, S and Hall, C (2011) *Feeling settled project: Guide for those involved in changing a service from residential care home to supported living, where the people stay in the same place.* Bath: National Development Team for Inclusion.

Sylvestri, A (2011) *Lessons for the coalition: An end of term report on New Labour and criminal justice.* The Hadley Trust. London: Centre for Crime and Justice Studies.

Taylor, I, Sharland, E, Sebba, J, Leriche, P with Keep, E and Orr, D (2006) *The learning, teaching and assessment of partnership work in social work education.* London: Social Care Institute for Excellence.

Teacher Development Agency (2011) *Strategy for the professional development of the children's workforce in schools 2009–12.* Manchester: TDA.

Teacher Training Agency (2005a) Handbook of guidance. Available at www.tda.gov.uk

Teacher Training Agency (2005b) Making a difference to every child's life. London: TTA. Available at www.tda.gov.uk

Teacher Training Agency (2005c) *Qualifying to teach. Professional standards for qualified teacher status and initial teacher training.* London: TTA.

Teasdale, S (2009) *Innovation in the homelessness field: How does social enterprise respond to the need of homeless people?* Barrow Cadbury UK Trust: Third Sector Research Centre.

Thangham, D (2011) Research: Evidence base on assessing risk in domestic violence cases. *Community Care,* 30/9/2011.

Thomas, J, Quinney, A and Whittington, C (2009) *Building relationships, establishing trust and working with others*. London: Social Care Institute for Excellence. Available at www.scie.org.uk

Timms, P and Borrell, T (2001) Doing the right thing – Ethical and practical dilemmas in working with homeless mentally ill people. *Journal of Mental Health,* 10(4): 419–26.

Townsend, P and Davidson, N (1982) *Inequalities in health: The Black report*. Harmondsworth: Penguin Books.

Toynbee, P and Walker, D (2001) *Did things get better? An audit of Labour's successes and failures*. London: Penguin.

Vernon, J and Sinclair, J (1998) *Maintaining children in school: The contribution of social services departments*. London: National Children's Bureau.

Voice UK (2001) *Behind closed doors*. London: Voice UK.

Wallcraft, J, Fleischmann, P and Schofield, P (2012) *The involvement of users and carers in social work education: A practice benchmarking study*. London: Social Care Institute for Excellence.

Wanless Report (2004). Available at www.hm-treasury.gov.uk

Warren, J (2007) *Service user and carer participation in social work*. Exeter: Learning Matters.

Watson, D and West, J (2006) *Social work process and practice*. Basingstoke: Palgrave.

Wheeler, B, Mitchell, R, Shaw, M and Dorling, D (2007) The geography of housing in Britain. *Geography Review,* 20(3): 2–6.

Whittington, C (2003) *Learning for collaborative practice with other professions and agencies. A study to inform the development of the degree in social work*. London Department of Health.

Whittington, C, Whittington, M, Thomas, J and Quinney, A (2009a) *Key policy and legislation with implications for interprofessional and interagency collaboration (IPIAC): A timeline of examples 1968-2008*. London: Social Care Institute for Excellence. Available at www.scie.org.uk

Whittington, C, Quinney, A and Thomas, J (2009b) *A model of practice and collaboration*. London: Social Care Institute for Excellence. Available at www.scie.org.uk

Whittington, C, Thomas J and Quinney, A (2009c) Professional identity and collaboration. London: Social Care Institute for Excellence. Available at www.scie.org.uk

Wintour P (2003) *Abbott defends indefensible in sending son to private school. The Guardian*, Saturday 1 Nov. Available at education.guardian.co.uk

Wintour, P (2010) David Cameron announces plan to end lifetime tenancies. *The Guardian*, 3/8/2010.

Withnall, A (2010) *Improving learning in later life*. London: Routledge.

Wolstenholme, D, Boylan, J and Roberts, D (2008) *Factors that assist early identification of children in need in integrated or inter-agency settings*. Research Briefing 27. London: Social Care Institute for Excellence.

YouGov (2010) *British social attitudes survey*. Available at http://research.yougov.co.uk

YoungMinds (2012) *Better mental health*. Available at www.youngminds.org.uk

Youth Justice Board for England and Wales (2010) *National standards for youth justice services*. London: Ministry of Justice.

Index